Multinational
Product Strategy

Georges Leroy

The Praeger Special Studies program—
utilizing the most modern and efficient book
production techniques and a selective
worldwide distribution network—makes
available to the academic, government, and
business communities significant, timely
research in U.S. and international economic, social, and political development.

Multinational Product Strategy

A Typology for Analysis of Worldwide Product Innovation and Diffusion

PRAEGER SPECIAL STUDIES IN INTERNATIONAL ECONOMICS AND DEVELOPMENT

Praeger Publishers   New York   Washington   London

Library of Congress Cataloging in Publication Data

Leroy, Georges.
    Multinational product strategy.

    (Praeger special studies in international economics
and development)
    Bibliography: p.
    Includes index.
    1. International business enterprises—Management.
2. Product management. I. Title.
HD69.I7L44   658.1'8   75-23980
ISBN 0-275-55990-4

PRAEGER PUBLISHERS
111 Fourth Avenue, New York, N.Y. 10003, U.S.A.

Published in the United States of America in 1976
by Praeger Publishers, Inc.

Printed in the United States of America

Over the last two decades, the flowering of the multinational corporation as an economic institution of major dimensions on the international scene has bred a variety of theories of international investment. Some are marked by a rather narrow explanatory base, emphasizing only one or two independent variables, while others are more comprehensive. Testing the hypotheses has commonly, but certainly not always, relied on macro data. Studies of individual companies, and individual products within companies, have been far more scarce.

Georges Leroy's study enriches our understanding of the foreign investment process by approaching the problem from the viewpoint of product strategy. "Product strategy" is defined here in a special sense--referring to the strategy for originating the product (or process) know-how, and determining the location of production and the geographic markets which will be addressed over time. Thus, little is said about product strategy in the marketing sense, that is, deciding on just what the configuration and attributes of the product should be in order to achieve the particular goals of the firm. By first spelling out the variety of alternative time-paths of product strategies which might conceivably be employed, Leroy clearly indicates the large number of options that might be open to the firm.

Perhaps the greatest contribution of the study, however, is the investigation into the actual history of particular products in a small group of unlike firms. The richness of the alternatives is immediately apparent, illustrating quite vividly the global scanning capacity of the mature international firm. Know-how can originate in several locations, manufacturing can be established in any of several alternative countries, and many geographic markets can be served. The experience these companies have acquired over time has clearly made them comfortable in operating in a variety of environments.

This suggests that the state of information these firms enjoy is such that they can be quite sure-footed in their international operations. For a firm based in the United States, with such knowledge, making a direct investment in Germany may be only slightly more complex than making a direct investment in a region in the United States where they have heretofore had no production.

This improved state of information may provide at least a part of the explanation for the expansion of U.S. firms abroad since the mid-1950s. The oligopoly theory of direct foreign investment emphasizes that direct investment results from the firm's interest in taking advantage, in one dimension or another, of some quasi-monopoly strength in its operations. But one can ask why American firms waited, in so many cases, until the 1950s or later to begin to move abroad in a vigorous way. Improved communication and transportation have often been cited as factors contributing to the surge in foreign direct investment. Surely this was reflected in corporate headquarters being able to obtain better and more current information about their international operations. Thus the mystery of international operations was reduced, and with it the perceived risk. Consequently, an important cost of international operations was decreased, so the American firm found international opportunities more attractive than they were previously.

The author's studies of the five companies included in this work impress one with the large number of products with which the multinational corporation deals. In time, the body of international operational know-how can clearly grow to the point where the firm can operate with a truly worldwide view, developing know-how here, constructing a plant there, and serving markets in several countries.

The scholar eager to seek out explanations of the behavior of firms in international business is, I believe, too frequently tempted to resort to a mailed questionnaire which is sent to dozens, if not hundreds of multinational companies. If the research questions are at all complex, the problem of maximizing the response rate is great, and too often the answers are ambiguous. Many responses to specific inquiries may puzzle the researcher, leading him to wish for further information which would clarify and expand on the answers received. Although results might be tabulated and presented in statistical form, the meaning of the results can be quite unclear and unreliable.

The alternative pursued in this study, namely eschewing the large sample approach in favor of personal interviews with a limited number of firms, is appealing on several counts. The researcher can learn about the company in some detail, and perhaps limit his work to one or two divisions of the company. Questions can be pursued sufficiently to minimize the problem of ambiguity. Conditions which might have made it difficult for the respondent to reply satisfactorily to a question in a mailed questionnaire can be comprehended by the researcher and recognized for their importance. Ideas which might not have occurred to the researcher beforehand can often surface, leading to new hypotheses.

The principal disadvantage of this approach, of course, is that it does not lend itself to statistical analysis. Thus generalizations and tested hypotheses are impossible, unless the funds available for the research are so great that indepth interviews can be arranged with a sufficiently large number of firms. Though lacking appropriate funding, the approach used by Leroy in this work is to be recommended to those who would truly enrich the literature in international business, since the flavor of international operations is so much more fully revealed. Studies of this sort are a much needed complement to the research based on larger bodies of quantitative data.

Richard H. Holton
Dean, School of Business Administration
University of California, Berkeley

Presented in this volume is an analysis of the growth strategies pursued by multinational firms. Incorporated in such growth strategies are the processes of innovation as well as the pattern governing the international diffusion of products either by exports or through technology transfer. The firm is seen as an entity that considers different methods called alternative multinational product strategies of promoting its products worldwide.

The originality of this study lies both in its unit of analysis, the product, thereby integrating various functional dimensions with particular focus on the development, production, and marketing aspects of the product; and the use of a dynamic framework, the concept of multinational product strategy, governing the product's international dissemination. The array of feasible multinational product strategies constitutes a typology of alternative strategies. The most familiar multinational product strategy is, of course, the international product cycle. This study indicates that this strategy is only one of the many possible multinational product strategies a manager may employ.

The empirical basis of the analysis is the pattern of multinational product strategies implemented by five North American-based multinational firms: the Hewlett-Packard Company, Massey-Ferguson Ltd., Alcan Aluminium Ltd., Dymo Industries, and the Gillette Company. Though the statistical base is limited, the variety of industries in which these firms operate, as well as their different degree of international involvement, suggests a number of generalizable propositions.

This research grew out of the need to develop a conceptual framework that will be unique to multinational firms, that will provide scholars with a better understanding of multinational firms, and that will help managers focus on international product planning, a key element of multinational operations. More specifically, researchers may be primarily interested in the new approach developed to analyze multinational operations at the strategic level, while international executives might find the discussion of alternative multinational strategies especially useful.

This study is divided into three parts. Part I presents the framework of analysis: possible multinational product strategies. In Chapter 1 we present the need for such a study, the objectives of this research, and our view of strategy. Chapter 2 presents the framework itself, the typology, in the case of two countries, the parent country and the host country. Chapter 3 provides a preliminary test of the typology by identifying strategies that correspond to those identified in the theories of foreign direct investment. As the multinational product strategies represent alternative ways of involvement abroad, it should be possible to match the hows (multinational product strategies) with the whys (the theories of private foreign direct investment). This results in classifying strategies in two groups: those that correspond to well-specified theories (that is, the theory makes explicit one or a very few corresponding strategies) and those that lack specificity as they are congruent with a relatively large subset of multinational product strategies.

Part II provides the test of the typology, by describing the behavior of the five firms in terms of the framework. Chapter 4 presents the objectives and methodology of the empirical study, while Chapter 5 provides an in-depth analysis of the strategies of each of the five firms. This analysis is done at two levels: first by product lines to obtain a comprehensive coverage of the activities of the firm--that is, the general pattern of multinational product strategies; and, second, by the analysis of a selected number of specific products--products that allow a better grasp of the variety of multinational product strategies implemented. The general pattern of strategies is presented historically for each firm as it evolved through time as well as for the present.

Part III analyzes the results of the investigation of the strategies for the five firms. Chapter 6 discusses the variety of strategies observed (the observed set) and compares it to the set defined in the typology (the feasible set). Chapter 7 presents the rationale behind the variety of multinational product strategies observed in the five firms. Particular emphasis is devoted to product and firm characteristics as determinants of the strategy selected. Finally, Chapter 8 appraises the usefulness of the typology which has been specifically constructed to analyze multinational firm operations.

This book, which originated as a Ph.D. dissertation at the University of California, Berkeley, would not have been possible without the help provided by numerous persons. First I would like to thank the members of my dissertation committee, Professors Richard H. Holton, James M. Carman, and John M. Letiche, for their guidance and encouragement throughout the length of this research. The research could not have been undertaken without the full cooperation of many executives with whom I talked at great length in order to understand the operations of their companies. In particular I would like to thank Robert Brunner of Hewlett-Packard, Ralph Ramsay of Massey-Ferguson, Roy Ansell of Alcan Aluminium, Thomas Fellner of Dymo Industries, and David Fausch of Gillette. They were always willing to respond to my numerous questions with ample information and revealing insights.

Many other persons have contributed to the completion of this research by providing funding for my studies. In particular I wish to thank the Ecole des Hautes Etudes Commerciales, and Roger Charbonneau, its director, for their generosity in providing the grant-in-aid to undertake the Ph.D. program. A Seagram Business Faculty Award provided me with assistance in the later stage of the research. I am grateful to my friends in the doctoral program at Berkeley and my colleagues in Montreal, in particular, my two friends and colleagues Martin Murenbeeld and Donald J. Patton with whom I had many fruitful discussions enriched by misunderstandings of a cultural and linguistic nature. The editing is theirs, but they should not be held responsible for any remaining shortcomings in this book.

Finally, my wife Michelle contributed to this book in many indirect ways by encouraging me throughout my studies, as well as the typing of a number of drafts.

CONTENTS

PART I: THE TYPOLOGY OF MULTINATIONAL
PRODUCT STRATEGIES

LIST OF TABLES

LIST OF FIGURES

LIST OF ABBREVIATIONS

EEC	European Economic Community
MNF	Multinational firm
MPS	Multinational product strategy
PFDI	Private foreign direct investment
R and D	Research and development
SIC	Standard Industrial Classification
SITC	Standard Industrial and Trade Classification

Abbreviations Used in the Typology

p	parent country
h	host country
	used in conjunction with:
K	indicates location of development of product know-how (the location is either Kp or Kh)
M	indicates location of markets in which product is sold (the location is Mp or Mh)
P	indicates location of the production of the product (the location is Pp or Ph)
S1, S2, . . . S8	are basic states of the firm's production and marketing activity related to the product. Example: S1 meaning (Kp, Mp, Pp)
MPS 1, MPS 2, . . . MPS 58	are multinational product strategies, defined in Appendix A. A multinational product strategy corresponds to the sequence of entries into new states. Example: MPS 7 = S1 (Kp, Mp, Pp) - S3(Kp, Mh, Pp)

THE TYPOLOGY
OF MULTINATIONAL
PRODUCT STRATEGIES

The growth of the multinational firms (MNFs) is clearly one of the important developments of the new "postindustrial" era. While there were only a handful of international companies at the turn of the century, the value of the assets of those firms abroad is now estimated at close to $150 billion, and some scholars predict that by the end of this century three to four hundred giant global enterprises will account for two-thirds of the world's production.

The bulk of the research into the phenomenon of the multinational enterprise has attempted to identify the main characteristics of these firms in terms of industrial structure, turnover, value of assets, profitability, research and development (R and D) outlays; and to study the impact of MNFs on nation-states. Comparatively little research has been devoted to the internal operations of these firms and to their strategies for growth.

The study of the MNF, like the study of most new phenomena, is hindered by conceptual difficulties. For example, one needs to identify the specific characteristics that distinguish the MNF from other large domestic corporations. Research along this line, conducted under the direction of Raymond Vernon of the Harvard Business School, has concluded that the U.S.-based MNFs in manufacturing are the largest and most profitable firms, and the most intensive users of advertising and R and D. These last two characteristics hint at some peculiarity that contributes to the strength of the MNFs but research to date has not explained how they are utilizing these distinctive assets.

Despite the importance of this question to business scholars, very few studies have been directed toward explaining how MNFs innovate and diffuse their innovations worldwide. In order to answer this question, the research objective here is to systematically analyze

the process of innovation and diffusion within the MNF by developing
a general framework of multinational corporate strategies for growth
and applying this framework to the worldwide activities of five MNFs.

The juxtaposition of the traditional or classic view of multinational strategies as presented in the literature prior to the early
1970s, with the newer view emerging out of a variety of later observations, highlights the need for a new conceptual framework for
proper comprehension and analysis of multinational strategies.

STRATEGIES OF MULTINATIONAL FIRMS: THE CLASSIC VIEW

Accounts of the early development of multinational firms show
that they generally developed a product in their country of origin, a
country that often had some unique features which made this development attractive. (The country of origin is in most cases the country
where the firm has its headquarters, and will be referred to as the
parent country of the firm, and the others as host countries for the
firm activities.) The development of products generated success and
growth in the parent country and led to some export orders from foreign countries. As export grew the interest of the firm in foreign
markets may have led to the setting up abroad of a warehouse, a selling branch, or some servicing facility for its products. Later the
firms would find it more economical to assemble or manufacture the
product in the host country. The commitment of resources abroad
has often been triggered by the threat, either real or perceived, to
an established export market. [1]

A variant of the above pattern has been proposed to explain the
investment behavior of U.S.-controlled multinational enterprises.
The main feature of this model--the international product cycle model
presented in further detail in Chapter 3--is that U.S. MNFs develop
products in response to the stimulus of their parent country environment. These innovations tend to be biased toward consumer goods for
high-income consumers and labor-saving equipment. When demand
develops abroad, the firms export to these markets and when their
export position is threatened and the production process has become
standardized, production will start abroad. As production abroad
increases and as production costs abroad are lower because of wage
rate differences, the product is likely to be imported back to the
United States, thereby completing the cycle. This model attempts to
explain the behavior of U.S. MNFs exclusively. The growth of
European- and Japanese-controlled MNFs does not necessarily con-
form to this model and even for some U.S.-based MNFs one finds that
proponents of the model show that its underlying assumptions do not

hold, thus throwing into question its explanatory power even for the
U.S.-based MNF.

STRATEGIES OF MULTINATIONAL FIRMS: THE NEWER VIEW

MNFs often do not develop a product for their parent country
market, but do so in response to the needs and opportunities of world
markets. Product specifications integrate inputs from these countries abroad and whenever possible one standardized product is developed to accommodate worldwide needs. As a corollary, the product specifications adopted are often those of the most advanced market where competition is strongest, be it the United States, Europe,
or Japan. MNFs generally have an intimate knowledge of their markets in Europe, in the United States, and elsewhere, and this knowledge in many cases is used to commercialize a product simultaneously worldwide. They know production costs in various locations and
this enables them to start production practically simultaneously in a
number of countries rather than gradually move the product abroad.
Lags are becoming shorter, as firms anticipate and react to competitive moves.

A number of MNFs are not only involved in marketing and producing their products abroad, but also in product development and in
basic research. While the share of R and D conducted outside the
parent country is still a relatively minor percentage of total R and D
for most MNFs, it appears to be growing.[2] It varies greatly across
firms and even across firms in the same industry. For example,
Class GmbH does all its R and D in Germany for combines, while
Massey-Ferguson Ltd. does a good deal of it in Europe; the Aluminum
Company of America (Alcoa) does all its R and D in its parent country, the United States, while Alcan Aluminium Ltd. shares it between
Canada, the United States, and the United Kingdom.

A sizable number of MNFs have made acquisitions outside their
parent country in order to acquire the know-how and other assets of
the host country firm. For example, Gillette acquired A. G. Braun
and S. T. Dupont, both European firms; Litton Industries acquired
the West German electric typewriter firm Triumph Adler because
the Litton subsidiary Royal had not been able to crack the U.S. market with its product. Other acquisitions of note included BASF, the
German chemicals firm, acquiring Wyandotte, the largest U.S. manufacturer of polyols; Plessey, a U.K. firm entering the alloys field by
buying the U.S. firm Alloys Unlimited; and CPC, the U.S. firm, entering the packaged soups business by acquiring Knorr, a German
firm. Numerous other examples of such acquisitions are presented
in Appendix B.

Two studies, one by Lawrence Franko and the other by John
D. Daniels, on the behavior of MNFs of European or Canadian parentage having made investments in the United States, indicate that a
number of firms diversified their operations upon entry into the
United States. Franko provides a number of examples where the
products sold in the United States differed from the products that
were manufactured elsewhere by these firms. He cites the case of
the British firm Plessey where "production in the U.S. is by and
large quite different from its production in the U.K."[3] and the example of a European pharmaceutical firm where one manager stated:
"We are now producing a product in the U.S., that we do not produce
anywhere else in the world, at least not yet. We may well bring it
back to Europe in the very near future."[4] From this Franko concludes that a major peculiarity of European acquisitions of firms in
the United States is the fact that a substantial number of acquisitions
have been made prior to achieving any significant export to the U.S.
market.[5] Daniels also adds credence to the newer view of MNF
strategies and presents the case of a manufacturer of needles as one
typical of the pattern of R and D acquisition:

> A manufacturer of needles and needle bearings
> felt that he needed to round out his line by be-
> ginning production of a high precision bearing.
> As the firm did not have the technical compe-
> tence to begin this production quickly, and since
> there were no firms producing them in its own
> country, the firm had to look outside.[6]

Daniels reports that 3 of the 40 firms which had recently invested in the United States decided that they wanted first to begin
operating in a foreign country and then set out to see what type of
product had the best market there.[7] He further notes that 22 of the
40 firms never exported or had exported negligibly to the United
States prior to investing there.[8] This would appear to be at odds
with the classic view that considers exports as a way to develop a
market. However, he also reports that of the 40 firms interviewed
30 of them had begun foreign operations by export.[9] This might indicate that as firms gain experience abroad they do not need to go
through the same steps each time they launch a product. It would be
of interest to know whether the experience was gained with different
products or with a single product, but Daniels did not investigate this.
The examples presented above indicate that the classic view is
not all-encompassing and that there are alternative ways to innovate
and diffuse a product internationally. This opinion appears to be
shared by Vernon, the major proponent of the international product

cycle, who has modified his stance by declaring that the international
product cycle model may not fit present reality as well as he had
first expected:

> The product cycle sequence relies heavily on the
> assumption that the special conditions of the U.S.
> environment--especially factor costs and con-
> sumer tastes in the United States--will set in
> train a sequence that leads, step by step, to in-
> ternational investment. Though this may be an
> efficient way to look at enterprises in the U.S.
> economy that are on the threshold of developing
> a foreign business, the model is losing some of
> its relevance for those enterprises that have long
> since acquired a global scanning capacity and a
> global habit of mind. [10]

It is clear then that a systematic study of alternative ways
used by firms to innovate and diffuse their products worldwide is
needed. Consequently, this is the main objective of the research
undertaken here. This study should be especially relevant for the
decision maker who is concerned with choosing the best of several
alternative product innovation and diffusion strategies. Our interests diverge here from those of economists. Whereas the economist
is interested in analyzing the main trends in order to make predic-
tions on, for example, the overall impact of foreign direct investments on a country's trade account, or capital account, this study
seeks to specify the set of feasible alternatives the executive should
consider before making a decision on product and market development strategy. It may well be that one alternative, even a rarely
used one, is the best one in the particular case.

OBJECTIVES OF THE RESEARCH

The main objective is to develop a framework that enables one
to categorize and analyze the alternative strategies that a firm can
employ as it decides on the country or countries in which to develop
product technology or know-how, to manufacture the product under
consideration, and to market this same product. Particular attention is paid in the sequencing of moves from one country to another.
This study therefore includes such aspects as where the firm
develops new products (in response to which opportunities) and
whether or not the firm will decide to import or produce that new
product where the product is marketed.

The set of alternative feasible strategies, selecting the product as the unit of analysis, constitutes the typology of multinational product strategies. The multinational product strategy is the central concept of this research; it describes the sequence of moves through time for a firm with a given product in terms of location of development and the various market and production centers.

A second objective is to indicate the usefulness of the typology in analyzing MNF strategies. In order to operationalize this method of analysis, we must show first that one can in fact describe the behavior of firms with this set of strategies, that the set is in fact an exhaustive one, and that it includes particular strategies not encompassed by the classic view of the MNF. We therefore apply the strategy analysis concept to a number of MNFs.

A third objective of this research is to relate the multinational product strategy selected to a set of product and firm characteristics which appear to have been judged important in the decision to select a specific strategy. This part of the study is exploratory and inductive in nature. We had no satisfactory theory a priori to guide us in order to select proper characteristics. A series of strategic decisions is a complex series of events that is often approached in an ill-defined way. We structure the study of those decisions insofar that here we hypothesize some critical elements in the decision process.

THE CONCEPTUAL FRAMEWORK: THE TYPOLOGY OF MULTINATIONAL PRODUCT STRATEGIES

Our goal is to define and classify alternative multinational strategies open to MNFs. Our framework will encompass the main product-related activities of the firm: product development, the production element, and the markets for the product. It will also be shown how international growth strategies can be classified along these three dimensions.

A review of the literature in international business strategy and in business policy shows that such a classification has not been attempted. Our framework borrows from the dynamic aspects which are present in the classic view and broadens this view by incorporating those aspects of the product-market grid often used to analyze corporate strategy.[11]

The classic view of international growth looks at the locations of production and markets, both dimensions we wish to incorporate in our framework along with the dynamics of this classic view. In addition, the product-market grid developed by H. Igor Ansoff indicates four strategies of growth open to the firm at any moment in time.

They are market penetration (the present product in the present market), market development (the present product in a new market), product development (a new product in the present market), and diversification (a new product in a new market). If we interpret the classic view from Ansoff's product-market grid viewpoint, we see that the firm follows first a market penetration strategy and then exports products to new markets; that is, it follows a market development strategy by tapping host country markets. Another version of the classic view, the international product cycle however cannot be incorporated in the product-market grid, for it adds a stage where market penetration of the parent country is accomplished by production abroad (in the host country) and the production dimension does not exist in Ansoff's framework.

The product-market grid is a general framework for corporate strategy analysis and it was not conceived for the case of MNFs. Consequently it needs to be modified to fit the circumstances faced by the MNF. Implicitly it assumes that the development and production locations for a given product are found in the same country; it is a two-dimensional diagram, not a multicountry framework. Multinational corporate strategists have more degrees of freedom than their counterparts operating inside the boundaries of any one country. Hence it is important to incorporate another dimension to describe MNF operations.

The typology of multinational product strategies for the MNF emerges as a framework incorporating the location of product innovation as well as the production and market locations. The multinational product strategy indicates the country where the product was developed (where innovation occurred), and the sequence of production and market entries in various countries (the diffusion process) over the life of the product. The typology is presented in Chapter 2.

SCOPE AND METHODOLOGY OF THE
EMPIRICAL STUDY

The empirical study was conceived as a way to test (modestly to be sure, for no statistical rigor is implied) the operationality and the usefulness of the typology. Preliminary work showed that in-depth knowledge of the firm was required in order to gain an adequate understanding of multinational product strategies. This information could only be gathered through interviews with managers of the selected firms.

While one could have looked only at the range of multinational product strategies implemented in those firms--this provides a test of the relevance of the typology--it would leave the reader and the

researcher still perplexed as to why these multinational product
strategies were chosen. The rationale for selecting a particular
multinational product strategy became therefore an important part
of the inquiry. In view of the present lack of knowledge of the rationale, this part of the study is exploratory: its objective is to develop propositions relating particular multinational product strategies to firm and product characteristics. Few working hypotheses
were initially developed; they emerged through interviews with the
managers of various firms and by considering different product lines.
However, one hypothesis is an exception to this and it holds that the
knowledge of host country markets is an important variable affecting
the choice of a particular multinational product strategy. Furthermore, this knowledge is likely to grow with the length of time the company is abroad. Firms that have been abroad for a long time are
therefore more likely to use a greater variety of multinational product strategies. In particular they are likely to develop or acquire
firms in order to develop new products abroad.

The five firms selected for the empirical study represented a
variety of manufacturing industries, lengths of experience as MNFs,
global sales, policies toward R and D, and intensity of R and D.
Each firm was known to have product development of one sort or another outside its parent country. This later aspect was considered
important as many moves presented in the newer view are of that type.

Interviews with a number of managers were conducted over a
period of several months leading to a good grasp of the main activities and profile of the firm over two decades (1955-75) for some, and
half a century for others. For convenience, the firms chosen were
North American-based ones but, as one can judge by looking at Appendix B, an equivalent sample of firms of European parentage could
be used instead if desired.

For each firm we obtained a profile of their growth and the
evolution of their main multinational product strategies. We analyze
in detail the general pattern of multinational product strategies presently implemented by these firms. Altogether the five firms were involved in 30 product lines that are analyzed in the general pattern of
multinational product strategies.

This is complemented by an in-depth analysis of a selected
number of products, 52 in total. These 52 products were diffused in
a number of countries by alternative means, resulting in total in
close to 200 multinational product strategies. The analysis of specific products allows us to obtain a better coverage of the variety of
multinational product strategies implemented by the five firms; and
it was used to analyze the rationale behind the variety of multinational product strategies encountered.

NOTES

1. See for example Raymond Vernon, Sovereignty at Bay (New York: Basic Books, 1971), pp. 72-74; and M. Z. Brooke and H. Lee Remmers, The Strategy of Multinational Enterprises (London: Longman, 1970), pp. 225-30.

2. See U.S., Congress, Senate, Committee on Finance, Implications of Multinational Firms for World Trade and Investment and for U.S. Trade and Labor (Washington, D.C.: Government Printing Office, 1973), p. 582. Other studies relating to various aspects of R and D are, for Canada, A. E. Safarian, Foreign Ownership of Canadian Industry (Toronto: University of Toronto Press, 1966), chap. 6; and for the United Kingdom, John H. Dunning, American Investment in British Manufacturing Industry (London: Allen and Unwin, 1958), chap. VI, especially pp. 168-75, 190. The only aggregate data available on R and D spending outside the parent country are for U.S. MNFs in manufacturing. On the average 8 percent of total corporate R and D expenditures were spent outside the United States in 1970. This ranged from plastics (24 percent), industrial machinery and equipment (21 percent), soaps and cosmetics (16 percent), nonelectrical machinery (12 percent), farm machinery and equipment (11 percent), electronic equipment (9 percent), and down to practically zero in primary and fabricated aluminum. Most of the foreign R and D by U.S. MNFs was performed in three countries: Canada (27 percent), United Kingdom (25 percent), West Germany (20 percent).

3. Lawrence G. Franko, European Business Strategies in the United States, Research Report 71-2 (Geneva: Business International, 1971), p. 22.

4. Ibid., p. 23.

5. Ibid., p. 43.

6. John D. Daniels, Recent Foreign Direct Manufacturing Investment in the United States (New York: Praeger, 1973), p. 79.

7. Ibid., pp. 70-71.

8. Ibid., p. 42.

9. Ibid., p. 52.

10. Vernon, op. cit., p. 107.

11. H. Igor Ansoff, Corporate Strategy (New York: McGraw-Hill, 1965), chap. 6.

2

MULTINATIONAL PRODUCT
STRATEGIES: A TYPOLOGY

In this chapter we present the central concept of the research, the multinational product strategy. First we present the concept of strategy and elaborate upon an operational definition of strategy. This is followed by an overview of the studies of multinational strategies, most of which analyze the activities of the MNF from a functional point of view. Then we introduce and develop the concept of multinational product strategy, first using a simple case, then introducing the various concepts, and later the generation of the typology itself. The product strategies are classified according to the origin of know-how, whether it is developed in the parent country or in a host country.

THE STRATEGY CONCEPT--ITS APPLICATION
TO THE MULTINATIONAL FIRM

The term "strategy" has been used in a variety of ways by military theorists, by business practitioners, and by management researchers. As the definitions of strategy used by these groups differ considerably, it is of great importance to clearly define the main features of the concept of strategy that we wish to use in this research.

Alternative Views on Strategy

Military theorists, the first users of this word "strategy," view strategy as the art of using military power to reach objectives set by governmental policy makers.[1] This usage is analogous to the view of game theorists[2] where strategy consists of a detailed

specification of action or set of rules covering all possible specific
circumstances that may arise.

In business policy, strategy is viewed as a guide to action, as
one cannot in most cases specify exhaustively the set of all strategies. Some authors view strategy as a plan to reach desired goals[3]
but others view it as encompassing the determination of the goals and
objectives of the enterprise.[4]

While the two issues above can be fairly easily settled in view
of the objectives of the researcher, less attention has been devoted
to the definition of strategy that is acceptable for both the decision
maker and the researcher. Does a pattern that is recognized by a
researcher constitute a strategy, irrespective of what the decision
maker himself perceives? Can one speak of a strategy ex post, or
the existence of some unconscious strategy in the decision maker's
mind? Here there are two schools of thought. The first sees the
decision maker as developing a strategy in a systematic way and
building an integrated plan of his future actions. As Henry Mintzberg
points out, this first view expressed by management theorists "treats
strategy as an explicit set of guidelines developed in advance of the
taking of specific decisions."[5] Mintzberg argues that the transposi-
tion of the theorists' views to empirical research limits its application: "so long as we view strategy as an explicit, prior set of guidelines we are restricted to studying strategy making in abstract, nor-
mative terms."[6]

Looking back, for example, at the classic view of MNF strategies, one could only speculate whether the pattern of moves identified
represents a strategy in the above sense. In many cases the answer
is likely to be that it will not qualify. The manager starts by export-
ing--he may even be asked to send some products abroad; he has not
yet devised any strategy as to where this is going to lead him. Will
this induce him to invest in that country three years from now? He
may look at the decisions one at a time and may not always develop
any explicitly stated plan over the next few years. In other cases,
he may, due to his experience, have developed beforehand an explicit strategy.

The second school of thought defines a strategy as "a pattern
in a stream of significant decisions."[7] This allows one to study a
broader range of strategies either as planned, prior guidelines, or
as resulting a posteriori from the decision maker's behavior. This
view is expressed by psychological theorists, Jerome S. Bruner,
Jacqueline J. Goodnow, and George A. Austin as they relate strategy
to efficiency on concept attainment:

> In studying concept attainment it has been our aim
> to externalize for observation as many of the

> decisions as could possibly be brought into the
> open, in the hope that regularities in these deci-
> sions might provide the basis for making infer-
> ence about the process involved in leaving or at-
> taining a concept. These regularities in decision
> making we shall call strategy. [8]

Herbert Simon, the well-known management theorist who developed the concept of limited rationality to describe managerial
behavior, stresses how a decision-making pattern arises out of successive commitments:

> Some decisions are irrevocable in the sense that
> they create a new situation which, in turn, in-
> fluences the decisions that follow them. . . . At
> each moment the behaving subject, or the organiza-
> tion composed of numbers of such individuals, is
> confronted with a large number of alternative be-
> haviors, some of which are present in conscious-
> ness and some of which are not. Decision, or
> choice, as the term is used here, is the process
> by which one of these alternatives for each mo-
> ment's behavior is selected to be carried out.
> The series of such decisions which determines
> behavior over some stretch of time may be called
> a strategy. [9]

The Strategy Concept Selected for This Research

In this research the second, more pragmatic, view of strategy
has been selected. Consequently, a strategy can be identified as a
sequence of decisions even if this strategy is not recognized explicitly by the manager as such. Furthermore, as Mintzberg points out,
what the manager states as his strategy is not such for a researcher
until he discovers a consistent pattern of decisions.

Several arguments can be advanced for preferring this definition of strategy. First, many firms have had extensive operations
abroad before developing any explicit strategy. Secondly, the notion
of multinational product strategy presented below encompasses a
number of major decisions made over the life of the product and
these decisions may extend over a time span that goes beyond the
planning horizon of the decision maker. This may be the case when
a product has a long life and decisions regarding entry into new
markets are made only progressively over a number of years.

We may choose to extend our concept of multinational product strategies and look at the growth pattern of MNFs over several product generations. In looking at a number of examples, one emerging pattern over the long run appears to be the establishment of research and development facilities abroad. Here the difference in time between the initial establishment of a manufacturing subsidiary abroad and the actual development of new products abroad may be in excess of five years. The pattern identified ex post by a researcher is unlikely therefore to have been explicitly planned as such by the manager. Rather, the pattern may have evolved through time as the result of successive commitments until it crystallized into a new set of product strategies that were implemented by the firm. Perhaps the activities of the U.S.-based MNFs of Ford or General Motors in the automobile industry, and Firestone and Goodyear in the tire industry, can be seen in this light. They first went abroad with their superior technology, but now they are in a position to export back to the United States some products or know-how from their European subsidiaries.

The approach to the concept of strategy used here is that a strategy is any pattern of significant decisions over time for a particular product. The particular types of decisions taken are presented below. Before turning to it, however, we want to show how this study relates to others that have looked at strategies from a multinational firm point of view.

Multinational Strategies: An Overview

As pointed out in Chapter 1, there is the classic view and the newer view of explaining how a product is diffused internationally. Research on particular aspects of multinational firm strategies has been extensive during the last decade and multinational firms have been studied from a variety of angles other than the one referred to above. These studies fall into two general categories.

The first category is the functional approach and is the most widely accepted method for analyzing MNF activities.[10] These studies look at marketing, or production, or finance, or organization strategies separately. They stress the distinguishing features of multinational strategies relative to corresponding domestic strategies. They focus on the diversity of the environments encountered and the complexity of operating simultaneously in more than one of these environments. In our study we will refer back to a number of these functional strategies when we build an integrated framework to approach multinational product strategies.

The other category of studies, represented by foreign investment theories developed by economists, deals with the question of
why firms invest abroad on a more aggregate level. These theories
will be studied in Chapter 3 where they are used as a preliminary
test of the typology of multinational product strategies.

THE TYPOLOGY OF MULTINATIONAL
PRODUCT STRATEGIES

The aim of this section is to develop a comprehensive list of
ways MNFs innovate and diffuse their know-how abroad. The whole
series of decisions related to these aspects is viewed as strategic
because of its vital importance for the firm, and the interdependence
of these decisions which requires top management attention above
that devoted to any of the functional disciplines (such as marketing,
finance, and production). The product constitutes the most visible
element created by the firm; this is why the product was chosen as
the unit of inquiry, and the central concept is the multinational
product strategy.

As a prerequisite to an understanding of the typology we present a number of definitions of the concepts used. As it is of primary importance to rise above the semantic maze characteristic of
much of the vocabulary in administration, we shall define "know-
how," "products," "product strategy" (to be used interchangeably
with "multinational product strategy"), and other constructs in a
manner as elegant and as operationally feasible as possible. This
is of critical importance as we may, for example, find that depending on our definition of "product" a theory may not be empirically
relevant (see Chapter 3, where the relevance of the international
product cycle theory is discussed).

First this section defines the basic dimensions that make up
the product strategy, and illustrates how the notion of product strategy emerges as an appropriate way to characterize the innovation-
diffusion process for a product. It concludes that the innovation resulting from the developmental activities of the firm generates product know-how, while the diffusion process involves primarily production and marketing activities. Therefore, a relevant definition
of product strategy must contain these three dimensions, namely,
know-how, production, and market. Because we look at the product
strategy in a dynamic way, the evolution of its location in different
countries through time appears of utmost importance and represents,
therefore, the crux of the concept of product strategy.

This section then presents systematically the nomenclature or
vocabulary that is used in the typology. And finally the typology of

multinational product strategies for the case of two countries is outlined. We present the constraints that were selected to determine
the feasible set of multinational product strategies.

The Concept of Multinational Product Strategy: Three Basic Dimensions

The literature on business strategy suggests that there are a
number of important aspects of multinational growth, but three considerations recur with great regularity. The first concerns the location of the market, that geographic entity in which some need is
uncovered which management determines can profitably be exploited
by the firm. The second consideration, not independent of the first,
concerns the technology necessary to profitably exploit such market
demand. Specifically, if such technology is available, management
must determine where it can be obtained. The third consideration
concerns production, specifically, the location of production.

These three considerations were early seen by John G.
McDonald, a partner in McKinsey and Company, as being of paramount importance in the operation of a truly global enterprise. It
is worth quoting at length from McDonald's speech before the American Management Association in 1960:

> This type of corporation (the world enterprise) re-
> quires a different management perspective from
> that of a company that operates purely domestically.
> As its business is global, so must management's
> perspective be global. By this we mean that man-
> agement decisions can be made only after consid-
> ering all the conditions and all the opportunities
> that exist throughout the world. Thus in such a
> global framework, the chief executive's responsi-
> bility is basically to decide:
>
> Where in the world should the corporation's
> time, money, and effort be invested to produce the
> best long-term results for the stockholders?
>
> In order to make such a decision, he must
> resolve many subsidiary problems that are also
> global in scope, such as:
>
> Where in the world can the company market
> its products most profitably?
>
> Where in the world can the company perform
> its research and development most effectively at
> the lowest cost?

From where, and from whom, in the world
should the company supply its market, to ensure
that it gets the best prices, delivery, quality, etc. ?
Where in the world should the company make
its products, so that it will be competitive in all its
major markets?
Now these types of problems obviously require
a perspective different from that of a domestic company. The main difference is that management of a
world enterprise addresses itself to answering where
in the world can the company carry out these things,
as opposed to where in the United States. For in-
stance, consider a company with an expanding market
in the United States and the need to build a new plant.
In the domestic company, the chief executive would
ask: where in the United States should we build this
plant? In the world enterprise, the executive would
ask: first, from where in the world, and from whom
in the world, would it be most advantageous to supply
this increased market; and second, if new production facilities are required, where in the world
would it be most advantageous to locate them?[11]

There are other questions of importance in the analysis of the
international development of the enterprise. Clearly such considerations regarding the flow of funds, the availability of competent managerial personnel and supplies, and the organizational structure are
vital to operational success. But these are of second-rank importance in the macroconsideration of the global strategy of the MNF.
We will now proceed to develop a typology with the following
three dimensions: (1) the location of the development of the product
know-how; (2) the location of the markets in which the product is
sold; and (3) the location of production of the product.
Without loss of generality we make the limiting assumption
that the firm operates in a two-country world, the parent country
(p) and the host country (h). (This nomenclature avoids the ethno-
centric connotation associated with home and foreign country and is
consistent with the fact that firms have in general a nationality of
origin.) The parent country (as noted previously) is the country
(or the nation-state) where a firm's headquarters is located. If we
further assume that the country where a product has been developed
is the parent country, we can represent the firm's production and
marketing activity related to this product with four states called
basic states, as follows.

In basic state S1 the product is produced and marketed in the parent country. By way of illustration, consider the razor blade which was developed in the United States. Production and marketing started in the United States. The razor blade is therefore initially in state S1. In basic state S2 the product is produced in the host country and exported back to the parent country. Using the same example, it may be that some razor blades are now manufactured in Europe or Mexico and imported to the United States. In basic state S3 the product is produced in the parent country, and is exported to the host country. Thus, the United States is likely to have exported razor blades to Canada or France. In basic state S4 the product is now produced in the host country for that market. Razor blades are presently manufactured in Canada for the Canadian market, and in France for the French market. Figure 2.1 depicts the four basic states.

During the life of the product several of these basic states will in all probability be encountered. For example, the classic view presented in Chapter 1 corresponds to two cases. The first case follows the pattern of states S1-S3-S4, that is, the firm develops and manufactures a product in its parent country for its parent market (basic state S1), subsequently it exports to a host country (basic state S3), and later manufactures that product in the host country to supply that market (basic state S4). The second case corresponds to the sequence S1-S3-S4-S2, that is, it adds toward the end of the life of the product the reimportation to the parent country (basic state S2) of the product. One can similarly devise a sequence such as S3-S4 if the firm develops a product in its parent country for another host country, and exports that product first from the parent country (basic state S3) before producing it in the host country, close to the market (basic state S4).

It is clear that at any time, the position of the firm for a given product can be characterized by what is called a state made up of a mix of basic states.

We have represented in Figure 2.2 the range of alternative feasible sets of states the firm may be in at any particular point in time. It is assumed in this that it is not feasible for a given product to be at the same time exported from and imported into the same country. Therefore the basic states S2 and S3 are mutually exclusive. Note that the representation of the firm activities with a sequence of basic states depicts the international innovation-diffusion process for a product. This sequence of basic states defines the firm multinational product strategy. This will become clear below where we rigorously define the specific concepts of the typology. This is necessary in order to generalize the typology to include those states corresponding to the case where the know-how for the product is developed in the host country.

FIGURE 2.1

The Four Basic States When the Know-how for a Product Is Developed in the Parent Country

		PRODUCTION LOCATIONS	
		Parent Country	Host Country
MARKET LOCATIONS	Parent Country	S1 (Kp, Mp, Pp) Parent country production for the parent country market	S2(Kp, Mp, Ph) Production in the host country is exported to supply the market of the parent country
	Host Country	S3(Kp, Mh, Pp) Parent country production exported to the host country market.	S4(Kp, Mh, Ph) Host country production for the host country market.

Note: Each basic state is represented by S followed by a digit (S3). It may be accompanied by an indication of the know-how location, in this case, the parent country Kp; the market location for this basic state, either parent Mp or host Mh; and an indication of the production location, either parent Pp or host Ph. For example, S3 (Kp, Mh, Pp) reminds the reader what the basic state S3 consists of.

Source: Compiled by the author.

FIGURE 2.2

Alternative Feasible Set of States of a Firm as a Mix
of Basic States for a Product Whose Know-how
Originates in the Parent Country

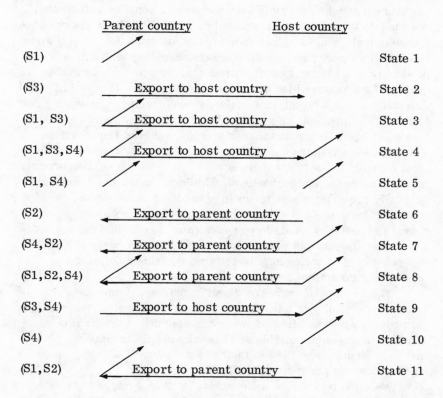

Note: The activity of the firm is represented symbolically by
arrows. An arrow of this type / means production and consumption of the product within a given country while a horizontal arrow
indicates the movement of a product from one country to the other
in the direction of the arrow.

Source: Compiled by the author.

The Concepts of the Typology

We note at the outset that the guiding principles in deciding on the proper definition of, for example, product, know-how, and product strategy are the relevance of the definition to the object of this study, the MNF, and the ability to operationalize the definition.

In dealing with the notion of product, specifically, we would like to be able to decide whether or not, for example, razor blades of the carbon coated variety developed in 1901 are similar to the stainless steel blades developed and marketed in the 1960s. The definition of a product as "a bundle of physical, service and symbolic particulars expected to yield satisfactions or benefits to the buyer"[12] does not do this, as no reference is made to the critical aspect of technological changes as per the razor blade example. A definition based on technology has implications for deciding what are new products and what are modified products. Improvements in the quality of a product which are aimed at increasing its reliability and durability through better materials and engineering may or may not lead to a new product. For example, the modification of the stainless steel blade to superstainless steel is a quality improvement which does not require a new technology whereas the modification from carbon blades to stainless steel blades, also a quality improvement, required a new technology. Similarly, a feature improvement generally requiring a new technology would be suggested by the move to twin-edge shaving blades or the change from mechanical lawn mowers, pushed by hand, to power lawn mowers. Styling improvements may or may not also include technological change. From this point of view technology is critical; hence our definition of product should reflect this.

The concept of know-how itself is elusive. Some know-how is related specifically to a product and is generally called technology[13] (as above), whereas other know-how is specific to the firm (for example, management policies and organizational structures which make the firm competitive in the marketplace). The latter know-how is, however, extremely difficult to measure.[14]

We shall now define the concepts used in the typology. The know-how used in the typology is product know-how. We therefore define know-how as a set of features crucial to the function of a particular product or the components of a product. The patent is the most obvious way to identify this know-how, although we do not limit the identification solely to patents. Some innovations cannot be patented yet they represent new know-how, and they therefore should not be excluded.

A product is defined as representing a set of technologies, or different elements of know-how. It is clear that two products incor-

porating the same elements of know-how are therefore identical.
For example, the engines of the Vega and Capri may incorporate the
same know-how and would therefore be identical products. In practice a number of products may differ only in size and shape; we
therefore can say that they are the same product. A product to be
considered as a new product must incorporate a new element of
know-how.

Any two products will be defined as being of the same product
line if there is a large intersection in the know-how structure of each
product. For example, if product A incorporates the know-how elements (or patents) P1, P2, P3, P4 and product B, the know-how
elements P2, P3, P4, P5, they are of the same product line. A
firm may modify a product for its market in country X, and patent
that modification, but the basic similarities of the product remain.

A product strategy space is defined as a space subtended by
the following three dimensions: the country of origin of the know-
how of the product (X_1), the country of sale (market) of that product (X_2), the country of production of the product (X_3). One should
note that it makes sense to speak about the country of origin of know-
how for a product only if all of the elements of know-how originate
in the same country; consequently, one may have to partition a product into product elements so that this property holds for each element. The three dimensions of the product strategy space are described further below.

The country of origin of know-how is the country where the
firm gained all the elements of the know-how. This know-how is
either developed* (internally) by the firm or acquired. For example,
if a U.S. firm develops a new process in one of its subsidiaries in
the United Kingdom we consider the origin of know-how to be the
United Kingdom. This would also be so if the U.S. firm acquired a
U.K. firm that had developed that process in the United Kingdom.
However, if the U.S. firm bought a license from an independent U.K.
firm, then the origin of know-how would be where the knowledge is
initially applied in the corporate system. The origin may therefore
be in the United States but it could also be in Germany if the knowledge was first exploited there. The rationale for this distinction
will become clear at a later point in the analysis. Suffice to say
here that we are looking at intrafirm know-how transfers and not
interfirm ones in our analysis of corporate strategy.

---

*We look at where the know-how was developed and not at
earlier phases of the development process. For example, we are
not concerned with the location of basic research but with the last
phase of the R and D process, the development phase.

The country of sale is the country in which the market for the
product is located. The country of production is where the product
is manufactured, the raw material extracted, or the service performed. For products made of components, one may treat the
assembly operation as a separate product with its specific know-how.

Any point in the product strategy space will be referred to as a
basic state for a firm with a given product. In the case of a world
with two countries, there are only two values on each axis of the
product strategy space, each corresponding to the location in the
parent country or the host country. We can represent in a symbolic way the product strategy space in a three-dimensional diagram,
as shown in Figure 2.3.

FIGURE 2.3

Representation of the Set of Basic States for a Product
in the Case of Two Countries

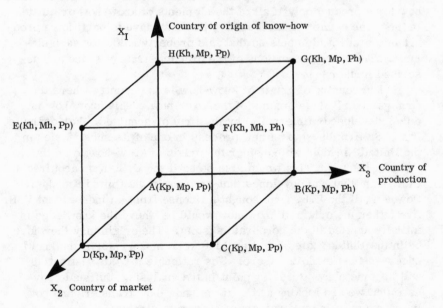

Source: Compiled by the author.

In this figure the origin of the axis is arbitrarily designated
as the location in the parent country. Any basic state defined as a
triplet (X_1, X_2, X_3) corresponds to a corner of the quadrangle.
Points A, B, C, D correspond to the four basic states viewed in
Figure 2.1, while the four other points (E, F, G, H) correspond to
those states where the know-how originated in the host country. An
alternative presentation of the eight basic states is given in Figure
2.4. In order to clarify the notation a basic state will in general be
followed by its triplet making explicit its meaning--for example, S1
(Kp, Mp, Pp), S3 (Kp, Mh, Pp).

A state is, as noted previously, a mix of basic states that
represents the position of the firm with respect to a given product
at a particular moment in time. The activity of the firm may, for
example, be characterized by one, two, or three basic states at any
one time.

We define the multinational product strategy, also called product strategy, as the sequential evolution of a firm with a given product through the basic states. A move from the basic state S1 (Kp,
Mp, Pp) to S2 (Kp, Mh, Ph), for example, is a product strategy, as
is a move such as from S1 (Kp, Mp, Pp) to S3 (Kp, Mh, Pp) and S4
(Kp, Mh, Ph). Product strategies generally will consist of a number of basic states, but one can also imagine a product strategy made
up of one basic state only. The difference between the concept of a
basic state and product strategy is therefore one of dynamics.

Successive entries into new basic states rather than successive
changes (that is, in terms of entries and discontinuations of basic
states) is the critical feature of a strategy because each entry represents a new commitment of resources. It follows, for example, that
the product strategy S1-S3 corresponds to the event a or b of case 1
in Figure 2.5. That is, despite the fact that at point in time t_3 for
a we are in state 2, while for b at point t_3 we are in state 3. In a
similar way the product strategy S2-S1 may correspond to the event
a or b of case 2 presented in Figure 2.5.

The Typology of Multinational Product Strategies

We can now present the typology of multinational product strategies for the case of two countries. A typology is what Milton
Friedman has called a "filing system" that must be exhaustive and
should be judged by the clarity and precision with which the categories are defined.[15] In keeping with this definition we will define

FIGURE 2.4

Typology of Basic States for a Product

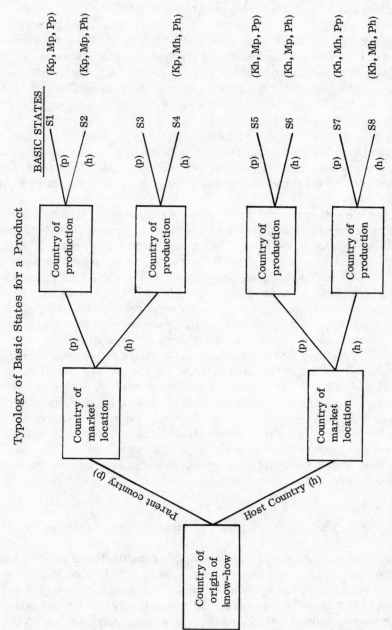

Source: Compiled by the author.

26

FIGURE 2.5

Relationship Between Basic States and Product Strategies

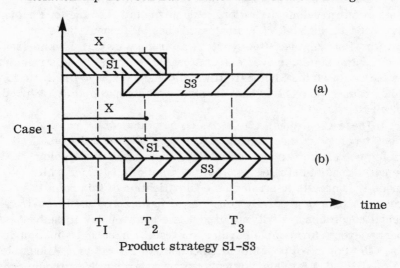

Product strategy S1-S3

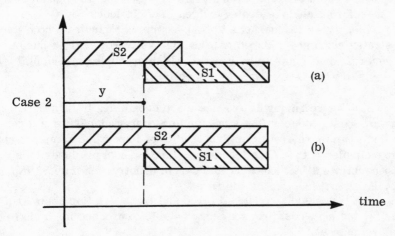

Product strategy S2-S1

Note: Inherent in the evolution of the product through various states are two types of lags, a market lag and a production lag.

   x = market lag; it represents the time lag between the initial demand in the first country and in the second country.

   y = production lag; it represents the time lag between the initial production in the first country and the production in the second country.

Source: Compiled by the author.

27

the total number of feasible product strategies from which we can derive an exhaustive typology.*

It should be clear that a great many strategies exist on the basis of our previous definition. Any permutation of the four basic states, S1 through S4, is a strategy; hence all permutations present us with 24 strategies. However, as a strategy may also comprise three or two states,or even one state,we have a total of 64 strategies for the set of states S1 to S4. If we allow know-how to originate in either country (parent or host country) we obtain a total of 128 product strategies.

These 128 product strategies do not, however, form the basis of our typology as they merely define the academic universe of all strategies determined by the states. The basis of our typology is the set of feasible strategies, that is, a set of strategies which excludes the unrealistic strategies. Clarification of this point is in order. A firm is generally constrained in its activities by environmental conditions. It will not export to a host country if the host country erects formidable barriers to trade. In such a situation S3 (Kp, Mh, Pp) is not possible for inclusion in a strategy. A feasible set of strategies for this particular firm regarding this product does not therefore include a strategy which itself includes S3.

Clearly we can construct other examples to indicate how a set of strategies can be reduced to a feasible set. However, a number of general conditions can be iterated which preclude an in-depth analysis of what is available to a specific firm:

1. One country will produce more economically than the other. The low-cost producer (the long-run low-cost producer for a given product) can therefore export but it will not import the same product. For example, if the parent country is the low-cost producer then the host country will not export to the parent country and state S2 (Kp, Mp, Ph) is not feasible in this case.

2. Given such barriers to trade as transportation costs and tariffs, the high-cost producer may be able to produce for a share of his own market.

3. While the initial producer may not be the low-cost producer, its lead in production may permit export of the new product for a

----

*In deriving this exhaustive typology, we must avoid two types of errors. The first error is to end up with a set of strategies some of which have no real existence because we have incorporated too few constraints in constructing the typology. The second error is to restrict the set of feasible strategies in the typology so much that some strategies exist that will fall outside the typology.

transitory period to the other country. This may be due to advantages in learning belonging to the initial producer, [16] or a small market in the other country, or other barriers that inhibit its start of production.

We study below the variety of feasible product strategies in four cases, depending on where the product is developed, and whether the parent country is a low cost producer or not.

Case 1: The product is developed in the parent country considering that the parent country is the low cost producer. The first environmental condition makes state S2 not feasible. The list of feasible product strategies is given below. We have labeled the product strategies MPS followed by a number. For example, the product strategy S1-S3-S4 is arbitrarily labeled MPS 1, and S3-S4-S1 is represented by MPS 2, and so on.

Three-State Product Strategies	Two-State Product Strategies	Single-State Product Strategies
MPS 1 = S1-S3-S4	MPS 7 = S1-S3	MPS 13 = S1
MPS 2 = S3-S4-S1	MPS 8 = S1-S4	MPS 14 = S3
MPS 3 = S4-S1-S3	MPS 9 = S3-S4	MPS 15 = S4
MPS 4 = S4-S3-S1	MPS 10 = S3-S1	
MPS 5 = S3-S1-S4	MPS 11 = S4-S1	
MPS 6 = S1-S4-S3	MPS 12 = S4-S3	

The product strategies that start with state S1 (Kp, Mp, Pp) correspond by definition to products developed in response to the needs of the parent country, while product strategies starting with the states S3 (Kp, Mh, Pp) or S4 (Kp, Mh, Ph) were developed in response to host country markets.

A few of the product strategies listed above start with states S4 (Kp, Mh, Ph). The initial location of production is in the host country which in this case is the high-cost country. Nevertheless temporary export in order to supply the parent country market is feasible according to our third environmental condition. We add therefore to the list of strategies above the following three multinational product strategies: MPS 28 = S4-S2-S1-S3, MPS 21 = S4-S2-S1, MPS 25 = S4-S2.*

---

*Note that MPS 25 = S4-S2 is a curtailed form of MPS 21 = S4-S2-S1 as production in the parent country did not materialize for any number of reasons; a likely one is a lack of sufficient demand for the product after its introduction. There are only three product

In Case 2, the product is developed in the parent country, and the host country is the low-cost producer. According to the first environmental condition state S3 is not feasible as the high-cost producer cannot export. The following product strategies are feasible:

Three-State Product Strategies	Two-State Product Strategies	Single-State Product Strategies
MPS 16 = S1-S2-S4	MPS 22 = S1-S2	MPS 13 = S1
MPS 17 = S1-S4-S2	MPS 8 = S1-S4	MPS 26 = S2
MPS 18 = S2-S1-S4	MPS 23 = S2-S1	MPS 15 = S4
MPS 19 = S2-S4-S1	MPS 24 = S2-S4	
MPS 20 = S4-S1-S2	MPS 11 = S4-S1	
MPS 21 = S4-S2-S1	MPS 25 = S4-S2	

The product strategies that start with state S1 (Kp, Mp, Pp) or S2 (Kp, Mp, Ph) correspond by definition to products developed in response to the needs of the parent country, while product strategies starting with state S3 (Kp, Mh, Pp) or S4 (Kp, Mh, Ph) are intended to first supply the host country market.

As in Case 1 above, the high-cost producer may temporarily export in order to develop the market in the other country. Therefore as a transition between states S1 and S4 one may find state S3. Consequently we obtain MPS 27 = S1-S3-S4-S2, MPS 1 = S1-S3-S4, MPS 7 = S1-S3. Table 2.1 gives the list of product strategies when the know-how originates in the parent country.

It should be noted that some product strategies are feasible whether or not it is the parent country or the host country that is the low-cost producer. Some examples are MPS 8 = S1-S4 or MPS 11 = S4-S1 or MPS 1 = S1-S3-S4 or MPS 21 = S4-S2-S1.

Case 3: Now consider the third case, where the product is developed in the host country, and the parent country is the low-cost producer. The first environmental condition eliminates state S6, that is, export from the high-cost producer to the parent country. The following product strategies are therefore feasible:

---

strategies, MPS 28, MPS 21, MPS 25, mentioned because state S2 is necessarily followed by state S1 and not S3 as one can reasonably assume that production in the parent country will be initially for the market (that is, state S1) rather than for export from the parent country (that is, state S3).

TABLE 2.1

Multinational Product Strategies for a Product Whose Know-how Originates in the Parent Country

Multinational Product Strategy (MPS)	Parent Country is Low-Cost Producer	Host Country is Low-Cost Producer
MPS 1 = S1-S3-S4	x	x
MPS 2 = S3-S4-S1	x	
MPS 3 = S4-S1-S3	x	
MPS 4 = S4-S3-S1	x	
MPS 5 = S3-S1-S4	x	
MPS 6 = S1-S4-S3	x	
MPS 7 = S1-S3	x	x
MPS 8 = S1-S4	x	x
MPS 9 = S3-S4	x	
MPS 10 = S3-S1	x	
MPS 11 = S4-S1	x	x
MPS 12 = S4-S3	x	
MPS 13 = S1	x	x
MPS 14 = S3	x	
MPS 15 = S4	x	x
MPS 16 = S1-S2-S4		x
MPS 17 = S1-S4-S2		x
MPS 18 = S2-S1-S4		x
MPS 19 = S2-S4-S1		x
MPS 20 = S4-S1-S2		x
MPS 21 = S4-S2-S1	x	x
MPS 22 = S1-S2		x
MPS 23 = S2-S1		x
MPS 24 = S2-S4		x
MPS 25 = S4-S2	x	x
MPS 26 = S2		x
MPS 27 = S1-S3-S4-S2		x
MPS 28 = S4-S2-S1-S3	x	
Total number of product strategies	18	18

Source: Compiled by the author.

Three-State Product Strategies	Two-State Product Strategies	Single-State Product Strategies
MPS 31 = S5-S7-S8	MPS 37 = S5-S7	MPS 43 = S5
MPS 32 = S5-S8-S7	MPS 38 = S7-S5	MPS 44 = S7
MPS 33 = S7-S5-S8	MPS 39 = S5-S8	MPS 45 = S8
MPS 34 = S7-S8-S5	MPS 40 = S8-S5	
MPS 35 = S8-S5-S7	MPS 41 = S7-S8	
MPS 36 = S8-S7-S5	MPS 42 = S8-S7	

Product strategies starting with state S5 (Kh, Mp, Pp) indicate that the product was initially developed for the parent country market, while product strategies starting with state S7 (Kh, Mh, Pp) or S8 (Kh, Mh, Ph) indicate that the first market is the host country one.

As we assumed that the initial producer, even if it is the high-cost producer in the long run, can temporarily export the product from the host country, we obtain two additional feasible strategies: MPS 51 = S8-S6-S5, MPS 57 = S8-S6-S5-S7, MPS 55 = S8-S6.

Case 4: Then we have the last case where the product is developed in the host country and where the host country is the low-cost producer. According to the first environmental condition, state S7, the export from the high-cost producer to the host country is ruled out. The following product strategies are feasible:

Three-State Product Strategies	Two-Stage Product Strategies	Single-State Product Strategies
MPS 46 = S5-S6-S8	MPS 52 = S5-S6	MPS 43 = S5
MPS 47 = S5-S8-S6	MPS 39 = S5-S8	MPS 56 = S6
MPS 48 = S6-S5-S8	MPS 53 = S6-S8	MPS 45 = S8
MPS 49 = S6-S8-S5	MPS 54 = S6-S5	
MPS 50 = S8-S5-S6	MPS 40 = S8-S5	
MPS 51 = S8-S6-S5	MPS 55 = S8-S6	

The product strategies that start with the state S5 (Kh, Mp, Pp) or state S6 (Kh, Mp, Ph) are by definition products developed in response to the needs of the parent country, while product strategies starting with state S7 (Kh, Mh, Pp) or S8 (Kh, Mh, Ph) are originally supplying the market of the host country.

If we assume again that the original producer may temporarily export to the long-run low-cost producer, that is, state S7 (Kh, Mh, Pp) may occur between state S5 (Kh, Mp, Pp) and state S8 (Kh, Mh, Ph), then the following additional product strategies are feasible: MPS 58 = S5-S7-S8-S6, MPS 31 = S5-S7-S8, MPS 37 = S5-S7.

Table 2.2 presents a list of the product strategies where the know-how originates in the host country.

TABLE 2.2

Multinational Product Strategies for a Product Whose
Know-how Originates in the Host Country

Multinational Product Strategy (MPS)	Parent Country is Low-Cost Producer	Host Country is Low-Cost Producer
MPS 31 = S5-S7-S8	x	x
MPS 32 = S5-S8-S7	x	
MPS 33 = S7-S5-S8	x	
MPS 34 = S7-S8-S5	x	
MPS 35 = S8-S5-S7	x	
MPS 36 = S8-S7-S5	x	
MPS 37 = S5-S7	x	x
MPS 38 = S7-S5	x	
MPS 39 = S5-S8	x	x
MPS 40 = S8-S5	x	x
MPS 41 = S7-S8	x	
MPS 42 = S8-S7	x	
MPS 43 = S5	x	x
MPS 44 = S7	x	
MPS 45 = S8	x	x
MPS 46 = S5-S6-S8		x
MPS 47 = S5-S8-S6		x
MPS 48 = S6-S5-S8		x
MPS 49 = S6-S8-S5		x
MPS 50 = S8-S5-S6		x
MPS 51 = S8-S6-S5	x	x
MPS 52 = S5-S6		x
MPS 53 = S6-S8		x
MPS 54 = S6-S5		x
MPS 55 = S8-S6	x	x
MPS 56 = S6		x
MPS 57 = S8-S6-S5-S7	x	
MPS 58 = S5-S7-S8-S6		x
Total number of product strategies	18	18

Source: Compiled by the author.

This typology of product strategies will be used to identify various moves made by multinational firms. There is quite obviously an element of risk involved in moving from one basic state to another; the nature of the risk can be seen as related to the particular states involved in the move. To explain, a firm moving from one basic state to the next may change the location of only one dimension of its product strategy space or several. For example, in moving from the basic state S1 (Kp, Mp, Pp) to S3 (Kp, Mh, Pp) the firm changes only one dimension, the market location. If on the other hand it moved directly from S1 (Kp, Mp, Pp) to S4 (Kp, Mh, Ph) this means moving simultaneously the location of the market and the production center. The typology identifies therefore three different degrees of risk depending on the number of dimensions shifted in moving from one basic state to the next. One can note that the strategies MPS 1 = S1-S3-S4 and MPS 27 = S1-S3-S4-S2 referred to as classic strategies in Chapter 1 are in fact risk minimizing ones. One could therefore use the framework to see whether as the firm gains experience abroad it increasingly uses the more risky product strategies. Obviously the firm's international experience compensates to some degree for the risk involved and a product strategy such as MPS 8 = S1-S4 may not be perceived by the experienced firm as any more risky than MPS 1 = S1-S3-S4 for an inexperienced one.

CONCLUSION

The typology of multinational product strategies presented in this chapter enables us to classify in a systematic way MNF activities in terms of worldwide innovation-diffusion at the product level. Instead of the handful of alternatives commonly referred to, we identify close to 60 multinational product strategies. The reader is referred to Appendix A where the list of these strategies and their description is presented. These multinational product strategies, constituting the feasible set, are made of a variety of states corresponding to those encountered over the life of the product. Four of these strategies are four-state strategies, 20 are three-state strategies, and the remainder are two-state and single-state strategies.

The typology is an important tool for analysis; it enables the researcher to identify and classify the activities of the MNF. We were able during the research to gather a number of examples of multinational product strategies from a variety of MNFs; for each

of the 28 MNFs, one or several examples of strategies are provided
in Appendix B. *

A tabulation of the variety of multinational product strategies
corresponding to these examples indicates that seven different multinational product strategies correspond to the case where the know-
how originates in the parent country and six when the know-how
originates in a host country. This later case, not identified in the
classic view, will be studied further. Another finding is that these
examples correspond to three-state, two-state, and single-state
product strategies, but none of them corresponds to four-state product strategies.

This variety of multinational product strategies raises some
questions as to the validity of a number of assumptions that have
traditionally been put forth. This large number of product strategies identified in the typology is the result of their relaxation. The
first assumption that we relaxed concerns the location of product
development. It is generally assumed that the firm develops a
product in response to parent market opportunities. Such a restrictive assumption is perhaps less necessary than it was in the past,
as firms have gained experience abroad and are now able to see
further and better. Also, their activities abroad are now relatively
and absolutely more important, making overseas operations worthy
of greater attention. The argument that other countries lag in terms
of income per capita behind the United States and will therefore
adopt, when they reach this income level, the same product is not
always a convincing one. Europe and Japan behave somewhat differ-
ently from the United States, because of physical, cultural, and
economic traits.

A second restrictive assumption found in the literature is that
the product needs to be developed close to the market as communication is of prime importance in the early stages of development.
In a number of cases, however, MNFs have gained enough experience

---

*These examples were gathered from the various business
journals. They are presented in Appendix B to illustrate the relevance of the typology. This is not a thorough research of a selected
number of publications to indicate the existence of a variety of multinational product strategies. These examples often lack the precision
to be interpreted without ambiguity as corresponding to a precise
product strategy; however, they indicate clearly the existence of
multinational product strategies that have not been dealt with in any
systematic way.

abroad with previous products so as to make long-distance communication more adequate, and they have developed appropriate organizational patterns[17] that allow them to relax the above assumptions.

A third assumption is that initially production and product development must be closely integrated. The experienced firm is
likely to increasingly trade off higher costs of communication regarding product development and production for lower costs of production abroad.

NOTES

1. See Liddell B. Hart, Strategy: the Indirect Approach
(London: Faber, 1967) and General Beaufre, Introduction a la
strategie (Paris: Librairie Armand Colin, 1965).

2. See R. Duncan Luce and Howard Raiffa, Games and Decisions: Introduction and Critical Survey (New York: John Wiley and
Sons, 1967).

3. Frank F. Gilmore and Richard G. Brandenburg, "Anatomy
of Corporate Planning," Harvard Business Review, November-
December 1962, pp. 61-72.

4. Alfred D. Chandler, Strategy and Structure (Cambridge:
M.I.T. Press, 1962).

5. Henry Mintzberg, "Research on Strategy Making" (Working paper, Faculty of Management, McGill University, March 1972).
Mintzberg stresses that while much work on the concept of strategy
has been done theoretically, few empirical studies have looked at the
strategy-making process.

6. Ibid., p. 2.

7. Ibid., p. 3.

8. Jerome S. Bruner, Jacqueline J. Goodnow, and George A.
Austin, A Study of Thinking (New York: John Wiley and Sons, 1956).

9. Herbert Simon, Administrative Behavior (New York:
Macmillan, 1947), pp. 66-68 (emphasis added).

10. See Richard D. Robinson, International Business Manage-
ment, A Guide to Decision Making (New York: Holt, Rinehart and
Winston, 1973); Michael Z. Brooke and H. Lee Remmers, The
Strategy of Multinational Enterprise: Organization and Finance
(London: Longman, 1970); William A. Dymsza, Multinational Busi-
ness Strategy (New York: McGraw-Hill, 1972). See, for multina-
tional marketing strategies, Vern Terpstra, International Marketing
(New York: Holt, Rinehart and Winston, 1972); Warren J. Keegan,
Multinational Marketing Management (Englewood Cliffs, N.J.:
Prentice-Hall, 1974); Richard H. Holton, "Marketing Policies in
Multinational Corporations," California Management Review 13,

no. 4 (Summer 1971): 57-67; and Robert D. Buzzel, "Can You
Standardize Multinational Marketing?" Harvard Business Review,
November-December 1968. In multinational production strategies
see Robert B. Stobaugh, "Where in the World Should We Put That
Plant?" Harvard Business Review, January-February 1969. In
international finance see David B. Zenoff and Jack Zwick, Interna-
tional Financial Management (New York: Prentice-Hall, 1969). In
multinational management the most interesting work is John M.
Stopford and Louis T. Wells, Managing the Multinational Enterprise
(New York: Basic Books, 1972).

11. John G. McDonald, "Organizing the Company As a World
Enterprise" (Speech presented at the American Management Association, New York, February 24, 1960.

12. Philip Kotler, Marketing Management, Analysis, Planning and Control, 2d ed. (Englewood Cliffs, N.J.: Prentice-Hall,
1967), p. 289.

13. See U.S., Congress, Senate, Committee on Finance,
Implications of Multinational Firms for World Trade and Investment and for U.S. Trade and Labor (Washington, D.C.: Government Printing Office, 1973), p. 552; technology is used here in its
most widely accepted sense, that is: "information or knowledge about
physical relationships that permits some task to be accomplished,
some service rendered, or some product produced. Conceptually
technology can be distinguished from 'science,' which organizes and
explains data and observations by means of theoretical relationships.
Technology translates scientific relationships into 'practical use.'"
The activities that are part of the technological process are generally called research and development (R and D). They include basic
and applied research in the sciences and engineering, and design and
development of prototypes and processes and exclude market research, product testing, economic research and other research in
the social science; for further details see National Science Foundation, Research and Development in Industry, NSF 68-20, 1966, and
E. Mansfield, Research and Innovation in the Modern Corporation
(New York: W. W. Norton, 1971).

14. For a study that deals with this question see Ralph Z.
Sorenson and Ulrich Wiechmann, "A Study of the International Stan-
dardization of Marketing Programs and the Transfer of Marketing
Skills Within Non-durable Consumer Goods Firms," mimeographed
(Preliminary presentation of findings, Harvard Business School,
Boston, 1973).

15. Milton Friedman, Essays in Positive Economics (Chicago:
University of Chicago Press, 1953), p. 7.

16. For more details on learning economies see William
Fellner, "Specific Interpretations of Learning by Doing," Journal of

Economic Theory 1 (August 1969): 119-40, and empirical evidence
in John E. Tilton, International Diffusion of Technology: The Case
of Semi-Conductors (Washington, D.C.: The Brookings Institution,
1971).

     17. Stopford and Wells, op. cit.

3

MOTIVES FOR FOREIGN
DIRECT INVESTMENT AS
A PRELIMINARY TEST OF
THE COMPREHENSIVENESS
OF THE TYPOLOGY

The pertinence of the typology of multinational product strategies can be assessed by considering those strategies that are consistent with the private foreign direct investment theories that have been formulated to explain this phenomenon. That is, we identify the motive for going abroad and move backward, assigning to each motive the corresponding product strategy. For each motive why, there is a corresponding way, or there is at least one way to respond to the stimulus.

In the literature on foreign investment we find two distinctly different types of studies: one is descriptive and empirical in nature and attempts to find out through questionnaires and interviews with top managers why firms invest abroad; the other type, theoretical in nature, attempts to develop a rationale through an analysis of macrodata as to why firms invest abroad.

The descriptive studies are of uneven quality. They are mentioned here because they represent a first attempt to understand why firms invest abroad through the perception of the investors themselves. The main test of the typology lies in the theories of foreign investments which have primarily been developed over the decade 1965-75.

EMPIRICAL STUDIES OF THE MOTIVES
FOR INVESTING ABROAD

Empirical studies of the motives for foreign direct investment have been undertaken periodically; the first study appeared in 1955 and presented the results of interviews with top executives in more than 400 firms, including 247 investors whose total foreign invest-

ment accounted for 70 percent of all U.S. corporate foreign investment. The researchers, E. R. Barlow and Ira Wender, asked the
following question: "What benefits or advantages does (would) your
company expect and seek before favorably considering a new investment or licensing operation abroad? (i.e. not profit only but specific
advantages which ultimately add up to better or more profitable company operations)."[1]

The respondents listed the following factors in descending order
of importance: (1) "favorable market or source of supply," (2) "con-
vertibility of currency," (3) "possibility of profit," (4) "stability of
foreign country," (5) "government encouragement to a company,"
(6) "favorable tax situation," (7) "forced to invest to maintain a market," (8) "favorable labor situation."[2] The ranking of these factors
is not markedly affected by the type of industry--extractive, manufacturing, or service and trade--as Table 3.1 indicates.

Three remarks are appropriate here. First there is a logical
problem: as the third reason cited "the possibility of profit" can
be achieved by various means such as a favorable market or source
of supply or tax situation which are also included in the questionnaire.
Secondly, it is not made explicit as to what is manufactured abroad in
comparison to what is manufactured in the home country of the firm.
It could be assumed that the firm invests when the market abroad for
its products is favorable, or to maintain a market that is already established. In both cases this can be seen as a market development
move in the sense that it is in response to a market opportunity for
the same product that was developed at home. Third, some firms
reported more than one reason for investing abroad. As can be seen
at the bottom of Table 3.1, the 247 companies interviewed reported
468 reasons for investing abroad.[3] One can question, therefore,
whether the relative importance of the motives is not biased as a result of the authors' allowance for multiple motives.

A further survey was conducted by Endel J. Kolde[4] in 1959
with 104 U.S. multinational companies, the results of which are presented in Table 3.2. In 1962, Jack N. Behrman[5] interviewed 72
firms and the summary of his results is reproduced in Table 3.3.

In a later study Raghbir Basi[6] solicited firms to indicate the
relative importance of a given list of motives for their investment
abroad. His results are presented in Table 3.4. The most recent
study of this type is a study by Michael Z. Brooke and H. Lee
Remmers[7] who interviewed some 80 manufacturing companies, several oil companies, and 30 banks originating in nine different countries. The results of their study are presented in Table 3.5.

In viewing the studies of Kolde, Behrman, Basi, and Brooke
and Remmers as well as that of Barlow and Wender, several main

TABLE 3.1

Motives for Foreign Direct Investment--1955 Survey by E. R. Barlow and Ira Wender
(number and percent of comments)

Reason for Investing	All Industries		Extractive		Manufacturing						Services and Trade	
					Producer Goods		Consumer Durables		Consumer Nondurables			
	Number	Percent	Number	Percent	Number	Percent	Number	Percent	Number	Percent	Number	Percent
Favorable market or source of supply	108	44	16	59	49	51	8	21	21	40	14	45
Convertibility of currency	66	27	8	30	18	19	11	28	21	40	8	26
Possibility of profit	59	24	5	19	26	27	11	28	10	19	7	23
Stability of foreign country	47	19	6	22	18	19	4	10	12	23	7	23
Government encouragement to a company	36	15	9	33	9	9	5	13	10	19	3	10
Favorable tax situation	35	14	7	26	11	11	6	15	5	9	6	19
Forced to invest to maintain a market	30	12	1	4	15	15	7	18	6	11	1	3
Favorable labor situation	16	6	1	4	8	8	4	10	2	4	1	3
Other	59	24	6	22	26	27	6	15	11	21	10	32
None	12	5	1	4	3	3	5	13	2	4	1	3
No comment	18	7	2	7	5	5	3	8	7	13	1	3
Companies interviewed	247	100	27	100	97	100	39	100	53	100	31	100
Total number of comments	468	100	60	100	183	100	67	100	100	100	58	100

Source: E. R. Barlow and Ira Wender, Foreign Investment and Taxation (Englewood Cliffs, N.J.: Prentice-Hall, 1955), p. 444.

conclusions can be drawn.* First, two motives for investing abroad come out repeatedly in these studies: a defensive motive, that is, a response to a threat such as fear of losing a market or being "forced to invest to maintain a market, " and an offensive motive which is in response to a favorable actual or potential market.

TABLE 3.2

Motives for Foreign Direct Investment--
1959 Survey by Endel J. Kolde

Primary Reason	Percent of Sample
Legal restrictions (tariffs, quotas, etc.)	21
Lower cost of production (savings on labor, raw materials, or processing)	20
Inefficiency of native marketing institutions	14
Competition	12
Dissatisfaction with international middlemen	11
Long-range expansion policy	7
Invitation by foreign companies or governments	6
Tax advantages	4
Other reasons	5
Total	100

Note: This survey was conducted as part of a study of foreign-based affiliates of 104 international companies and their 533 affiliates. The responses to the survey were tabulated in terms of the primary reason for establishing foreign-based affiliates. Kolde did a follow-up survey in 1965 that probed into the reasons for continued growth of a company's international involvement. This later list of motives does not contain any classification of their relative importance.

Source: Endel J. Kolde, International Business Enterprise (Englewood Cliffs, N.J.: Prentice-Hall, 1965), p. 233.

---

*Numerous difficulties are involved in comparing these studies one with the other. The sample used in each differs in terms of size, type of industry, method of inquiry (either interviews or questionnaires, or both), selection of motives (either from a list or left to the discretion of the respondent) and because the time of the studies differs from the mid-1950s when few currencies were freely convertible through the 1960s when most such restriction had been relaxed.

TABLE 3.3

Motives for Foreign Direct Investment--
1959 Survey by Jack N. Behrman

Motive	Number of Companies
Increased profits	20
Expanded foreign demand or market	19
Nationalism and foreign restrictions	14
To obtain raw materials	12
Lower costs abroad (labor and better technology)	7
Diversification	5
Shortage of dollars for imports in host country	4
Maintain supplier relation with customer	4
Poor performance of local distributors	3
Necessity to adapt product to foreign demands	3
To protect patents by working them	2
To develop private enterprise abroad	2
To raise living standards abroad	1
To protect the U.S. market	1

Note: The 72 companies questioned responded that their motives were complex and not singularly "profit-directed." For example, increased profits was the single reported motive for only 8
companies out of 20 that reported it.

Source: Jack N. Behrman, "Foreign Associates and Their
Financing," in U.S. Private and Government Investment Abroad, ed.
R. F. Mikesell (Eugene: University of Oregon Press, 1962), p. 89.

This dichotomy sheds some light on the behavior of firms and
the triggering force in foreign investment, but it does not lead deeply
into the analysis of the longer-term motives. If one were to do this
one would have to break down the decision to invest into its several
components--the decision to look abroad, the investigation process,
and the decision to invest, [8] and analyze each step in detail. Clearly
the firm's initial decision to venture abroad may arise "from some
chance, almost freakish event," [9] but it would be a mistake to ex-
trapolate that line of reasoning to the total $150 billion that is now
invested abroad. The motive for the initial investment and the decision process is markedly different in nature from the next steps. [10]
The sort of triggering encountered may or may not have a decisive
impact on the response that is forthcoming. For example, in

TABLE 3.4

Motives for Foreign Direct Investment--
1963 Survey by Raghbir S. Basi
(number of companies)

Possible Motive	Crucially Important	Fairly Important	Not Important
Fear of losing a foreign market[a]	57	69	30
Foreign government's favorable attitude toward U.S. investments	76	69	13
Availability of suitable local manpower at lower wages	10	93	55
Familiarity with the foreign country[b]	30	70	56
Political stability in the foreign country[c]	101	58	1
Present extent of the market[d]	53	88	13
The extent of the potential market[d]	126	32	2
Tax structure in the foreign country	30	101	27
Stability of the country's foreign exchange position	61	90	8
Inflationary trends in the foreign country	35	99	21
Existence of local complementary engineering facilities	9	51	93
Utilization of available patents or licenses in the foreign country	8	44	95
Expected higher profitability[e]	55	89	10
Raw materials availability	41	73	40
Availability of capital and other assistance from local businessmen	27	51	72

Note: The study included 160 companies.

[a]Market may be lost either through local competition or governmental restrictions.

[b]Familiarity here implies a favorable image.

[c]Political stability does not connote a democratic form of government or the absence of it.

[d]Market refers to the available market within, as well as outside, the national boundaries of a country.

[e]Higher profitability implies profits that are higher than those of the United States.

Source: Raghbir S. Basi, Determinants of United States Private Direct Investments in Foreign Countries (Kent, Ohio: Bureau of Economic and Business Research, Kent State University, 1963), p. 10.

TABLE 3.5

Motives for Foreign Operations--1970 Survey by Michael Z. Brooke and H. Lee Remmers

Motive	Frequency Encountered
Defensive strategies	
A company is operating abroad to defend its existing business as a result of:	
Government action in establishing or increasing:	
Tariff barriers	A
Import controls	D
Legislation (at home or abroad) against monopolies or trade agreements	C
Demands for local manufacture and other problems of nationalism in overseas markets	B
Transport costs and delays	A
Difficulties with agents	B
Difficulties with licensees	C
Troubles with after-sales service and other technical difficulties abroad	C
The need to protect patents	C
The need to ensure supplies of raw materials and components	B
The need to go international when competitors, suppliers, or customers do so	B
The need to protect shareholders at home from trade recessions at home by:	
A geographical spread	C
Product group diversification (which may involve geographical as well)	D
Aggressive strategies	
The search for:	
More profitable uses for underemployed resources at home in:	
Capital and equipment	B
Personnel	D
Know-how	C
The more effective use of opportunities by the development of global plans and strategies for resources and markets	C
Access to foreign knowledge or methods	D
The need to expand when this can only be abroad	D
The possibility of escaping from constraints at home	E
Other pressures	
Influence of governments, for example:	
By general encouragement to foreign investment	E
Tax concessions	D
Cheap loans	D
Grants or guarantees	D
Buildings	E
Influence of other companies, for example, approach for know-how	C
Internal to company, such as pressure groups advocating overseas manufacture because of the expertise and insights of members	C

Note: The symbols used represent the judgment of the authors as to the frequency of a given motive as follows: (A) motive mentioned in practically all the firms investigated; (B) motive mentioned in over half of the firms investigated; (C) motive mentioned in less than half of the firms investigated; (D) motive mentioned once or twice by the firms investigated; (E) motive not mentioned at all by the firms investigated, but referred to in the literature.

Source: Michael Z. Brooke and H. Lee Remmers, The Strategy of Multinational Enterprise: Organization and Finance (London: Longman, 1970), pp. 227-29.

response to the intervention of a foreign government to raise its tariffs, the firm must decide whether or not to keep its position by exporting and thereby reducing its profits, or to invest locally, find a licensee, or withdraw totally from the market.

Another conclusion we can draw from these five studies is that they do not question what is accomplished by these investments. The implicit hypothesis is that firms conduct the same business abroad that they were successfully conducting at home. That is, all the motives mentioned in the studies above lead to a market development move except in the case where investment is to take advantage of a favorable source of supply. In that case, as in the market development move, there is a transfer of technology abroad but the product is likely to be exported to the parent country instead of exports from the parent country.

A third observation on these studies is that the motives they reported relate to the environment of the firm in terms of markets, government stability, and other characteristics of the receiving country. They practically exclude factors relating to the firm itself, the characteristics of its products, and its country of origin. In this sense the question asked in these studies is not why the firm invests abroad but rather what are the characteristics of the host countries that invite investment by the firm. Only Brooke and Remmers perceived that difference and included as motives the search for more profitable uses of underemployed resources at home in capital, equipment, personnel, and know-how. Investment abroad was properly viewed by these authors in the context of a firm's overall growth strategy.[11] We will expand that line of thought in this research.

THEORIES OF PRIVATE FOREIGN DIRECT INVESTMENT

Since 1955 private direct foreign investment (PFDI) has become increasingly important and a number of theories have been proposed to explain this phenomenon. We will examine the various theories to interpret them in terms of the typology, that is, to match each theory with the corresponding set of product strategies.

It should be mentioned here that the theories of PFDI were conceived to explain the establishment of production facilities abroad, and not always the steps leading to it, or stemming from it. In contrast, the framework developed in the typology encompasses not only production abroad, but also marketing and product development. Nevertheless in many of the theories of PFDI, reference is made to the marketing and product development aspects, and furthermore they clearly indicate the important role of intermediary stages such as exports before production abroad (international trade and international production are closely intertwined in practice). The theories of PFDI do provide a preliminary test of the relevance and comprehensiveness of the typology as they are concerned with the main features that distinguish the MNF from other traditional firms.

Before discussing the major theories of PFDI and their corresponding product strategies, we should note that the interpretation of these theories has proven to be a difficult task in those cases where the theories lack specificity in terms of the typology of product strategies. The position adopted here is to interpret the theories in their main, or most likely sense, rather than in a loose sense. Consequently, depending on their specificity, some theories are interpreted as corresponding to one specific product strategy, others to a few product strategies, and still others to a large subset, or in one case to the entire feasible set defined in the typology. To repeat, the important aspect of this discussion is to appraise the relevance and comprehensiveness of the typology.

Theory of International Capital Movements

The theory of international capital movements was first developed to explain portfolio investments but later was applied to direct investments. It views PFDI as a transfer of capital that is motivated by international differences in yields of assets. A criticism of the theory is that it does not adequately explain why there is a difference in behavior between portfolio investment and PFDI. At present, direct investment accounts for 75 percent of the private capital outflows of the leading industrial nations[12] compared with less than 10 percent in 1914. Table 3.6 illustrates this in the case of the United States.

In the table it can be seen that from 1946 to 1970 U.S. long-term portfolio investment abroad increased fivefold while direct investment abroad increased tenfold. Furthermore, in 1970 the United States was a net exporter of direct investment by $64.9 billion while it was a net importer of portfolio investment of $6.9 billion. Such opposing capital movements cannot be entirely explained by the interest rate theory. The existence of risk and uncertainty, however, make cross-movements likely.

A number of additional factors weaken the explanatory power of the portfolio theory. First, PFDI can occur without any net international transfer of capital but not without a net flow of equity capital. Second, PFDI is not concentrated in particular countries as the portfolio theory would imply, but rather in particular industries. Third, the distribution of assets and liabilities of the U.S. multi-

TABLE 3.6

International Investment Position of the United States in Selected Years, 1914–70
(billions of dollars at year end)

Position	1914	1919	1930	1939	1946	1957	1965	1970
Total U.S. investments abroad	3.5	7.0	17.2	11.4	18.7	54.2	106.6	155.5
Private	3.5	7.0	17.2	11.4	13.5	36.8	81.6	119.9
Long-term	3.5	6.5	15.2	10.8	12.3	33.6	71.4	104.7
Direct	2.6	3.9	8.0	7.0	7.2	25.3	49.5	78.1
Portfolio	0.9	2.6	7.2	3.8	5.1	8.3	21.9	26.6
Short-term	--	0.5	2.0	0.6	1.3	3.2	10.2	15.2
U.S. government	--	--	--	--	5.2	17.4	25.0	35.6
Total foreign investments in the								
United States	7.2	4.0	8.4	9.6	15.9	31.4	58.8	97.5
Long-term	6.7	3.2	5.7	6.3	7.0	12.8	28.3	46.7
Direct	1.3	0.9	1.4	2.0	2.5	4.8	8.8	13.2
Portfolio	5.4	2.3	4.3	4.3	4.5	8.0	19.5	33.5
Short-term	0.5	0.8	2.7	3.3	8.9	18.5	30.6	50.7
U.S. net creditor position	-3.7	3.0	8.8	1.8	2.8	22.8	47.7	58.1
Net long-term	-3.2	3.3	9.5	4.5	10.3	36.3	63.3	87.7
Net short-term	-0.5	-0.3	-0.7	-2.7	-7.4	-13.5	-15.6	-29.6

Source: U.S. Department of Commerce, Survey of Current Business (Washington, D.C.: Government Printing Office, various issues).

national firms are such that the liabilities are mostly in the rest of
the world whereas marketable securities and cash are mostly in the
United States, contrary to the fact that interest rates are high in the
United States. Fourth, cross-investments often occur within indus-
tries--for example, similar industries in Europe and the United
States do invest abroad, even in each other's territories, as it were![13]

    The weaknesses of the portfolio theory cited above show the lack
of understanding of the true nature of these investments abroad. A
related hypothesis suggested by Richard Caves is that net flows of
direct investment move from countries well endowed with equity capital, to those poorly endowed, although he then notes:

> Yet a superficial review of the evidence hardly un-
> covers compelling support: capital seems to flow
> toward high profit countries (or industries, at
> least), but the countries which export large flows
> are not obviously low-profit areas. One should
> not prejudge a test of the capital-abundance hypoth-
> esis before it has been performed, but reference
> to the role of the international corporation would
> at least render its failure unsurprising.[14]

    It is sufficient to say that this theory, whatever its particular
form, has not grasped several of the important characteristics of
the foreign investment phenomenon. The transfer of capital is not,
as thought initially, the critical variable; rather other components
of the package such as entrepreneurship and technological or other
productive knowledge appear to determine its form. Capital is only
an accompanying variable. In terms of the typology the theory is
not of great interest because it does not guide one to any particular
move or preferred product strategy. Any product strategy may be
consistent with a move in response to higher profitability abroad.

Theory of Imperfect International
Transfer of Know-how

    The characteristic of PFDI singled out in the theory of im-
perfect international transfer of know-how[15] is the distinctive competence or know-how possessed by the investing firm that gives it an
edge over its competitors. The advantage may be in the form of
administrative know-how or technological know-how and is necessary
to permit the firm to develop new markets overseas. But the existence of these advantages is not a sufficient condition for the establishment of production facilities abroad. The firm will do so only if

exporting and licensing agreements are insufficient means of extracting a rent. According to Caves:

> Here is the link to the basis for direct investment:
> the successful firm producing a differentiated prod-
> uct controls knowledge about serving the market that
> can be transferred to other national markets for this
> product at little or no cost. This is clearly so for
> the patented good or product embodying a particu-
> larly apt bundle of traits.[16]

The alternative of licensing a foreign producer may yield an
adequate return to the innovator in cases where it is a one-shot innovation, where this innovation has a short life and can be imitated
easily, and where an acceptable partner can be found. Where the
value of the patent cannot be fully recovered by the innovator foreign
investment is likely to take place.[17]
    The advantages enjoyed by the firm that makes a direct in-
vestment must be strong enough to compensate for its initial lack of
knowledge about economic, social, and legal conditions in the foreign market and be protected relatively well from entry by competitors.[18] Empirical evidence for U.S. MNFs in manufacturing
appears to be consistent with this theory: (1) the industries that
spend a large percentage of their sales on research and development
export a high percentage of sales and are high investors abroad (see
Table 3.7); (2) the industries that sell differentiated products (using
as an index of product differentiation the advertising-to-sales ratio)
are high investors abroad.[19]
    In terms of our typology of product strategies this theory is
consistent with the subset of strategies that start with state   S1
(Kp, Mp, Pp) and end up with state S4 (Kp, Mh, Ph).

The International Product Cycle Theory

The international product cycle theory[20] was developed to explain the pattern of international trade and investment of the United
States. The model considers the evolution of a product in terms of
technology, capital intensity, and industry structure and is presented
in Figure 3.1. The international product cycle stems from a number of factors including leads and lags in demand in various countries, tariffs and transportation costs, problems of communication,
and diseconomies in the external sector.

TABLE 3.7

Research Effort and World Performance by U.S. Industries, in Terms of
Exports and Foreign Direct Investments, 1962

Industry and SIC Number	Research and Development Intensity	Export Performance (as percentage of sale)	Sales by Direct Foreign Investments ($1,000)
Transportation (37)	10.0	5.5	7,960
Aircraft (372)	27.2	8.4	--
Other than aircraft	2.8	4.2	--
Electrical machinery (36)	7.3	4.1	3,220
Instruments (38)	7.1	6.7	--
Chemicals (28)	3.9	6.2	4,245
Drugs (283)	4.4	6.0	--
Chemicals (other than drugs)	3.8	6.2	--
Machines (nonelectrical) (35)	3.2	13.3	3,311
Rubber and plastic (30)	1.4	2.0	1,367
Stone, clay, and glass (32)	1.1	1.9	--
Petroleum and coal (29)	0.9	1.2	--
Fabricated metal (34)	0.8	2.1	2,333
Primary metal (33)	0.6	3.1	--
Nonferrous metal (333)	0.8	4.2	--
Ferrous metal	0.5	2.5	--
Leather (31)	0.6	1.7	--
Printing and publishing (27)	0.6	1.7	--
Tobacco (21)	0.3	2.2	--
Food (20)	0.2	0.9	3,385
Textile (22)	0.2	3.4	--
Furniture and fixtures (25)	0.1	0.7	--
Lumber and wood (24)	0.1	2.0	--
Paper (26)	0.1	2.1	1,160
Apparel (23)	0.1	0.7	--
All 19 industries	2.0	3.2	--
5 industries with highest research effort	6.3	7.2	--
14 other industries	0.5	1.8	--

Note: Industries arranged in descending order of R and D intensity, defined by R and D expenditures as a percentage of sales.

Sources: W. Gruber, D. Mehta, and R. Vernon, "The R and D Factor in International Trade and International Investment of the United States Industries," Journal of Political Economy, February 1967, p. 23; Survey of Current Business, October 1964, p. 11.

FIGURE 3.1

The International Product Cycle Theory

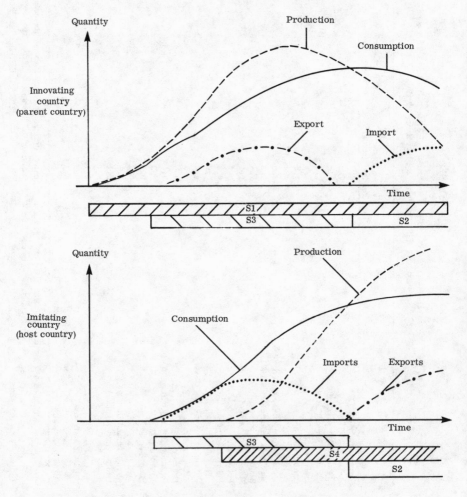

THE INTERNATIONAL PRODUCT CYCLE THEORY

Multinational Product strategy S1-S3-S4-S2

Source: Compiled by the author.

The stages of the international innovation-diffusion sequence for a product innovated in the United States are as follows. First, a new product is developed in response to market needs in the United States stemming from the high personal disposable income and high labor costs characteristic of this country. Entrepreneurs in the United States are first aware of these new wants and this is especially true if there is very effective communication between the potential market and suppliers. The first production site will also be located in the United States not so much because of cost considerations but because of the need at the early stage of development of the product to have continuous communications between those responsible for production and development on one side, and purchasers and suppliers on the other. Some demand develops abroad that will be supplied by export from the United States.

In the maturing product stage demand expands and the most important features of the product become standardized. Concern about production costs and increased foreign demand leads to some production abroad. In this stage the United States is still an exporter but production abroad supplies an increasing share of world demand.

As the product becomes standardized the low cost of production necessary to remain competitive leads the firm to minimize labor costs by moving production to low-wage countries. At this stage the product is imported back into the United States.

The international product cycle theory has gained increased acceptance for application at the microlevel of the firm,[21] yet it is clear that one important class of variables relative to the firm and its experience at home and abroad has not been taken into consideration. The international product cycle emphasizes the product rather than the dynamics of the firm's international growth.

Empirical evidence gathered for the electronics industry by Seev Hirsch[22] (and subsequently by John E. Tilton)[23] is consistent with the theory as outlined above. Hirsch shows that the growth sectors of this industry (that is, government and industrial components and accessories, special purpose tubes) have positive trade balance while the three mature sectors of this industry (consumer products, receiving tubes, cathode ray tubes) show negative trade balance in the balance-of-payments accounts of the United States. A 1971 econometric study on U.S. data compared the explanatory power of various theories of international trade and confirmed "the product cycle as a fairly good general description of the life of products in trade in manufactured goods."[24]

In terms of the typology the international product cycle theory corresponds to the product strategy MPS 27 = S1-S3-S4-S2.

Theory of Industrial Structure

The theory of industrial structure, also known as the oligopoly theory, of foreign investment suggests that the prime motivation for a firm going abroad is "to remove competition between that foreign enterprise and enterprises in other countries."[25] Empirical evidence indicates that large firms predominate among MNFs and more specifically, a few large firms dominate certain industries--the transportation industry, the petroleum industry, and the aluminum industry for example. In such industries centralization of decision making is preferable to independent decision centers and results in "horizontal" or "vertical" investments[26] on an international scale. The few large firms which dominate these industries invariably compete in the same market with the result that independent action of one of the oligopolists generally elicits similar responses from its competitors.[27] The response is termed a follow-the-leader strategy. If, for example, the initiating firm makes an investment in order to bring in lower production costs competitors will match the move.

The oligopoly theory provides, however, neither necessary nor sufficient conditions for direct investment abroad. Not all large firms have invested abroad (this is especially true for firms in the steel, cement, and machine tools industries) and those that have are not necessarily oligopolists. The theory provides a rationale for foreign direct investment for some firms in particular industries, but there the generalization ends. The theory of imperfect transfer of know-how combined with the theory of industrial structure is seen by Caves as providing a better explanation of foreign direct investment. "Oligopoly with product differentiation," he maintains, "normally prevails where corporations make horizontal investments to produce abroad the same line of goods as they produce in the home market."[28]

The interpretation of the oligopoly theory in terms of the product strategy framework is best made by using the distinction above between horizontal and vertical international investments. Horizontal investments as mentioned above, correspond to MPS 1, that is, a sequence including S1 (Kp, Mp, Pp)-S3 (Kp, Mh, Pp)-S4 (Kp, Mh, Ph) as the firm penetrates foreign markets with products it developed in the parent country. The oligopolist may also react by acquiring a competing firm selling a close substitute; this would be strategy MPS 45 = S8 (Kh, Mh, Ph) as the product know-how, market, and production activities of the firm being acquired take place abroad (seen from the acquiring firm point of view). Alternatively the acquiring firm may buy a firm that exports already toward its parent country, that is, MPS 55 = S8 (Kh, Mh, Ph)-S6 (Kh, Mp, Ph). If the

acquired firm produces in the parent country of the acquiring firm
this leads to MPS 51=S8 (Kh, Mh, Ph)-S6 (Kh, Mp, Ph)-S5 (Kh, Mp,
Pp). Vertical international investments, to produce abroad a raw
material or other input to their production process at home, correspond either to the case where the product know-how developed by
the firm in the parent country is transferred abroad and the product
imported back to the parent country, that is, MPS 22 = S1 (Kp, Mp,
Pp)-S2 (Kp, Mp, Ph); or to the development of acquisition of know-
how in the host country, that is, MPS 45 = S8 (Kh, Mh, Ph), or
MPS 55 = S8 (Kh, Mh, Ph)-S6 (Kh, Mp, Ph), or even MPS 51 = S8
(Kh, Mh, Ph)-S6 (Kh, Mp, Ph)-S5 (Kh, Mp, Pp). The product strategies MPS 23 = S2-S1 or MPS 26 = S2 could also be included if one
were using a looser interpretation of the oligopoly theory. That is,
the firm develops know-how in the parent country to produce the
product abroad to be used as an input in its parent country.

Theory of Tariffs and Other Barriers to Trade

Barriers to international movement of goods, such as tariffs,
transportation costs, "buy national" policies, and xenophobic atti-
tudes of consumers, diminish the flow of goods internationally.
There is a body of empirical evidence which indicates that such barriers threaten the market position of a firm and are therefore a
powerful galvanizing force compelling the firm to react.[29] As the
firm generally has committed resources to that market and has
accumulated goodwill, the establishment of a tariff is likely to induce
the firm to react by manufacturing locally. This is particularly so
if the export stage is seen as less than satisfactory in terms of
learning customer needs and after-sale servicing.

The theory of tariffs has nothing per se to say about which
firms will invest abroad, and the form the investment will take: the
exporting firm may license its former agents and depending upon the
nature of the tariff, the firm may build a factory in response to
tariff restrictions. The theory of tariffs has relevance at the macro-
level; it is not a theory of the firm.

The product strategies corresponding to the theory of tariffs
(the know-how originates in country 1, say, and country 2 is the importing country with tariffs) are the subset that includes the sequence of states S3 (Kp, Mh, Pp)-S4 (Kp, Mh, Ph). If the know-how
originates in the country 2 this corresponds to the subset of product
strategies including the sequence of states S5 (Kh, Mp, Pp)-S8 (Kh,
Mh, Ph).

Theory of Currency Areas

According to Robert Aliber, the proponent of the theory of currency areas:

> The key factor in the explanation of the pattern of
> direct investment is that the world is divided into
> different currency areas and that there is a bias
> in the market's estimate of exchange risk. The
> bias in the evaluation of the exchange risk deter-
> mines whether a country is likely to be a source
> country or a host country for foreign investment.[30]

Separate currency areas mean that interest rates on similar assets denominated in different currencies may differ because exchange rates may change. Source country firms are those able to capitalize a given stream of expected earnings at a higher rate than a host country firm. Because of the currency premium, host country firms may issue debt denominated in the currency of the source country. The reader may note that there is a strong parallel between this theory and the theory of the capital movements where the source country is the supplier of capital. We saw in the theory of capital movements that only a small amount of the capital necessary for the operations of U.S. MNFs is sourced in the United States.

For Aliber a currency premium is a necessary but not sufficient condition to explain the pattern of foreign investment: "The second element in the hypothesis is that the market applies a higher capitalization rate to the same income stream generated in the host country when received by a source country firm than by a host-country firm."[31]

This bias in the market gives an edge to MNFs. But why is that so? Why do MNFs perform this role of financial intermediaries and substitute for the financial institutions themselves? Aliber attempts to answer this question when he argues that the source country firm might be more efficient in hedging the exchange risk,[32] and it might provide the investor with a diversified portfolio at a lower cost than he could acquire on his own. The investor might also be ignorant of the share of earnings coming from abroad. It may well be the case that MNFs are truly superior to purely financial institutions but as banks and other financial institutions have followed the multinational trend, it is difficult to accept the argument that the strength of the MNFs is solely a financial one.

Financial theories of direct investment such as the currency areas theory of Aliber do not appear to go to the heart of the matter. A currency is preferred because it belongs to a strong economy, which means that it also has a high level of foreign currency reserves and a healthy balance of payments. These attributes characterize an economy with comparative strength vis-a-vis other countries. But we noted that industries which were highly competitive in terms of export potential were technology intensive. Therefore a theory of currency areas is not directed at the true cause of strength of an economy, but rather at one of its consequences, a strong currency.

Notwithstanding these drawbacks, a link between this theory and the typology can be made. The currency area theory postulates that as the market grows the firm will shift from export to foreign investment to serve the market; we now obtain the traditional sequence S1 (Kp, Mp, Pp)-S3 (Kp, Mh, Pp)-S4 (Kp, Mh, Ph). However, other moves are feasible as Aliber claims that his theory also explains foreign take-overs and thus it is consistent with any of the product strategies made up of states S5 to S8.

Matching Product Strategies and Investment Theories

This discussion of the literature on the motives that lie behind the level and pattern of foreign direct investment indicates that managers of MNFs perceive their decision to be influenced by numerous factors. In the first group of studies cited above we saw that the most important factors are, from the managers' view, the tariff barriers and other environmental constraints that "forced them" to invest abroad, that is, in terms of our typology to move from state S3 (Kp, Mh, Pp) to state S4 (Kp, Mh, Ph). This move has not been studied from the broader point of view of the strategy of expansion of the firm, a point to which we address ourselves in this research.

The second group of studies cited, the theories of PFDI, focus on one or a few specific aspects of the firm or the environment. The results of the interpretation of these theories in terms of the typology noted above show that the typology adequately covers the variety of moves corresponding to the theories. We did not encounter any case falling outside the feasible set defined in the typology of multinational product strategies.

This discussion also reveals that the theories vary a great deal in their specificity in terms of our framework. In some cases broad subsets of product strategies are consistent with one theory, in a few others a theory identifies a product strategy, or a few of them in particular. One theory dealing with the international capital movements is consistent with the entire set of feasible strategies in the typology. Some theories like the theory of tariffs, or the theory of imperfect international transfer of know-how (excluding the international product cycle theory), specify some intermediate steps in the product strategy (for example, the move from state S3 [Kp, Mh, Pp] to state S4 [Kp, Mh, Ph]). This is because many theories look at one particular step in the expansion of the firm, but not, say, an earlier step such as production for the parent country market. Finally, a last group of theories, the theory of industrial structure and of the international product cycle, are well specified as they identify a precise multinational product strategy. From our point of view one would have hoped that more theories were specific. In view of the lack of specificity of many of the theories it is difficult to isolate the subset of product strategies that were included as part of the feasible set identified in the typology but were not referred to in the PFDI theories. Rather it is the objective of the remainder of our research to show that MNFs implement a great variety of multinational product strategies some of which were not adequately specified in the literature on foreign direct investment. One particular subset that received little attention in the literature corresponds to multinational product strategies whose know-how originates in the host country. We shall pay particular attention to this.

The following empirical study will therefore not only establish the shortcomings of the theories as they apply to an individual firm's behavior but it will also indicate the firm's rationale for following a variety of strategies we will encounter in the subsequent chapters.

NOTES

1. E. R. Barlow and Ira Wender, Foreign Investment and Taxation (Englewood Cliffs, N.J.: Prentice-Hall, 1955), p. 147.

2. Ibid., p. 444.

3. Ibid., p. 432.

4. Endel J. Kolde, International Business Enterprise (Englewood Cliffs, N.J.: Prentice-Hall, 1968), p. 233.

5. Jack N. Behrman, "Foreign Associates and Their Financing," in U.S. Private and Government Investment Abroad, ed. Raymond Mikesell (Eugene: University of Oregon Press, 1962), pp. 77-112.

6. Raghbir S. Basi, Determinants of United States Private Direct Investment in Foreign Countries (Kent, Ohio: Bureau of Business and Economic Research, Kent State University, 1963).

7. Michael Z. Brooke and H. Lee Remmers, The Strategy of Multinational Enterprise: Organization and Finance (London: Longman, 1970), p. 224.

8. Yair Aharoni, The Foreign Investment Decision Process (Boston: Harvard University, Graduate School of Business Administration, 1966), p. 42.

9. Brooke and Remmers, op. cit., p. 224.

10. This distinction is made in Edith T. Penrose, "Foreign Investment and the Growth of the Firm," Economic Journal 66 (June 1956): 220-35.

11. Ibid.; the linking of foreign investment and a firm's strategy for growth was first carried in this work.

12. International Monetary Fund, Balance of Payments Yearbook, vol. 21, 1970.

13. These criticisms of the portfolio theory as an explanation of PFDI were made by Stephen Hymer in "The International Operations of National Firms: a Study of Direct Foreign Investment" (Ph.D. diss., Massachusetts Institute of Technology, 1960), pp. 17-22.

14. Richard E. Caves, "International Corporations: The Industrial Economics of Foreign Investment," Economica, February 1971, p. 4.

15. Hymer, in op. cit., appears to be the first to develop this theory, followed by C. P. Kindelberger, in American Business Abroad (New Haven: Yale University Press, 1969), and Harry G. Johnson, "The Efficiency and Welfare Implication," in The International Corporation, ed. C. P. Kindelberger (Cambridge: MIT Press, 1970), pp. 35-56.

16. Caves, op. cit., p. 6.

17. On this question of licensing versus foreign investment, see Jack Baranson, "Technology Transfer Through the International Firm," American Economic Review, May 1970; and R. F. Mikesell, ed., U.S. Private and Government Investment Abroad (Eugene: University of Oregon Press, 1962).

18. J. S. Bain, Barriers to New Competition (Cambridge: Harvard University Press, 1956). Bain's analysis devoted to the advantages that established firms have relative to new firms is applicable to the advantages possessed by firms of one country relative to another.

19. For some figures on this question see Raymond Vernon, Sovereignty at Bay (New York: Basic Books, 1971), p. 9. A differentiated product is a collection of functionally similar goods produced by competing sellers, but with each seller's product distinguishable from its rivals by minor physical variations--brand name and subjective distinction created by advertising.

20. This theory was first proposed by M. V. Posner in "International Trade and Technical Change," Oxford Economic Papers, October 1961, in order to explain trade caused by the existence of some technical know-how in one country, not available elsewhere--independent of the classical causes of trade in terms of comparative cost differences. This led to empirical research by a number

of authors: G. C. Hufbauer, Synthetic Materials and the Theory of International Trade (Boston: Harvard University Press, 1966); Seev Hirsch, "The United States Electronic Industry in International Trade," National Institute Economic Review, no. 5, November 1965. This research led to a more precise definition of the concept of the international product cycle by Raymond Vernon, in "International Investment and International Trade in the Product Cycle," Quarterly Journal of Economics, May 1966; and in William Gruber, Dileep Mehta, and Raymond Vernon, "The R and D Factor in International Investment of the United States Industries," Journal of Political Economy, February 1967. And a further test was made in Louis T. Wells, "Test of a Product Cycle Model of International Trade:U.S. Exports of Consumer Durables," Quarterly Journal of Economics, February 1969.

21. An example of the widespread acceptance of this theory as a prescription for business firms can be found in Warren J. Keegan Multinational Marketing Management (Englewood Cliffs, N.J.: Prentice-Hall, 1974), p. 218: "A new approach to international trade that offers promise to business executives concerned with formulating a long range product strategy is closely related to the product life cycle concept in marketing. The trade cycle model suggests that many products go through a cycle. . ." (emphasis added).

22. Seev Hirsch, "The United States Electronics Industry in International Trade," National Institute Economic Review, no. 5 (1965): 92-97.

23. John E. Tilton, International Diffusion of Technology: The Case of Semi-Conductors (Washington, D.C.: The Brookings Institution, 1971).

24. William H. Branson and Helen B. Junz, Brookings Papers on Economic Activity 2 (1971). The measure of the "age" of a good used here is the date at which this particular seven digit SITC category first appeared in the export schedule.

25. Hymer, op. cit., p. 24.

26. Caves, op. cit., p. 10.

27. Frederick T. Knickerbocker, Oligopolistic Reaction and Multinational Enterprise (Boston: Harvard University Press, 1973).

28. See Caves, op. cit., pp. 1-6. He speaks of differentiated product, a notion that differs somewhat from know-how. In certain cases some forms of know-how such as process innovations may not create differentiation in the consumer's mind. And some differentiation may be created by promotion that is not reflected in the product.

29. The notion of defensive investment is developed in Yair Aharoni, op. cit., p. 64, and in J. Polk, W. Meister, and L. Veit,

U.S. Production Abroad and the Balance of Payment: A Survey of
Corporate Investment Experience (New York: National Industrial
Conference Board, 1966), pp. 43-52.

30. Robert Z. Aliber, "A Theory of Direct Foreign Investment," in The International Corporation, ed. C. P. Kindelberger,
op. cit., p. 34.

31. Ibid., p. 30.

32. Robert Z. Aliber, "The Multinational Enterprise in a
Multiple Currency World," in The Multinational Enterprise, ed.
John Dunning (London: George Allen and Unwin, 1970), pp. 49-56.

II

MULTINATIONAL
PRODUCT STRATEGIES:
THE BEHAVIOR
OF FIVE FIRMS

4

THE EMPIRICAL STUDY: OBJECTIVES AND METHODOLOGY

OBJECTIVES

In the early stage of this research, it was judged that the empirical study would be designed only for an empirical test of the typology, that is to say, the observation of as many different types of product strategies as possible. The validation of the typology (its power) is to a great extent a function of how many of these product strategies are encountered (that is, the observed set), relative to the total set identified in the typology (that is, the feasible set).

Ideally, this should be done by first identifying a number of products corresponding to a large spectrum of product strategies, complemented by an in-depth study of a sample of cases. The first part would have required the sending out of a mail questionnaire that was simple enough to be answered by a large number of MNF executives. Such a questionnaire could have listed the set of product strategies, and asked them to give an example of products where that product strategy was used. In a second stage, some of these products would be selected for further analysis. This approach was rejected for a number of reasons. First, the list of product strategies (see Appendix A) included 56 product strategies (36 of them would be relevant for a firm whose parent country is considered a high-cost producer), and it would require careful analysis on a manager's part to thoroughly grasp the meaning of each of these. Secondly, it would have required quite extensive funding and a great deal of time to analyze the selected products further as they would belong to a variety of firms. Finally, as we hypothesized that firm characteristics play an important role in determining the pattern of the product strategies, each firm responsible for a product would have required extensive study, involving a task exceeding the time and financial limits of this work.

Instead, the approach selected consists of first choosing the firms to be investigated and then studying the general pattern of their product strategies. It is further complemented by an in-depth study of the product strategies of a selected number of their products. The five firms chosen were selected so as to maximize the chances of uncovering a wide variety of product strategies, especially those that were not specified adequately in Chapter 3.

This empirical study is therefore one of an exploratory nature, the objective being first to test the typology by classifying the product strategies observed and second, to explore a manager's rationale for preferring one product strategy over another. The second objective is a difficult one to tackle. Any research that studies the rationale for decision making is confronted with a multiplicity of factors that are taken into account, compounded in many cases by the limited rationality of the decision maker himself when faced with complexity. Nevertheless, no previous studies have been done for a large number of the product strategies, and the studies relating to classic product strategies have not been focusing on a manager's rationale from a product or firm point of view; rather they looked at the behavior of the firm in response to host country environment. * It is necessary then, in the first stage, to determine the sort of variables that have influenced the choice of a particular product strategy. It is hoped that the generation of a list of such factors will make a sizable contribution in itself.

One a priori hypothesis has been formulated relating to why the diversity of product strategies implemented now might be greater than in the early years of the multinational era. That is, the experience of the firm has, we thought, likely played an important role in determining the selection of product strategies by that firm. Therefore, the study of the growth process of the firm is a crucial step in this inquiry.

The presentation of the empirical findings takes the following two-pronged approach: first, for each of the five firms in the sample, a profile of their evolution through time is presented including the main product strategies for each of their product lines; secondly, this profile is complemented by a detailed study of a selected number of products for each firm using a product questionnaire developed for that purpose. The results presented in Chapters 6 and 7 show the variety of product strategies implemented by the five MNFs selected

---

*By country environment we mean that the variables looked at were among others the stability of the host country's foreign exchange reserves, tax structure, and availability of raw materials. Chapter 3 presents a number of examples of this sort.

and provide a list of variables that lead managers to select a given product strategy. In addition, the sample is used to derive propositions relating product strategies to a number of variables that influence the manager's choice.

THE SELECTION OF THE FIRMS

Two criteria were used in selecting the firms. First, a broad range of product strategies was sought and secondly, we wanted to pay particular attention to the product strategies where the know-how originates in the host country.

In the absence of any knowledge about the pattern of product strategies likely to be implemented by a firm, we selected firms having characteristics as diverse as possible. This appeared to be the best way to fulfill our first objective of encountering a broad range of product strategies. On an a priori basis, the characteristics that were thought to be relevant were the types of products manufactured--either consumer or industrial goods--the size of the firm, the length of experience as an MNF, the percentage of sales outside the parent country, the type of industry in terms of R and D intensity, and the policy of the firm toward R and D (that is, by acquisition or internal development).

We achieved our second objective by selecting firms that we knew had developed some products in host countries. For the U.S. or Canadian MNFs it means that they had R and D capability in Europe mainly, and in some other host countries. As Appendix B shows, a number of examples of firms that have made such types of moves could be gleaned from the literature.

We decided to choose firms from the manufacturing sector exclusively and select products that could be classified as final products, or components thereof, for the firm. Excluded, then, are intermediary products such as machinery used in a production process, or management know-how. The simplifications were believed desirable to minimize problems of identifying know-how elements.

A practical constraint was also added. Due to financial limitations and availability of information, qualifying firms had to be U.S.- or Canadian-based so that numerous interviews could be arranged at reasonable cost. Experience with the first firms selected showed that each firm required a large investment in time in order to fully understand its operations and thus it would not be feasible to interview more than four or five firms.

The five firms finally selected on the basis of these criteria are presented in Table 4.1. Together the companies chosen represent a fair spectrum of MNF types. The smallest firm, Dymo

TABLE 4.1

Main Characteristics of Firms Selected for Study

Firm	Type of Goods Manufactured	Worldwide Sales Volume, 1972 ($ million)	Length of Experience Outside Parent Country (year[s] international division was set up)	Research and Development (R & D)		
				Corporate R & D as Percent of Sales	Percent of R & D Outlays Outside Parent Country	Internal Development or Acquisition
Alcan*	Aluminum products mainly (industrial goods)	1,456	1930s	1.7	27.0 outside North America	Development in smelting and acquisitions in fabricating
Gillette	Razors, toiletries, appliances (consumer goods)	870	1920s	2.6	32.0	Primarily acquisitions
Hewlett-Packard	Electronic instruments (industrial goods)	480	1959	9.2	3.0	Primarily development
Dymo Industries	Visual communication: labeling, marking (industrial and consumer goods)	94	1964	3.0	Not available	Development and acquisitions
Massey-Ferguson*	Agricultural, industrial, and construction machinery (industrial goods)	1,200	1908	2.5	50.0 outside North America	Acquisitions

*Has its headquarters in Canada (that is, Canada is the parent country).

Source: Compiled by the author.

Industries, has sales of less than $100 million while the largest,
Alcan, had sales of a billion-and-a-half dollars in 1972. All are
heavily oriented toward international markets, deriving a minimum
of 40 percent of their sales from outside their parent country. Two
of the firms, Hewlett-Packard and Dymo Industries, have gone
abroad since 1959; two others, Gillette and Massey-Ferguson, have
been multinational since the 1920s. At least one is a high-technology
firm (Hewlett-Packard) while two others (Alcan and Massey-Ferguson)
can be classified as low-technology firms in terms of the ratio of R
and D expenses to sales. Some have diversified by acquisition
(Massey-Ferguson); others (Hewlett-Packard) have made few acquisitions to increase their technological know-how. These firms, as
indicated above, are all based in North America; three have the
United States as their parent country; two are of Canadian parentage,
one of which, Alcan, is of U.S. descent.

THE SELECTION OF PRODUCTS AND
PRODUCT STRATEGIES

After grasping the broad characteristics and developments in
the various product lines within each of the firms we decided, with
the aid of the appropriate manager, which products should be studied
in detail. In most cases, the manager concerned was the international marketing director, or the product manager with international
or worldwide responsibility, or the international product coordinator.
The following criteria were used in selecting the products. First,
the product had to be old enough to be at the end of its life cycle so
that one could observe all the stages of its cycle; for some firms
such as Hewlett-Packard the product's life averages five years; for
others (Massey-Ferguson), eight to ten years with a midlife upgrade;
or 20 years, as with the Ferguson transaxle. Secondly, the manager
concerned had to be familiar enough with that product to be able to
answer the questionnaire.

Our selected group of products is voluntarily biased. The first
bias is toward products that have major know-how components that
are identifiable; minor product changes were of little interest. The
second bias is toward products that have been transferred internationally, that is, they are either exported or produced with imported
know-how.

It will be recalled that the typology of product strategies presented in Chapter 2 involves a two-country world. We will now show
how the typology has been operationalized to allow its application in
a world with many countries.

In the two-country typology the parent country is determined automatically by the country of headquarters of the firm and the host country is in fact not a single country but rather encompasses the entire rest of the world (ROW). Obviously the host country is very heterogeneous in terms of culture, politics, and socioeconomic factors. This variety in the ROW's environment has a bearing on the type of product strategy actually selected by a firm. This means that a very detailed study of product strategies would have to break down the ROW into its component countries demanding far too much of the managers' time and yielding only marginal benefits for the purpose of our study. As a realistic compromise we selected a number of geographic areas which were believed to provide the researcher with a fair spectrum of product strategies. In order to accomplish this, the ROW (or the host country) was broken down into the United States, Canada, Europe, Latin America, Australia, and Japan. The grouping of European countries together and Latin America as a bloc, however crude it may look, corresponds in most cases to the way the MNFs studied have organized their international departmentalization.

The breakdown of the host country into a number of areas has some important consequences for the study. First, we are not limited to one product strategy for a given product; several product strategies for each product may occur. Each product strategy has as its initial state the first state of the product, and the sequence of states that were encountered when the product was diffused in another geographic area or country. If the product is diffused in more than one geographic area, more than one product strategy is implemented for that product. For example, product 1 of Alcan (as presented in Chapter 5) has S1 as its first state as it was developed in Canada, the parent country, and produced and marketed there first. It was diffused in Europe initially by export (state S3) and later was produced in Europe (state S4). The product strategy Canada-Europe is therefore MPS 1 = S1-S3-S4. In a similar manner, the product strategy Canada-Japan is MPS 1 = S1-S3-S4. If the product had been only exported to the United States the product strategy Canada-United States would have been MPS 7 = S1(Kp, Mp, Pp)-S3 (Kp, Mh, Pp). Hence there are, in fact, two strategies for this Alcan product. Another important consequence of the breakdown of the host country into a number of countries is that it biases the type of product strategy encountered toward repeated use of the product strategy MPS 45 = S8 (Kh, Mh, Ph). This is so because any trade between two host countries is designated by S8. An example of this bias is given (in Chapter 5) with product 11 of Massey-Ferguson. Produced in Italy initially, this product was first introduced into the European market by production in Europe (that is, state S8 [Kh, Mh, Ph]). It was later introduced in the United States (that is, state S8 as Italy and the

United States are two host countries). The product strategy Europe-United States is therefore S8 as is the product strategy Europe-Australia, and Europe-Latin America. The strategy Europe-Canada for this product is MPS 55 = S8 (Kh, Mh, Ph)-S6 (Kh, Mp, Ph) as it involves Canada, the parent country of Massey-Ferguson.

These two examples indicate the reasoning behind the product strategy assignment for the products to be investigated in Chapter 5.

THE CONSTRUCTION OF THE INTERVIEW GUIDES

The general information on the growth of the firms selected for this study was obtained through annual reports, articles, and publications of the particular firms, complemented by interviews using as a guide the general firm questionnaire (see Appendix C). This was a relatively long task but by and large presented no major obstacles.

The construction of the product questionnaire (Appendix D) to guide the inquiry regarding specific products was of a more difficult nature. Preliminary interviews with managers led to the development of a product questionnaire that was readapted several times to meet new circumstances encountered in the various firms. This is particularly important and cannot be avoided in an exploratory study. It was found that in the initial questionnaire, competition was a posteriori not looked at carefully enough. When interviews revealed that it had a marked effect on the product strategy selected, the number of questions related to competition was increased. We had to determine timing and location of competition. An average intensity of competition was not enough. This may still leave the market researcher unsatisfied as various other aspects of competition could have been looked at. However, this would have necessitated reducing the time spent on investigating other matters and would have increased the difficulty of reaching the properly informed manager. Our objective here is to get an overall view of the variables affecting the selection of product strategies. In-depth study of any one of them is left for further research.

Broadly speaking, in order to gain an understanding of managers' rationale for choosing a particular product strategy we were led to inquire into the main features of the product in terms of technology, performance, the nature and origin of product specifications; the policy of the firm toward product standardization; the characteristics of the demand; the nature of competition; the characteristics of the production process.

As the characteristics of the firm had been probed earlier, we did further research on the firm per se only as regards particularly relevant aspects such as the planning for a particular product.

We chose to compare product strategies of firms that are believed to have little in common, such as Massey-Ferguson, Gillette, and Alcan, to cite only those three. This could be achieved only by using indexes, measurements that cut across all of these firms. We know from the literature that, for example, the decision of the firm to export or to manufacture a product in the host countries is related to a number of variables, among them the level of demand, tariff rates, the intrinsic ability of the product to be traded, and economies of scale in production. To measure these variables, economists have used indexes to compare various products based on objective measures in monetary and real terms, such as capital-to-output ratios. But these measures were unavailable for many of the characteristics that interest us, and managers might not know the figures, or would want to keep them confidential. It has been my experience that asking managers to give a precise figure takes a lot of time that could be more profitably spent on gaining an understanding of their operations. Therefore substitute indexes had to be developed to do so.

It was felt necessary to make a number of assumptions in order to facilitate this development. First, as noted above, it is assumed the manager has a good understanding of the various product lines in his firm and is able to make comparisons among them. Therefore our point of reference is his firm rather than the average of the firms in the industry or some other external point of reference. Second, subjective indexes in the form of a semantic differential judgment of a phenomenon are sufficient for this exploratory study. That is why a question such as the following is asked: How do you rank the labor intensity of the production process for this product relative to other products of your firm--high, medium, low?

The interviews were conducted in the spring and summer months of 1973 and 1974. The initial interview was usually conducted with the international marketing director and was devoted to an overview of the main activities of the firm in terms of products and markets. As the information in the product questionnaire requires that it be administered to managers who were in close contact with the life of the product, further interviews were arranged with product managers with worldwide responsibility (or those knowledgeable in international operations), or with international product coordinators.

5

THE PATTERN
OF MULTINATIONAL
PRODUCT STRATEGIES,
BY FIRM

This chapter deals with the five firms we studied, their product lines and a selection of products from those lines. The objective
of the analysis is to present the growth of these firms, particularly
as it relates to the evolution of the variety of multinational product
strategies each of them employed. The analysis of the variety of
multinational product strategies implemented altogether by the five
firms is contained in Chapters 6 and 7.

In order to grasp the dynamics of the firm, we present each of
the major phases of the firm's growth in terms of product diversification and international commitments, in addition to providing an understanding for these moves.

These firms are well known ones; this enables us to limit the
presentation to the events and management decisions that are viewed
as having a most important impact on the strategy to be selected.
Despite the fact that some of the firms are relatively new internationally there emerges, from each of them, a profile characteristic
of their international growth.

Each of the firms we have chosen markets a tremendous variety
of products, and it is beyond the scope of this study to make a definitive statement on the product strategy employed for each and every
product. We therefore are forced to obtain an adequate coverage of
the firm's behavior by analyzing its general pattern of multinational
product strategies with a reduced set of data--data specific to product lines. This broad coverage of the strategies has been complemented in each firm by our analysis of a selected number of specific
products of the firm's line. The product strategy for a given product
line corresponds to the one used most often. There are variations
around that trend that we picked up by focusing on specific products.
The data by product line are a better index of the frequency, the data

by products a better index of the variety of product strategies. The
selected products and their corresponding strategies are presented
as a table for each firm; while both sets of data are presented in this
chapter, most attention is paid here to the evolution of the general
pattern of product strategies.

HEWLETT-PACKARD COMPANY

The Hewlett-Packard Company is a young and dynamic MNF
founded in 1939 when William R. Hewlett and David Packard successfully designed such instruments as an electronic harmonica tuner and
a resistance capacity oscillator that was bought by Walt Disney for
his movie Fantasia. Hewlett-Packard is now the world's largest
manufacturer of precision electronic measuring instruments with
worldwide sales amounting to three-quarters of a billion dollars.
    The firm's leadership in the field of electronic measuring in-
struments was achieved through high engineering skills in close contact with the market needs. Hewlett-Packard spends 10 percent of
its sales revenues on R and D. These R and D expenditures are used
first to diversify Hewlett-Packard activity into other electronic ap-
plications covering a broad range of fields including instruments and
systems for chemical research and medicine, agriculture, communications, and the growing field of electronic computation[1] (Hewlett-
Packard entered some of these fields by buying out a number of small
U.S. companies as can be seen in Table 5.1). Secondly, the firm
spends part of its R and D to develop components for its products in
order to insure a quality edge over its competitors. It now has several divisions for exclusive development of proprietary components
such as solid-state devices, integrated circuits, and hybrid micro-
circuitry (instruments cannot be patented but the uniqueness of some
of the components can make imitation by competitors difficult).
    Presently Hewlett-Packard operations are organized into four
product groups with the following sales breakdown:

Group	Percent of Total Sales
Electronics products	50
Data products	35
Medical electronics	10
Chemical analysis	5

TABLE 5.1

Hewlett-Packard Co.--Chronology of the Main Acquisitions

Year	Acquisition
1956	Dymec Inc. (U.S.): a firm specializing in radar simulators and digital data systems.
1958	F. L. Moseley Company (U.S.): a manufacturer of high quality graphic recorders used in many applications with Hewlett-Packard instruments.
1959	Boonton Radio Corporation (U.S.): prominent manufacturer of instruments to test electronic circuit quality.
1961	Sanborn Company (U.S.): manufacturer of medical diagnosis apparatus and precision instruments.
1961	Harrison Laboratories (U.S.): manufacturer of top quality power supplies.
1964	Mechrolab Inc. (U.S.): manufacturer of vapor pressure and automatic membrane-type osmometers.
1964	International Control Machines (U.S.): firm specializing in the development of data handling systems.
1965	Datamec Corporation (U.S.): manufacturer of digital magnetic tape units and other electrochemical equipment.
1965	F and M (U.S.): a highly respected manufacturer of gas chromatographs.
1972	Vertek (U.S.): a small medical electronics company specializing in pulmonary test equipment.

Source: Hewlett-Packard, Annual Report, various issues.

International Growth

The origin of Hewlett-Packard's international activity goes back to the late 1940s when the company began selling a few of its products outside the United States. Over the next several years, international orders grew to the point where they reached 10 percent of sales volume in the late 1950s. At that point, Hewlett-Packard decided to commit more resources to its international activity, especially in Europe, which resulted in a marked increase of international orders reaching $100 million in 1969. International sales have doubled since then to a point where they now account for over 40

percent of total sales. About three-fourths of this international
sales volume represents exports from the firm's American factories.[2]

Due to the fact that Hewlett-Packard products are highly
sophisticated industrial products, demand abroad is still largely
concentrated in a few developed European countries which accounted
for close to 70 percent of international sales in 1972. Japan and
Canada account for most of the balance.

The Export Stage

Hewlett-Packard's European involvement has been selected to
illustrate the steps followed by the company through this export
stage.[3] Initially exports to Europe were handled through local export agents. With increased activities, this distribution method was
no longer appropriate and Hewlett-Packard took over the direct contact of these representatives who were to become the backbone of its
international marketing organization. It viewed the forming of the
European Economic Community (EEC) as creating an opportunity for
European competition which would threaten its position in this important market. It responded in 1959 with a European marketing
headquarters in Geneva and a wholly owned field sales organization
plus its first manufacturing subsidiary outside the United States.

The nature of the threat posed by the formation of the EEC can
be understood when the distinctive advantages that Hewlett-Packard
enjoyed over its European competitors become known. One can
classify Hewlett-Packard's products into two categories: products
that are basically an assembly of standard component parts that competitors can duplicate, and products that require a great many special and precision parts which need expensive and extensive tooling
and hence require a large and significant market. The formation of
one European mass market can give rise to a large instrumentation
company which, viewing the European market as a whole (a viewpoint
Hewlett-Packard held from the start) would be capable of competing
with Hewlett-Packard for products of the second category.

Establishment of Production
Facilities Abroad

To forestall this diverting of trade and to avoid the subsequent
loss of its competitive advantage, the decision was made to begin
manufacturing in the Common Market, and a German factory was established in 1959. Soon thereafter the United Kingdom increased
duties on electronic measurement products, thereby eroding the
Hewlett-Packard position in that market. This led the company to

its second factory, established in the United Kingdom early in 1961.
At that time, it was believed that the United Kingdom would enter the
Common Market; thus Hewlett-Packard avoided duplication of production facilities by selecting products to meet the differing needs of the
respective EEC and U.K. markets.

The firm discovered that setting up its own marketing and production facilities abroad resulted in markedly increased penetration
of the European market. Its European regional organization based
in Lausanne, Switzerland, initiated a training program for its representatives' sales engineers comparable to the one in the United
States.[4]

A second element contributing to a sales increase was the setting up of a local warehouse, as noted by Hewlett, president of the
company:

> Customers like the idea of being able to get de-
> livery of equipment on short notice and not wait
> for it to be shipped from a foreign country
> 8,000 miles away. In a sense, the fact that
> stock is maintained locally is a symbol that you
> are really interested in helping them, and they
> react accordingly.[5]

The result was that during the first year of operation of the
Swiss company, European orders increased 72 percent. Hewlett
notes:

> In all, I think we as a company should be deeply
> grateful for the Treaty of Rome and the Euro-
> pean Common Market, which developed from it.
> Its establishment has forced us into an interna-
> tional expansion program that was long overdue
> and, judging from results to date, gives every
> indication of becoming a vital part of our total
> corporate operation.[6]

The evolution of Hewlett-Packard's international activities in
Europe is a classic case of international expansion. First products
are developed for the parent country market, manufactured and sold
there, then exported, and later produced close to the host country
market. Note that it may take the firm several generations of products to shift from a purely export stage, that is, product strategy
MPS 7 = S1 (Kp, Mp, Pp)-S3 (Kp, Mh, Pp) to the product strategy
MPS 1 = S1 (Kp, Mp, Pp)-S3 (Kp, Mh, Pp)-S4 (Kp, Mh, Ph).

TABLE 5.2

Hewlett-Packard Co.--General Pattern of Product Strategies, by Product Lines

Product Line	Main Know-how Centers	Main Markets	Main Production Centers	Main Set of Product Strategies Presently Implemented
Electronic products group Instruments	United States, Germany, United Kingdom, Japan	Worldwide	United States, Germany, United Kingdom, Japan	MPS 1 = S1-S3-S4 } from the United States to host countries MPS 7 = S1-S3 MPS 8 = S1-S4 whenever competition is high MPS 51 = S8-S6-S5 } from any host country to the United States MPS 55 = S8-S6 MPS 45 = S8 from any host country to any other host country
Systems	United States	Large developed countries	United States, Germany, Japan	MPS 7 = S1-S3 } from the United States to host countries MPS 1 = S1-S3-S4
Components	United States	United States, Europe, Japan, other primarily in Asia	United States, Singapore, Malaysia	MPS 7 = S1-S3 for components produced in the United States only MPS 29 = S1-S3-S2-S4 for components later produced in Singapore and Malaysia
Data products group Data systems	United States	Worldwide	United States, France, Japan	MPS 7 = S1-S3 } from the United States to host countries MPS 1 = S1-S3-S4
Calculators	United States	Worldwide	United States, Germany, Japan	MPS 7 = S1-S3 } from the United States to host countries MPS 1 = S1-S3-S4
Advanced products (components)	United States	Worldwide	United States, Singapore	MPS 7 = S1-S3 for components produced in the United States only MPS 29 = S1-S3-S2-S4 for components later produced in Singapore
Medical electronics group	United States, Germany, Japan	Worldwide	United States, Germany, Japan	MPS 7 = S1-S3 } from the United States to host countries MPS 1 = S1-S3-S4 MPS 55 = S8-S6 MPS 51 = S8-S6-S5 } from any host country to the United States MPS 45 = S8 from any host country to any other host country
Chemical analysis group	United States, Germany	Worldwide	United States, Germany	MPS 7 = S1-S3 } from the United States to host countries MPS 1 = S1-S3-S4 MPS 55 = S8-S6 MPS 51 = S8-S6-S5 } from any host country to the United States MPS 45 = S8 from any host country to any other host country

Source: Compiled by the author.

Now that Hewlett-Packard has acquired experience with its European operations it does not mean that the company introduces every product internationally using product strategy MPS 1. There are a number of important characteristics of its products that explain the general pattern of product strategies presented in Table 5.2. First, for electronic instruments which are highly complex, close contact between the development center and the production center is required. Therefore the initial state of any product strategy is such that production and development activities are at the same manufacturing center (that is, the state must have Kp, Pp, or Kh, Ph). At Hewlett-Packard every development center has its corresponding manufacturing facilities under the same roof. As the United States is the most advanced and the single most important market, Hewlett-Packard products are likely to be developed and marketed first in the United States. The first state in the majority of cases is therefore S1. Production abroad (that is, away from the development center) is undertaken only for the least sophisticated elements of any product. For example, in the case of the frequency counter the complex elements of the product are exported only from the United States (that is, product strategy MPS 7 = S1-S3). The less sophisticated elements are exported first but are then produced abroad (that is, product strategy MPS 1 = S1-S3-S4. This can be seen in Table 5.3 as a number of the products selected for in-depth study followed that pattern. Note that this in effect precludes the observation of the international product cycle strategy, as a product developed in the United States will toward the completion of its life cycle be manufactured in one center only, a place where its complex element has always been manufactured, and this is the United States itself. In addition, most products are capital rather than labor intensive (that is, labor generally accounts for only 20 percent of the cost of the product).

The second important product characteristic that affects the type of product strategy selected is the size of demand for the instruments. Some Hewlett-Packard instruments are highly specialized and have a low worldwide demand amounting to only a few hundred units; such is the case for the Fourier analyzer. Other instruments are general purpose instruments and have a high worldwide demand as is the case for the oscilloscopes. These may be produced in more than one production center while the low-volume instruments are exported. The company's products have high value-to-weight ratios (called the trade-ability index in this study) implying that shipping costs can be absorbed in the price of the product.

The pattern of product strategies described above has been altered somewhat as the result of a 1968 organizational change. Traditionally the transfer abroad of the production of instruments was the result of an estimation of the increased profit such a move would

TABLE 5.3

Hewlett-Packard Co.--Selected Products and Their Product Strategies

Product Number	First State — Country of: Development Know-how	First Market	First Production	First State	Diffusion of Product Worldwide United States — States	Market Lag	Production Lag
1	United States	Worldwide	United States	S1 S3	S1	0	0
2	United States	Europe	United States	S3	S1	2	0
3	United States	United States	United States	S1	S1	0	0
4	United States	United States & Canada	United States	S1 S3	S1	0	0
5	United States	United States & Canada	United States	S1 S3	S1	0	0
6	United States	United States & Canada	United States	S1 S3	S1	0	0
7	United States	United States & Canada	United States	S1 S3	S1	0	0
8	United States	Worldwide	United States	S1 S3	S1	0	0
9	United States	Worldwide	United States	S1 S3	S1	0	0
10	United States	United States & Canada	United States	S1 S3	S1	0	0
11	United States	Worldwide	United States	S1 S3	S1	0	0
12	United States	Worldwide	United States	S1 S3	S1	0	0
13	United States	United States & Canada	United States	S1 S3	S1	0	0
14	United States	United States & Canada	United States	S1 S3	S1	0	0
15	United States	United States	United States	S1	S1	0	0
16	United States	United States & Canada & Europe	United States	S1 S3	S1	0	0
17	United States	Japan & Europe	Japan & Europe & United States	S4* S3	S1 S1	2 2	2 0
18	United Kingdom	United Kingdom	United Kingdom	S8	S6	1	INF
19	United Kingdom	United Kingdom	United Kingdom	S8	S6-S5	3	24
20	United Kingdom	Worldwide	United Kingdom	S8 S6	S6	0	INF
21	United States	United States	United States	S1 S3	S1	0	0
22	United States	United States	United States	S1	S1-S2	0	0-36
23	United States	Worldwide	United States	S1 S3	S1-S2	0	0-6
24	United States	Worldwide	United States	S1 S3	S1-S2	0	0-6

*The transfer of production to Europe, Japan, or the United States involves only the part of the product that is less sophisticated in terms of technology.

Explanatory notes:
    a) The "S1" corresponds to the particular state encountered for each product.
    b) Market lags and production lags are expressed in number of months since the first introduction of the product.
    c) Dash indicates that there was neither marketing nor production for that product in this particular country.
    d) The term "INF" (Infinite) means that production did not take place and is not foreseen.

	Canada			Europe			Japan			Latin America		
States	Market Lag	Production Lag	States	Market Lag	Production Lag	States	Market Lag	Production Lag	States	Market Lag	Production Lag
	Diffusion of Product Worldwide											
S3	0	INF	S3-S4*	0	6	S3-S4*	0	6	S3	0	INF
S3	2	INF	S3-S4*	0	12	S3	4	INF	S3	4	INF
S3	12	INF	S3-S4*	60	180	S3-S4*	60	204	--	--	--
S3	0	INF	S3	3	INF	S3	3	INF	S3	3	INF
S3	0	INF	S3-S4*	5	30	S3	3	INF	S3	3	INF
S3	0	INF	S3-S4*	3	36	S3-S4*	3	36	S3	3	INF
S3	0	INF	S3	3	INF	S3	5	INF	S3	3	INF
S3	0	INF	S3	0	INF	S3-S4*	0	12	S3	0	INF
S3	0	INF	S3	0	INF	S3-S4*	0	12	S3	0	INF
S3	0	INF	S3	3	INF	S3	5	INF	S3	3	INF
S3	0	INF	S3	0	INF	S3	0	INF	S3	0	INF
S3	0	INF	S3-S4*	0	18	S3-S4*	0	18	S3	0	INF
S3	0	INF	S3-S4*	6	28	S3-S4*	6	36	S3	6	INF
S3	0	INF	S3	3	INF	S3	3	INF	--	--	--
S3	6	INF	S3	6	INF	S3	26	INF	--	--	--
S3	0	INF	S3	0	INF	S3	0	INF	S3	0	INF
S3	4	INF	S4*	0	0	S4*	0	0	--	--	--
S3	4	INF	S3	0	INF	S3	0	INF	--	--	--
S8	6	INF	S8	0	0	S8	6	INF	S8	6	INF
S8	3	INF	S8	0	0	S8	4	INF	S8	3	INF
S8	0	INF	S8	0	0	S8	0	INF	S8	0	INF
S3	0	INF	S3	0	INF	S3	0	INF	--	--	--
S3-S4	24	INF	S3-S4	24	INF	S3-S4	24	INF	--	--	--
S3-S4	0	INF	S3-S4	0	INF	S3-S4	0	INF	--	--	--
S3-S4	0	INF	S3-S4	0	INF	S3-S4	0	INF	--	--	--

Source: Compiled by the author.

generate. In practice this meant that the U.S. product division lost some production and part of the R and D budget, due to the fact that the marketing subsidiary was allowed part of the R and D recovery included in the price. It also led to suboptimization, because the U.S. development center had little incentive to develop an instrument with worldwide specifications. The company's major organizational change in 1968 gave product managers worldwide responsibility resulting in transfers of production abroad sooner than otherwise would have been the case. In fact it may result in the employment of product strategy MPS 8 = S1 (Kp, Mp, Pp)-S4 (Kp, Mh, Ph) as the benefits from selecting this strategy (omitting the export stage) are great when competition in the host country is fierce. For one thing the competitor's market dominance is reduced with Hewlett-Packard's presence in the form of a manufacturing center.

There is one addition to the pattern of product strategies presented above, and this concerns high labor intensive components. Hewlett-Packard decided in the early 1960s to start researching and manufacturing solid-state components in order to keep significant competitive edge in its instruments. This led the company, in the early 1970s, to establish an assembly operation in Singapore for its core memories used in computer products. Now Hewlett-Packard Singapore and a newly formed subsidiary in Malaysia assemble and package a number of high-technology components. Most of the parts come from the United States, with the assembly and testing done in Singapore and then the completed items are shipped back as finished components to Hewlett-Packard divisions. It pays the company to do assembly and some manufacture in Singapore as these are very high volume items (that is, a few hundred thousand items a year), price competition is intense, and labor represents such a great share of the product cost that production in Singapore may cost one-fourth of that in the United States. The general pattern of product strategies for these components is, first, state S1 (Kp, Mp, Pp) as the components are developed in the United States, initially produced in the United States for the U.S. market and, soon after, state S3 (Kp, Mh, Pp) as they are exported from the United States to various overseas subsidiaries. After a few months when production is running smoothly, it is transferred partly or fully to Singapore. Components are shipped back to the United States where testing is done (that is, state S2 [Kp, Mp, Ph]). For highly complex components, testing is always performed in the United States, for others it is transferred and leads to state S4 (Kp, Mh, Ph) as Singapore directly supplies the world market outside the United States with these components. The corresponding product strategy is MPS 29 = S1 (Kp, Mp, Pp)-S3 (Kp, Mh,

Pp)-S2 (Kp, Mp, Ph)-S4 (Kp, Mh, Ph).* As can be observed in Table
5.2, Hewlett-Packard develops and manufactures components for
electronics products and data products. In both these cases the general pattern of product strategies implemented is either product
strategy MPS 29 noted above, or MPS 7 = S1 (Kp, Mp, Pp)-S3 (Kp,
Mh, Pp) whenever the component is produced in the United States
only and exported.

International Product Developments
at Hewlett-Packard

The development of new products by the company's subsidiaries
in Europe took place rapidly as a result of the company policy to permit the subsidiary managers abroad to spend certain designated sums
on development activities. These funds were first used to adapt transferred designs to local market requirements, but soon enabled them
to embark on programs of developments that led to products of their
own. According to Bill Doolittle, the company's vice president-
international:

> At the present time, 15 to 30% of our overseas
> production of each of our international manufac-
> turing facilities consists of products developed
> by the international manufacturing subsidiaries.
> This percentage should continue to rise in the
> future due to an ever-increasing emphasis on the
> production of locally developed products. [7]

Initial product developments abroad were left largely to the subsidiary. This meant that the subsidiaries worked out improvements
or variations of U.S.-designed products in response to the particular
characteristics of the host country market. For example, the high
level of competition in the United Kingdom against the company's frequency counters led its U.K. division to develop a low-cost version.
However, soon thereafter the U.S. parent developed a better product
which undercut the improvement. This internally competitive situation led Hewlett-Packard to encourage its subsidiaries abroad to
"create and market their own proprietary items in product areas determined by themselves and not duplicated by [the] U.S. divisions."[8]

---

*Due to the constraints imposed on the typology this product
strategy is not on the list of product strategies given in Table 2.6.
It is noteworthy that this exception is the only product strategy observed that was not included in the feasible set.

This has induced the main subsidiaries (those in the United Kingdom, Germany, and Japan) to develop products in response to their own particular market needs, with the help of researchers available locally.

The U.K. subsidiary in response to a very progressive U.K. market in the postal service developed, in 1967, a microwave link analyzer, followed by up-and-down converters, and digital testing equipment. The microwave link analyzer received wide acclaim throughout the world from the microwave communications industry (80 percent of the production is exported, 50 percent goes to the U.S. market) and was deemed to be of such technological importance as to win the coveted Queen's Award in 1969. The product strategy selected in that case is MPS 55 = S8 (Kh, Mh, Ph)-S6 (Kh, Mp, Ph) as the product was exported from the United Kingdom to world markets. Several products for statistical measurements and analysis were developed by engineers that came from the University of Edinburgh where the technique is highly developed. However, the world market for such instruments did not develop and consequently no further R and D funds were invested.

The evolution of the activities of the German subsidiary parallel very closely those of the U.K. subsidiary. Initially, in response to the fast-growing European market, the German plant assembled oscilloscopes, oscillators, voltmeters, and power meters designed by the U.S. parent. However, it soon adapted U.S.-designed products and started to develop its own in response to German and European needs and distinctive German competence. It has now developed products in three product areas: pulse generators, acoustics, and fetal heart monitoring. Though the parent company was doing some work in the area, the high quality of the German team led the company to decide to establish Boblingen, Germany as its worldwide development center for pulse generators. The team's capabilities are such that "they have produced a number of significant pulse generators and, moreover, through the sharing of their knowledge, have contributed to the division that has been engaged in pulse generation work."[9]

In 1966 the German subsidiary entered a second area, acoustics, an area where European theoretical work is ahead of that of the United States. As in the case of the pulse generator: "Work in this area has been stimulated through close association with theoretical work carried out at the University of Stuttgart, an institution at which several of the German subsidiary's development engineers have trained."[10]

It was a technical success, but the company found that it did not sell in the U.S. airports as it did in Europe, and decided to discontinue that product line.

A third product, the fetal heart monitor, was developed by the German subsidiary in close association with a prominent German physician. It has sold quite well worldwide and is now manufactured in the United States as well as in Germany. The corresponding multinational product strategy is MPS 51 = S8 (Kh, Mh, Ph)-S6 (Kh, Mp, Ph)-S5 (Kh, Mp, Pp) between Germany (the host country) and the United States (the parent country), and product strategy MPS 45 = S8 between Germany and any other host country (that is, any country excluding the United States).

The third major subsidiary, Yokogawa-Hewlett-Packard (a joint venture in Japan), has also developed a number of products. In close cooperation with U.S. product management, it developed a new battery-powered cardiograph. It was anticipated that the major market would be in those countries where more expensive, fixed-station cardiographs are not feasible, but it is finding good acceptance in the United States and Europe as well.[11] Several other significant products developed in response to Japanese interest in the measurement of component parameters have centered around bridges, Q-meters, and similar devices. The subsidiary's most significant product has been a universal bridge which, because of its unique design, has captured a large portion of the world market.[12] (This product corresponds to product strategies MPS 51 = S8-S6-S5 between Japan and the United States, and MPS 45 = S8 otherwise.)

The experience of Hewlett-Packard product developments outside the United States, while still a small share of company activity, indicates that the company has been highly successful in recognizing the particular needs and opportunities of the host countries in Europe and Japan. Hewlett-Packard followed the example of its plant locations in the United States (that is, in the vicinity of universities such as Stanford and MIT) and was able to benefit from local talent at the universities of Stuttgart and Edinburgh. Its first experience with products developed abroad clearly indicated the need to have the host country divisions look at the worldwide market for their products rather than at their own particular (small) market. This is especially true of the U.S. market that represents a large share of the world market for electronic instruments. In order to help host country subsidiaries sell products in other countries and particularly in the United States, Hewlett-Packard created the position of import marketing manager, with responsibility for marketing all the products developed by overseas factories.[13] A subsequent improvement has been to make selected U.S. divisions the marketing licensees for imported products, thus bringing factory support functions into play on behalf of the imported products.

Summary of Growth and Product Strategies

The growth of Hewlett-Packard over the period 1955-75 has been accompanied by a marked shift in the pattern of product strategies implemented. From a U.S. firm oriented primarily toward the U.S. market, with little export (that is, relying only occasionally on MPS 7 = S1-S3), Hewlett-Packard is now a young multinational firm (with 40 percent of its sales recorded internationally) and implementing a diversity of product strategies.

The relative frequency of utilization of these product strategies reflects this involvement abroad. The subset of product strategies whose know-how originates in the United States represents the bulk of the product strategies as it dates back to the origin of the firm. We showed how the subset of product strategies originating abroad is the result of successive commitments: first increased exports, later followed by production activities abroad, that finally led to the development of new products in response to the recognition of host country market needs and opportunities, initially in Europe and later in Japan. The subset of product strategies originating abroad represents clearly a new trend in the company's activities. The last step, the development of products, was fostered by the company's management philosophy, particularly its policy regarding research and development. Product development abroad occurred in the three product groups where the company is most experienced: electronics, medical electronics, and chemical analysis. It entered the data products field only in 1967. It just established manufacturing facilities abroad and this explains why there is no product developed abroad yet as one stage follows the other.

We saw that the particular product strategy implemented was either export only from the center where the product was developed (that is, MPS 7 = S1-S3 and MPS 55 = S8-S6) or export first, then production in a few other countries (that is, MPS 1 = S1-S3-S4 and MPS 51 = S8-S6-S5) depending primarily on the level of demand and the complexity of the production process. In some cases competition or a good knowledge of host country markets, and a shift toward worldwide product managers were instrumental in having the export stage skipped resulting in the utilization of MPS 8 = S1-S4. Finally some components, the labor intensive ones, followed a particular product strategy MPS 29 = S1-S3-S2-S4.

This general pattern of product strategies presented above by product-lines was complemented by the analysis of 24 selected products from the electronics production group. Twenty are instruments and four are components. Their international diffusion was presented in Table 5.3. All are from the electronics products group within the most important group of Hewlett-Packard.

MASSEY-FERGUSON LTD.

Both the Massey Company and the Harris Company, forerun-
ners of Massey-Ferguson Ltd., started operations around 1850 in
Ontario, Canada. By the time they merged in 1891 the Massey and
Harris companies accounted for over half of all farm implements
sales in Canada.[14] The new firm grew with the development and
mechanization of the farm machinery industry and its leadership in
tractors and combines gained recognition. The company's name was
adopted in 1953 when it merged with Ferguson of the United Kingdom.
Massey-Ferguson is now the third largest farm equipment manufacturer in the world with $1.5 billion sales in 1973, after two U.S.-
based firms (International Harvester and John Deere). Its main
product groups are:

Group	Percent of Total Sales
Farm machinery	72
Industrial and construction machinery	15
Engine group	13

The Massey Company's international orientation started as
early as 1867 when it was awarded two gold medals at the International Exposition in Paris. It established a branch company in London in 1887, with Fred Massey as its manager, and also in France
and Adelaide, Australia, in 1887. In 1908, 48 percent of its sales
and as high a proportion of its profits were derived from outside its
own Canadian market and this was before it had developed a market
in the United States. Between 1910 and 1947, the company extended
its assembly and manufacturing facilities--in response to tariff and
foreign exchange restrictions--to Batavia, New York, and to France,
Germany, Australia, the United Kingdom, and South Africa. Note
that Massey-Ferguson implemented the classic pattern of product
strategies (that is, MPS 1 = S1 [Kp, Mp, Pp]-S3 [Kp, Mh, Pp]-S4
[Kp, Mh, Ph]) at a very early stage. The company has since capitalized on its presence and knowledge of foreign markets with a number
of acquisitions, thereby implementing a number of other product
strategies. The chronology of these acquisitions is presented in
Table 5.4, and the strategies presently implemented, in Table 5.5.
The company's international orientation is now more pronounced than
at any other time in its history as 92 percent of company sales are
outside Canada (65 percent outside North America), and close to 50
percent of its research and development and production capacity is
outside North America.

TABLE 5.4

Massey-Ferguson Ltd.--Chronology of the Main Acquisitions

Year	Acquisition

Farm Machinery Group

1953   Harry Ferguson Ltd. (U.K.): this firm, merging with Massey-Harris, had built a worldwide reputation for revolutionizing the farm tractor with its three-point linkage and hydraulic command of implements developed by Harry Ferguson. By 1953, more Ferguson tractors had been sold throughout the world than any other kind.

1955   H. V. McKay-Massey Harris Proprietary Ltd. (Australia): full acquisition was realized after an interest in it of 26 percent since 1930. McKay is the leading farm implement manufacturer in Australia, and was one of the early developers of the harvesting-combine.

1960   Landini-S.P.A. (Italy): Landini is the leading farm equipment manufacturer in Italy.

1961   Tractors and Farm Equipment Ltd. (India): Massey-Ferguson acquired a 49 percent interest in this company which manufactures tractors.

1961   Safim Manufacturing Ltd. (South Africa): Massey-Ferguson has a controlling interest in this jointly owned manufacturer of farm implements.

1965   Solar Aircraft (U.S.): acquired by Massey-Ferguson, this plant was used to relocate the executive offices of Massey-Ferguson's subsidiary and converted into a new farm implement plant.

1965   M.F. Farm Services Ltd. (U.K.): the new name of this British firm acquired by Massey-Ferguson, it manufactures and markets farmstead equipment in the U.K.

1965   Badger Northland Inc. (U.S.): a farm equipment manufacturer, this company produces forage harvesting and farm material handling equipment.

1965   Motor Iberica S.A. (Spain): Massey-Ferguson acquired 37 percent interest in this firm which is a major manufacturer of trucks, tractors, diesel engines, and other agricultural and industrial equipment.

1966   Crichton Industries Pty. (Australia): Massey-Ferguson entered the sugar cane harvester market with this acquisition.

1967   A new plant was acquired in Detroit, where production of transmissions and axles was realized.

1967   A controlling interest was acquired in a firm of Porto Alegre (Brazil) which produces farm implements.

1968   Langeskov Plovfabrik A/S (Denmark): this 75-year-old company specializes in the manufacture of plows and cultivators.

1969   Ransomes de Mexico S.A. (Mexico): this subsidiary of an English firm is the largest manufacturer of agricultural implements in Mexico. It became the principal source for a full range of Massey-Ferguson implements and enabled the company to offer the most complete line of Mexican-made agricultural machinery available in the country.

Year	Acquisition
1969	Rheinstahl Hanomag A.G. (Argentina): Massey-Ferguson has a controlling interest in this tractor manufacturer. The plant occupies 215,000 square feet and has a capacity of 4,000 tractors a year.
1970	Eicher GmbH (Germany): Massey-Ferguson has a minority interest in Eicher, which produces tractors, especially machines adapted for vineyard work.
1972	Slattery Group (South Africa): this firm manufactures corn harvesting equipment as well as other farm machinery.

Industrial and Construction Machinery Group

1957	Davis Co. (U.S.): Davis is the leading and largest American manufacturer of industrial and construction attachments to suit tractors (loaders and backhoes).
1960	Landini and Figli (Italy): this Italian firm produces farm tractors and crawler tractors.
1968	A new factory was opened in Aprilia, Italy, for the ICM group to supply the European market.
1969	Simmel S.P.A. (Italy): Massey-Ferguson acquired a 33 percent interest in this large Italian manufacturer of crawler tractor components, thus assuring an improved supply source for Italian industrial and construction machinery operations.
1972	Beltrami S.P.A. (Italy): Massey-Ferguson acquired a 50 percent interest in this firm, which manufactures industrial and construction machinery components and already supplied Massey-Ferguson for a number of years.

Engines Group

1959	F. Perkins Ltd. (U.K.): with this acquisition Massey-Ferguson started its integration in engines. Perkins is one of the world's largest producers of high-speed diesel engines with uses going from motor boats to trucks and tractors.
1959	Standard Motor Co. (U.K.): this company is a large British automobile manufacturer and had formerly the license to manufacture the Ferguson tractor outside North America. Included in the purchase were two plants of Standard's French subsidiary.
1964	Perkins Hispania (Spain): a further interest was acquired in this company, which manufactures Perkins engines.
1968	Motores Perkins S.A. (Mexico): a 21 percent interest in this company assured Massey-Ferguson of Perkins engines production in Mexico.
1970	Agreement was reached with Yanmar Diesel Engine Co. of Japan. Yanmar is the leading manufacturer of its class in Japan. Perkins industrial and marine engines are completed by Yanmar with Japanese components.
1973	Diesel Nacional (Mexico): a 21 percent interest was acquired and this firm manufactures engines.

Source: Massey-Ferguson Ltd., Annual Report, various issues.

The Farm Machinery Group

The company's farm machinery group consists of three product lines: implements, tractors, and harvesting equipment. Whereas at one time farm implements were the mainstay of the Massey Company, the advent of the internal combustion engine led to the development of the tractor and numerous self-propelled farm machinery equipment such as the harvester combine--basically a harvesting implement with an engine.

Implements

During the late nineteenth century the Massey-Harris success was more than anything else due to its position of leadership in farm implement technology in Canada. In fact this technology was a replication of prevailing U.S. technology and the company simply secured access to the best U.S. machines and modified them to suit local conditions. Such was the case for the Ketchem mower, the Manny (a combined hand rake and mower), and the Kirby mower for which manufacturing rights were purchased in the 1860s.[15] Massey-Ferguson's leadership in farm implements and its internationally minded management successfully transferred their acquired technology to Europe, Australia, and Latin America. This was done first by export from Canada and then by production in these countries (that is, MPS 1 = S1 [Kp, Mp, Pp]-S3 [Kp, Mh, Pp]-S4 [Kp, Mh, Ph]). With time, however, strong competition in this product line (where there are few barriers to entry in terms of development and production) has diminished the profitability of implements for a large firm such as Massey-Ferguson.

Presently the company's policy with respect to farm implements is to let each operating subsidiary develop, produce, or acquire rights to sell those implements needed to support tractor sales. Due to few economies of scale in production and a low value-to-weight ratio, implements are manufactured close to the market. This means that the main pattern of product strategies for implements is MPS 13 = S1 (Kp, Mp, Pp) and MPS 45 = S8 (Kh, Mh, Ph). Whenever the product's know-how is transferred, it means that MPS 8 = S1 (Kp, Mp, Pp)-S4 (Kp, Mh, Ph) or MPS 40 = S8 (Kh, Mh, Ph)-S5 (Kh, Mp, Pp) are implemented. On the average, according to Ralph Ramsay, director, product management, tractor and implement systems, between 40 and 50 percent of implements that are put into production have been designed at some other operating unit. Because of the proximity of the United States and Canada, the absence of tariffs between the two countries, and quite similar climatic and soil conditions, product strategy MPS 13 = S1 (Kp, Mp, Pp) seldom occurs.

Rather, whenever an implement is developed in Canada it is likely to be exported to the United States, that is, MPS 7 = S1 (Kp, Mp, Pp)-S3 (Kp, Mh, Pp).* The main know-how centers, markets, production centers, and the list of product strategies for the farm implements is given in Table 5.5.

Tractors

After years of unsuccessful attempts to acquire tractor technology, Massey-Ferguson finally became a leader in the tractor industry as a result of its 1953 merger with Harry Ferguson Ltd. Ferguson had revolutionized farm machinery with its invention of the three-point linkage and related hydraulic developments that converted the tractor from a pure power source used to pull implements into an agent capable of controlling the implements.

This invention and related technology were later transferred to Detroit where Massey-Ferguson decided to establish its worldwide corporate design center for tractors. The decision of Massey-Ferguson to centralize its tractor design was made in response to a worldwide trend toward similar agricultural requirements for tractors (mainly higher horsepower tractors in response to increased labor shortage).†

Prior to this decision Massey-Ferguson designed tractors in five development centers, each located in a main market. Massey-Ferguson's present pattern of product strategies begins therefore with S8 (Kh, Mh, Ph),for no development occurs in Canada. Canada is supplied by export from the Detroit plant, leading to product strategy MPS 55 = S8 (Kh, Mh, Ph)-S6 (Kh, Mp, Ph). Europe and other countries are supplied either through production in the market or

_____

*One product from this product line was selected for further study, see Table 5.6. The product strategy employed differs somewhat in this particular case as it was developed in the United States, produced in Canada and introduced in both the United States and Canada simultaneously.

†Massey-Ferguson still has its parent design center for small tractors in the United Kingdom, but as worldwide standardization takes place its importance will decrease as the following example illustrates: The MF 185 tractor, a medium-size tractor, was designed in Detroit, but first produced and marketed in the United Kingdom. It was first introduced in France by export from the United Kingdom, then in Mexico, North America, and Brazil. The United Kingdom is the main manufacturing center of Massey-Ferguson tractors for exports outside North America.

TABLE 5.5

Massey-Ferguson Ltd. --General Pattern of Product Strategies, by Product Lines

Product Line	Main Know-how Centers	Main Markets	Main Production Centers	Main Set of Product Strategies Presently Implemented
Farm machinery group				
Tractors	United States, United Kingdom	Worldwide	United States, United Kingdom, Italy, Brazil, Argentina, Mexico	MPS 55 = S8–S6 between the United States and Canada MPS 45 = S8 in other cases
Implements	United States, Canada, Europe	Worldwide	Worldwide	MPS 7 = S1–S3 between Canada and the United States MPS 8 = S1–S4 between Canada and a number of other countries MPS 40 = S8–S5 between the rest of the world and Canada MPS 45 = S8 in other cases
Harvesting	Canada, France, Australia, Brazil	Worldwide	Canada, France, Brazil, Australia	MPS 7 = S1–S3 between Canada and particularly the United States MPS 8 = S1–S4 between Canada and some other host countries MPS 1 = S1–S3–S4 between Canada and some other host countries MPS 45 = S8 in other cases
Industrial and construction machinery group				
Crawler tractors	Italy	Worldwide	Italy	MPS 55 = S8–S6 between Italy and Canada MPS 45 = S8 in other cases
Industrial tractors	United States	Worldwide	United States, United Kingdom	MPS 55 = S8–S6 between United States and Canada MPS 45 = S8 in other cases
Four wheel drive loader	United States	Worldwide	United States, Italy	MPS 55 = S8–S6 between United States and Canada MPS 45 = S8 in other cases
Hydraulic excavators	Italy	Worldwide	Italy	MPS 55 = S8–S6 between Italy and Canada MPS 45 = S8 in other cases
Engine group				
Engines	United Kingdom	Worldwide	United Kingdom, France, Australia, Italy, Brazil	MPS 55 = S8–S6 between United Kingdom and Canada MPS 45 = S8 in other cases

Note: "In other cases" implies the parent country is deleted from the strategy.
Source: Compiled by the author.

92

export from any one of the seven host countries, that is, product strategy MPS 45 = S8 (Kh, Mh, Ph).

Tractors are high-technology items with very large economies of scale in production which enables them to be shipped economically due to their high value-to-weight ratio.

Harvesting Equipment

Massey-Ferguson's early success in this product line contrasts with its difficulties in finding an adequate tractor technology. Massey-Ferguson developments in harvesting illustrate how, due to early expansion abroad with its implements (particularly in Australia and Argentina), the company seized unique opportunities in the stripper harvester and the self-propelled combine. The first example is related by E. P. Neufeld:

> Massey Harris by the turn of the century had a good market in Australia, saw the need for a stripper harvester and, borrowing heavily from various Australian machines, designed one by 1901 for the Australian market. In 1910 it introduced its No. 1 reaper thresher which depended not on a stripping mechanism but on the North American type of cutter bar to cut the straw. . . . Initially sold extensively in Australia and Argentina they were introduced into North America in 1917.[16]

The self-propelled combine was developed in 1938 and proved to be an innovation that was to revolutionize harvesting. Tom Caroll, who joined the Massey Harris organization as a distributor in Argentina,. convinced his headquarters of the future of the self-propelled combine idea. He developed it in Argentina, had it built in Toronto, and had the combines sent to Argentina. Further refinements gave birth to the famous Massey Harris No. 21 self-propelled combine that was later to be known for its use in the "harvest brigade." This event marked the first serious penetration of the U.S. market by Massey-Ferguson.

Since these early days Massey-Ferguson has decentralized its development activities for combines to five locations (Australia, North America, Germany, France, and Brazil). Each center developed combines particularly adapted to crop, soil, and the climatic conditions of each of these countries. However, in response to a trend toward increased similarity in crop types on a worldwide scale, its North American development center, located in Toronto, has

become the corporate harvesting engineering center. (The corresponding pattern of product strategies in this product line is presented in Table 5.5.)

Massey-Ferguson entered the sugar cane harvester market
with the acquisition in 1966 of the Australian firm Crichton Industries
Pty. Ltd.: "We [Massey-Ferguson] thought at that time we could help
them [Crichton] put an industrialized and reliable product on the market."[17] A model was developed and introduced in 1968 with initial
aim at the Australian market. Later on, however, Massey-Ferguson
succeeded in opening up other markets in the United States and the
Caribbean to the point that now half of the Australian production is
exported. This example adds further credence to the argument that
the company's presence in the Australian market was instrumental
in recognizing opportunities that fitted into the company's objectives.

The example of the baler is also relevant to our study. The
company's position in the market was relatively weak and it was
facing strong competition, especially in Europe. As other MNFs
that design one basic product with worldwide specification, Massey-
Ferguson decided to develop a product geared to the most sophisticated market, the European one. Having a high level of engineering
in several countries, the company has substantial flexibility as to
where to develop a product and where to produce it. It therefore decided to have it developed in the United Kingdom and started production in France first.

Industrial and Construction Machinery Group

The industrial and construction machinery (ICM) group represents a later addition to the farm machinery business. However, this
product group is not entirely new to Massey-Ferguson as some of the
product lines (for example, the industrial tractors) of the ICM group
have a technology that resembles that of the farm machinery group.
Massey-Ferguson entered the business by acquiring in 1957 the Davis
Company, a leading U.S. manufacturer of attachments to tractors.
One such attachment was a backhoe loader. Massey-Ferguson,
helped by its experience in Europe with the farm machinery, was
quickly able to perceive business opportunities there with its new
product line. In the early 1960s, it decided to transfer its U.S. technology and establish production facilities in the United Kingdom. It
discovered, however, that U.S.-designed products were not suited
to the working conditions of Europe and in view of a high failure rate
it established some engineering facilities in the United Kingdom to
design a product that fitted these more exacting requirements. The
result is that presently there is little commonality of parts between

the U.K. and U.S. versions of a product. This, Massey-Ferguson would prefer to change in view of its belief that it should achieve worldwide standardization in the ICM product group (as does Caterpillar, the leader in the field). Standardization of products worldwide would require it to adopt the product specifications demanded in Europe, the most stringent market.

In view of the technology that the company has in tractors and loaders in the United States (as the result of its acquisition of the Davis Company) the development of products in these two product lines will remain in the United States. Production and marketing are furthermore likely to occur first in the United States, that is, the first state is S8 (Kh, Mh, Ph). The ICM products are sold in somewhat lower quantities than the farm machinery products, hence for many ICM products it is not economical to manufacture them at a second plant. The product strategies employed are therefore MPS 45 = S8 (Kh, Mh, Ph) whenever the product is produced and traded among host countries, such as for example between the United States and Europe, and MPS 55 = S8 (Kh, Mh, Ph)-S6 (Kh, Mp, Ph) whenever the product is produced in one of the manufacturing centers (that is, in the United States, the United Kingdom, or Italy) and exported to Canada.

Massey-Ferguson activities in the ICM product group include two other product lines. They are the crawler tractors and hydraulic excavators, both developed in Italy. The company entered the crawler tractor product line by acquiring the Italian firm Landini. It then proceeded to increase its Italian operation when the profitability of this line had been established, by building a factory in Aprilia with the help of financial incentives from the Italian government. It further increased its Italian activities by giving the operation worldwide responsibility for a new product line, the hydraulic excavator product line. The selection of Italy as the company's worldwide center for hydraulic excavators stems from the fact that the European market for hydraulic excavators is large, fast growing, and more advanced than in the United States. The multinational product strategies for these two product lines are identical to those referred to for the other two ICM product lines; that is, MPS 55 = S8 (Kh, Mh, Ph)-S6 (Kh, Mp, Ph) and MPS 45 = S8 (Kh, Mh, Ph).

Engine Group

Another step toward vertical integration at Massey-Ferguson was taken in 1959 when it bought the leading manufacturer of high-speed diesel engines, Perkins Ltd., based in England. Perkins was already a multinational company with manufacturing facilities in England,

TABLE 5.6

Massey-Ferguson Ltd. --Selected Products and Their Product Strategies

| Product Number | First State — Country of: | | | | | Diffusion of Product Worldwide — United States | |
	Development Know-how	First Market	First Production	First State	States	Market Lag	Production Lag
1	United States	United States & Canada	Canada	S7 S5	S7	0	INF
2	United States	United Kingdom	United Kingdom	S8	S8	18	INF
3	United States	United States & Europe	United States & Europe	S8	S8	0	0
4	United Kingdom	United Kingdom	United Kingdom	S8	S8	24	24
5	Germany	Italy	Germany	S8	S8	2	INF
6	United States	Europe	France	S8	S7	6	INF
7	France	Finland	France	S8	--	--	--
8	Canada	Canada & United States	Canada	S1 S3	S3	0	INF
9	Australia	Australia	Australia	S8	S8	48	INF
10	United Kingdom	Europe	United Kingdom	S8	S8	2	INF
11	Italy	Europe	Italy	S8	S8	4	INF
12	United States	United States & Canada	United States	S8 S6	S8	0	0
13	United States & Italy	Worldwide	United States & Italy	S8 S6	S8	0	0

Explanatory notes:

a) The "S1" corresponds to the particular state encountered for each product.
b) Market lags and production lags are expressed in number of months since the first introduction of the product.
c) Dash indicates that there was neither marketing nor production for that product in this particular country.
d) The term "INF" (infinite) means that production did not take place and is not envisaged.

96

Diffusion of Product Worldwide											
Canada			Europe			Australia			Latin America		
States	Market Lag	Production Lag	States	Market Lag	Production Lag	States	Market Lag	Production Lag	States	Market Lag	Production Lag
S5	0	0	--	--	--	S8	84	84	S8	132	132
S6	12	INF	S8	0	0	S8	4	INF	S8	18	108
S6	2	INF	S8	0	0	S8	3	INF	S8	72	72
S6	12	INF	S8	0	0	S8	24	INF	S8	96	156
S6	2	INF	S8	0	0	S8	4	INF	S8	2	INF
S5	6	6	S8	0	0	S7	18	INF	--	--	--
--	--	--	S8	0	0	--	--	--	--	--	--
S1	0	0	S3-S4	12	48	S3	18	INF	S3	24	INF
--	--	--	--	--	--	S8	0	0	S8	24	INF
S6	2	INF	S8	0	0	S8	12	INF	S8	3	INF
S6	4	INF	S8	0	0	S8	12	INF	S8	4	INF
S6	0	INF	S8	36	36	S8	24	INF	S8	48	INF
S6	0	INF	S8	0	0	S8	18	24	S8	10	10

Source: Compiled by the author.

France, Australia, Italy, and Brazil, and a number of associated
companies in India, Argentina, Spain, and Mexico. The Perkins
division is run independently from others (Massey-Ferguson supplies
some of its competition with Perkins engines). Perkins' development
of engines is located in the United Kingdom where much of the manufacturing activity does take place; the first state of any product strategy is therefore S8 (Kh, Mh, Ph). The general pattern of product
strategies in the engine group is similar to other product lines of the
ICM product group, that is, MPS 55 = S8 (Kh, Mh, Ph)-S6 (Kh, Mp,
Ph) and MPS 45 = S8 (Kh, Mh, Ph).

Summary of Growth and Product Strategies

Massey-Ferguson has evolved over 100 years (1875-75) from
a leader in farm implements acquiring U.S. farm technology and exploiting it inside its protected market in Canada, to a fully integrated
farm and industrial construction machinery firm. This growth process started with the exporting of implements and was followed with
the establishment of production facilities abroad to supply those markets (that is, MPS 1 = S1-S3-S4). Later on affiliates modified the
equipment in response to the needs of their own environments (we saw
this happening for the tractors and harvester combines) and were able
to detect new developments such as those in harvesting (for example,
as it happened in Australia and Argentina). By and large this is because the company has always stressed the importance of good communication with the market in the belief that farmers are an important source of innovations which can be commercialized.

In the 1950s Massey-Ferguson responded to a decrease in profitability by integrating backward into the engines and tractors. Its
worldwide experience in manufacturing and distribution enabled it to
search for and acquire world leaders in their respective technologies.
During the 1960s Massey-Ferguson diversified into the industrial and
construction machinery through acquisitions in the United States and
the United Kingdom of firms that were leaders in their own markets.
As a result of these acquisitions in various countries, the company's
development centers are widely dispersed abroad (as the list of its
main know-how centers, by product line, indicates in Table 5.5).
This results in a pattern of product strategies of the type MPS 55 =
S8-S6 and MPS 45 = S8. As with the other firms studied, we selected
a number of products for further study. Of the thirteen products,
three are from the tractor product line, one is an implement, four belong to the harvesting product line, one is a component for the farm
machinery group, and four are from the ICM group. Their international innovation-diffusion is presented in Table 5.6.

ALCAN ALUMINIUM LTD.

Alcan Aluminium Ltd., following a plan of reorganization of
its parent company, Aluminum Company of America (Alcoa), became
incorporated in 1928; its assets were initially those controlled by
Alcoa outside the United States making Alcan a multinational company from its birth. It was in Shawinigan (Quebec) that, in 1900, the
first Canadian aluminum smelter was built, and by 1940 Alcan had
subsidiaries in 18 countries and sales amounting to $80 million.
Alcan's sales have since grown to reach $1,456 million in 1972,
making Alcan the second aluminum giant of the world behind Alcoa.

Presently Alcan is extracting bauxite in 8 countries; has primary smelters in 10 countries, fabricating operations in 33 countries; and is selling aluminum products in more than 100 countries.

This growth occurred through the development of new bauxite
deposits, and increased efficiency in the production of aluminum
ingots coupled with developments in rolling technology and vertical
integration forward into fabricated aluminum products. The forward
vertical integration represented a major turning point in Alcan activities, for as late as 1958 aluminum ingots represented 70 percent
of company sales; today they represent only 30 percent with fabricated products accounting for the remainder. The increased size
and complexity of Alcan activities led to the reorganization of the
company in 1968 into three divisions that correspond to the three
product groups--raw materials (that is, ore), smelting, and fabri-
cating--and to a number of changes in its research and development
organization. These major developments are presented below and
are followed by an analysis of the pattern of multinational product
strategies at Alcan for the three main fabricated aluminum product
lines--building products, foil and packaging products, and electrical
products.

Developments at Alcan: Canada's Role
and Forward Integration

Due to its abundant energy resources, Canada has played a key
role in Alcan growth. Alcan Canada represented two-thirds of Alcan's smelter capacity as late as 1965[18] and was exporting a large
part of its production to the United States and Europe. With increased
primary smelting capacity in Norway, Australia, Brazil, Japan, and
the United States, Canada now represents approximately half of Alcan's capacity.[19]

The second key element in Alcan's growth has been its decision
to integrate forward in response to a long period of surplus smelter

capacity in the industry that started in 1957 and had destabilizing effects on the profitability of the company. Without sufficient captive outlets for its ingots, Alcan was vulnerable and decided to buy out its customers in a number of key markets and to develop integrated facilities to produce finished products in these markets.

In order to do this, Alcan embarked on a series of acquisitions (see Table 5.7) and committed extensive capital outlays of $600 million in fabricating facilities during the 1960s. In 1974, Alcan planned to spend half of its capital expenditures on fabricating facilities.

Fabricating operations include rolling, extrusion, and the development of new alloys in order to serve the various end uses of aluminum--from aeronautics to building products, electric cables to household foil. As success in these many product categories requires quite different skills than those used to extract bauxite and manufacture aluminum ingots, Alcan had to decide how it wanted to master these new techniques. Due to the characteristics of the fabricated aluminum products, Alcan growth in this sector could only be assured with operations close to the markets to be served, for two reasons. The first stems from the low transportability of aluminum products in general, as their weight or bulk/value ratio is such that it quickly becomes uneconomical to ship semifinished, or finished products, and tariffs compound the problem. The second reason is the need to be close to the construction people, the canners, or any other local user to ensure that the product is suited to their specifications.

Therefore, Alcan's activities in the fabricating area lead to the building up of relatively autonomous operations in strategic locations in a variety of countries. Alcan decided to build major integrated sheet mill systems in Canada, the United States, the United Kingdom, and Germany to make acquisitions downstream in order to control aluminum uses and protect itself with these captive outlets. Alcan bought out a large number of firms during the 1960s in the United States, Canada, the United Kingdom, and other countries, which led to a trebling of fabricated sales in the decade after 1963. In each of these markets, Alcan consolidated, rationalized, and expanded its activities, setting up geographic area headquarters as profit centers.

It is worth mentioning here that Alcan's move forward to the market was more successful in some areas than others due to the strength of companies that were already established. For example, Alcan was not able to integrate forward in continental Europe the way it was able to do elsewhere, because of the greater sophistication and strength of local aluminum companies such as Vereinigte Aluminium Werke in Germany, Pechiney in France, and Alusuisse in Switzerland. In these countries it was difficult to build as strong an image as Alcan has had in Canada and in the United Kingdom, and as it is slowly

achieving in the United States. In Japan, Alcan is involved in a number of joint ventures and has been quite successful; developments in
fabricating also have occurred in Brazil and Spain.

   This rapid growth and diversification from a basic metal manufacturer to a leading producer of finished products has built up a
need to adapt the organization to these new developments. The heavy
reliance on centralization and direct reporting of each country to company headquarters in Montreal has been replaced in the late 1960s by
a policy of decentralization. One of the main features of this new
structure is the grouping of countries into eight geographical areas,
the rationale for which has been explained by Culver, the company's
executive vice president for fabricating and sales:

> So we have an open system, we have high ethic,
> we cooperate, we share knowledge. This is what
> a multinational enterprise is. And there is
> nothing in that definition that conflicts with the
> idea of eight areas of initiative and drive, areas
> that stand on their own feet, that develop their
> business as they think best all within these gen-
> eral principles. [20]

   This management philosophy has a direct bearing on how technology is going to be generated and transferred internationally.
Since each geographical unit is a profit center, it is paramount to
encourage the various area managers to keep up with the latest developments in their fields worldwide.

   The research and development function at Alcan is not completely decentralized and Alcan has corporate research facilities
that do basic research in practically all of the fields in which it is
involved. This research is complemented by development of products in the various operations centers in the eight geographical areas.
The more basic research program is initiated by the research center
management, and is aimed at providing the knowledge required to
assure the technical success of the development programs.

   The basic research is done in three laboratories. One, in
Arvida (Canada), is involved with ore and smelter research and some
rolling of ingots. The other two, one in Kingston (Canada), the other
in Banbury (Britain), are conducting research in the fabricating field.
Alcan spends close to $15 million a year in research and development
at these three laboratories. Development done in the operating divisions is excluded from the figure; thus the figure underestimates
somewhat the true R and D spending of Alcan. This research effort
is divided approximately as follows: 15 percent ore, 30 percent
smelting, 55 percent fabricating. As for the R and D effort in the

TABLE 5.7

Alcan Aluminium Ltd.--Chronology of the Main Acquisitions

Year	Acquisition
	Foil and Packaging
1958	33 1/3 percent interest in Fabrique d'emballages metalliques, S.A. (Fribourg, Switzerland), the leading maker of aluminum cans in Europe.
1960	Supreme Aluminum Industries Ltd. (Canada): a substantial utensil company in Toronto. Aluminum Goods Ltd., a Canadian subsidiary of Alcan, licensed that company to produce Wear-ever cooking utensils instead of continuing these activities itself.
1961	Majority interest in Antonio Vernocchi S.A., a long-established manufacturer of foil in Argentina.
1963	Cochrane Foil Works (Canada): a manufacturer of high plates, was also involved on a small scale in TV dinner trays.
1964	Fisher's Foil Ltd. (United Kingdom): one of the principal aluminum foil rollers and packaging firms in the United Kingdom.
1965	Morfoils Ltd. (Canada): a large manufacturer of rigid aluminum foil containers. This represented Alcan entry into the frozen food business.
1965	Alanco Ltd. (Canada): a producer of aluminum extrusions.
1965	Polyfoil Papers Ltd. (United Kingdom): Britain's leading supplier of household foil, and a traditional customer of Fisher's Foil Ltd.
1966	Acquired full control of Metcan Products Ltd. (Canada), a producer of collapsible tubes and closures for containers in Toronto.
1968	A 50 percent interest in J. Booth Aluminum Ltd. (United Kingdom), which later led to a merger, to become the largest unit in the U.K. fabricating industry.
1968	Alcan acquired a leading manufacturer in frozen food business in Canada.
1968	Hueck und Buren K.G. (Germany): an important German firm in extrusion and aluminum foil.
1969	Canada Foil (Canada): a leader in foil rolling and flexible packaging, was a subsidiary of Imperial Tobacco.
1970	Chicago Metallic: a U.S. producer of flexible packaging and bakery products.
1970	Acquired a German foil roller which became Alcan Folienwerke GMBH.
1970	Majority control and direction of the sheet rolling and extrusion company, Angeletti and Ciucani Fonderia Laminatorio S.P.A. (Italy). This firm has a cold rolling mill, a modern line of aluminum and steel sheet painting, and a subsidiary in extrusions.
	Electrical Products
1963	Central Cable Corp. (United States), with capacity to produce 18,000 tons of aluminum wire and cable. It marked the entry of Alcan into the cable business and energy transport.
1964	25 percent interest in Unidare Ltd. (Ireland), manufacturing a wide range of electrical cables and equipment from aluminum and copper, and aluminum foil, extrusion strips, and circles.
1965	Alcan acquired two plants, in Ohio and Virginia, where sheets and coils are manufactured. These plants belonged to its former U.S. partners (Bridgeport Brass Co., Cerro Corp., and Scovill Manufacturing Co.) in a joint venture.
	Building Products
1961	Flexalum Corp. (United States): Alcan entry into siding business.
1963	Fabral Corp. (United States): 50 percent interest. This company manufactures roofing, siding materials, and accessories for industrial, commercial, and agricultural buildings.
1963	Metals Disintegrating Co. (United States): producer of aluminum powder and paste. This company innovated in the manufacture of extra fine powder. It also developed a process that is used worldwide to manufacture aluminum pigments.

Year	Acquisition
1964	Almetco Manufacturing Group Ltd. (Canada): it is the largest fabricator of aluminum windows in western Canada, with a plant near Vancouver.
1965	Alcan acquired two plants in New Jersey and California where production of siding and other building products is taking place. These plants were acquired from its former U.S. partners in a joint venture (Bridgeport Brass Co., Cerro Corp., and Scoville Manufacturing Co.).
1965	Pillar Holdings Ltd. (United Kingdom) and Alindustries joined forces in a new company, Architectural Aluminum (or Archital). This arrangement provided access for Alindustries metal to the building industries, as Archital included units operating in the fields of aluminum doors, windows, shopfronts, curtain walling, and related products.
1966	Formation of Alcan Building Products Limited (Canada) to achieve the identity of company sales in the residential building market. It encompasses the activities of Roselyn Metal Products Ltd., Alme and Co. Manufacturing Group Ltd., and the company's siding division in Toronto and Montreal.
1966	Joint venture to form Alcan Pipe Ltd. (Canada), which was to build a plant at Vernon (B.C.) to produce pipes and tubing. The company was expected to contribute substantially to the enlargement of Alcan activities in the field of irrigation.
1967	Schwartz-Haumont (France): an expanding French extrusion anodizing enterprise. This controlling interest was taken in order to acquire know-how in "the fast anodizing process with wide potential applications in the architectural field that holds a trump card in this growing market," according to Alcan officials.
1968	J. Booth Aluminum Ltd. (United Kingdom): Alcan acquired a 50 percent interest in that firm which later led to a merger, resulting in the largest unit in the U.K. fabricating industry.
1970	Kawneer (Australia): a major fabricator of aluminum architectural products.
1972	Majority interest in V.E. Anderson Manufacturing Co. (United States): entry into aluminum and door business in United States.
1973	Airmaster (Canada): a manufacturer of windows and doors.
1973	Renalex Inc. (Canada): a siding supplier and installer to the new housing industry.
1973	An Alcan subsidiary, Aluminum Building Systems Canada, formed with Del Zotto Enterprises. The objective is to market a unique aluminum forming system for the placement of concrete in high-rise buildings.

Others

Year	Acquisition
1950	Aluminio Do Brasil S.A.: a fabricating enterprise.
1960	Participation in Supreme Aluminum Industries Ltd. (Canada), a substantial utensil company. Aluminum Foods Ltd., a Canadian subsidiary, licensed that company to produce and market Wear-ever cooking utensils instead of continuing with these activities itself.
1960	Joint venture to form Alcan Enfield Alloys Ltd. (United Kingdom). The new company produces a large range of foundry alloys from scrap and primary aluminum.
1961	A controlling interest was acquired in a partially completed extrusion plant in Belgium, the company's second such plant in the European Common Market.
1966	Simalex Aluminum Co. Ltd. (Canada), from which Alcan bought an extrusion plant.
1968	A 25 percent interest in Empresa Nacional Del Aluminio, S.A. (Spain). This firm is the main aluminum fabricating and transforming unit in Spain.
1969	Metal Goods Corp. (United States): a large distributor of metallic products that insures outlets to Alcan for semifabricated and fabricated products.
1972	Joint venture with E. H. Price Ltd. (Canada) involving an extrusion and finishing operation in Winnipeg, and the setting up of a new plant in Calgary, Alberta.

Source: Alcan Aluminium Ltd., Annual Report, various issues.

fabricating division, it is distributed in smelting and casting, rolling, and extrusion, and these represent the bulk of the spending in the laboratories. Other R and D in building products, anodizing, coil coating, foil conversion, and electrical and lithosheet products is done in both the operating divisions and the two fabricating laboratories. Development is closely related to problems encountered in operations and operating managers have a major say in deciding which project to pursue. The interface between them is organized through regular committee meetings of key technical people of the various operating divisions in each of the product areas. For example, the extrusion committee is composed of representatives of the major countries having extrusions facilities. The definition of a program of development usually takes place through discussions involving the business managers of the country concerned, the researchers in the laboratories, and the appropriate technical committee. Usually on any one program there is one operating division that is more enthusiastic about it than the others. Because the laboratory will have to work closely with one of the operating companies in order to transform the research into a workable product, there is a tendency to allocate the research program to the laboratory that is closest to that operating facility.

The result is that in some fields Kingston has most expertise, in others Banbury, and in still others they both may be involved in a similar type of research for product areas where markets are quite similar. For example, in extrusion the need for development is much greater in Europe; therefore much of the research is done in Banbury. In anodizing and lithosheet, the Europeans being most interested, the development is done in Banbury. In rolling and casting, it is done in Kingston because the main smelter is in Arvida, and large rolling mills are installed at Kingston and nearby, at Oswego (New York). For building products, where technical assistance is heavily market oriented, Kingston helps the North American companies while Banbury helps the European ones. It should be emphasized that in opposition to research that is more process oriented, much product development occurs in the operating divisions with some technical support from the research centers.

The transfer of product technology from one research center to an operating division or among operating divisions is encouraged by corporate staff coordinators. They play an important role to foster exchanges between operating companies inside the Alcan group. The fact that developments in one operating company are available free to other operating companies is not enough to create efficient transfers. Confidence based on personal relationship is necessary, so that no operating company feels it has to be on the defensive. Each operating company is a profit center, so it has to be convinced that the proposed product is worth the investment.

Our center of interest in this study is related to the end result of the research and development activities, that is, the product. If a new process is used the product is judged here to be new, as it incorporates new technology. We chose in this study not to look at intermediary products at Alcan (that is, products that are inputs for further manufacturing operations inside the firm). This excludes from the analysis the ore and smelting divisions and means that in terms of fabricating we looked at the following product lines: building products, foil and packaging, and electrical products. Semi-fabricated items such as rolled products were excluded.

Building Products

The initial major involvement of Alcan in building products started in the early 1960s in the United States, when it acquired Flexalum, a company in the siding and awning business.

Alcan Canada entered this same area shortly thereafter through the acquisition of several Canadian firms that were already selling building products such as aluminum siding and window frames.

In the United Kingdom, entry into this field resulted from the acquisition of James Booth Aluminum Ltd. in 1970. In Australia, Alcan got started in architecture and building products with the acquisition of Kawneer. Within Japan, Alcan is involved through its joint venture partners. Alcan's involvement in the building and construction business has increased steadily; these activities are now accounting for roughly one-third of Alcan's sales of fabricated products.

In accordance with the management philosophy noted above, each of the markets develops its own product. The main centers of development are therefore the main markets where Alcan is present, that is, the United States, Canada, and the United Kingdom, and to a lesser extent Japan, and Europe. Each market area develops the products that it sees best suited to local demand pattern. The corresponding product strategies are MPS 13 = S1 (Kp, Mp, Pp) whenever a product is developed in Canada for the Canadian market exclusively, and MPS 45 = S8 (Kh, Mh, Ph) whenever it is developed in one of the host countries for that market. The potential efficiency that flows from being a multinational firm is not utilized in this case as no transfer takes place.

We mentioned earlier that at Alcan contacts between specialists and managers are encouraged on an international scale. International product line coordinators from the corporate staff foster these exchanges through international building product committee meetings once a year where the technical and marketing people, and managers of subsidiaries in each country are introduced to new product innovations, and exchange ideas on the success and failure of their colleagues. Transfer of product know-how is therefore done on a case-by-case basis in a relatively unstructured manner, rather than through a deliberate grand plan. The exchange may result in a modified product, or one may find that a product from one country is not suitable to another. The transfers of product know-how occur using market testing, an approach that appears economical because it requires very low capital investment. As mentioned by one executive: "$20,000 worth of equipment can put a firm in the window business." For example, one subsidiary in the United States decided to try to sell its windows around the world, and with the help of Alcan's worldwide organization it discovered that its design was not suitable for all climates. A successful example has been the transfer of a design to Brazil; some windows designed in Vancouver may fit the European market, and so on. In each case, it pays to produce close to the market due to the high weight/value ratio. Product strategies in use are therefore either MPS 40 = S8 (Kh, Mh, Ph)-S5 (Kh, Mp, Pp) whenever the know-how is developed in any host country and the know-how is transferred to Canada, or MPS 8 = S1 (Kp, MP, Pp)-S4 (Kp, Mh, Ph) whenever the know-how originates in Canada and later is transferred to other countries.

There has seldom been the need to have the cooperation of two or more countries to develop a particular product because the cost of development is low. In one case, however, it was found that it would be worthwhile in order to share the high costs of development of a panel system. The product that was developed with international specifications from the main four markets (the United States, Canada, the United Kingdom, and Europe) was quite successful and was used as a vehicle to bring managers together. This experience is unique within the company.

Foil and Packaging Products

The company's foil and packaging products are either convenience products for the housewife and sold directly to her, such as household foil and numerous containers, or they are products used by food companies in packaging meats, precooked bakery products, and frozen foods.

Alcan's entry into foil at the consumer product level dates back only as far as its decision to integrate forward in 1958. There is one exception to this, however, as Alcan had been in foil and packaging since the 1930s in Switzerland with its small but very successful subsidiary Aluminium A. G. Rohrschach. Alcan entered foil and packaging in Canada during the 1960s by a series of acquisitions and in the United Kingdom, Germany, the United States, and Japan in a similar manner. Its penetration of these markets varies according to the specific product considered.

Thus Alcan's first venture in this field occurred in 1960 with household foil in Canada, where the objective was to launch the Alcan name into the public forum with a mass market type of product. As Alcan had great experience in foil rolling, such a move did not require any major development in technological know-how but it had to learn to develop marketing know-how in the consumer products area. After ten years of heavy promotion expenditures Alcan succeeded in making this a commercial success and captured more than one-third of the Canadian market. In the United Kingdom, Alcan entered the household foil market in 1965 by acquiring Polyfoil Papers Ltd. Alcan has not tried to enter the U.S. market in this area as it would mean competing against Reynolds, which has over half of the U.S. market, which in turn would require tremendous fixed costs for promotion with the possibility of carving out only a small share of that market. Alcan is not in continental Europe in any extensive way and not under the Alcan brand name because competition is very strong there, too. In 1970 Alcan bought know-how in bakery containers (pots and pans) with the acquisition of the U.S. firm Chicago Metallic and has been able to diffuse it now in a number of countries.

Alcan entered the flexible packaging business in Canada in 1969 with the acquisition of Canada Foils Ltd. This product requires close contact with customers, as its composition is adapted to meet particular needs of customers (that is, in terms of the number of layers, printing to customer specification). Produced in small batches, this product does not enter into international trade.

Alcan specializes in sophisticated multilayer coatings of foil and packaging products where there are fewer competitors. This job requires sophisticated equipment such as extruders that laminate and coat foil. Alcan Canada acquired such a machine when it bought Canada Foils Ltd. in 1969; subsequently Alcan installed an extruder in the United Kingdom and one in Switzerland. There was a transfer of know-how in order to have an efficient process and Alcan is beginning to go further in terms of using its experience and success in one country as demonstration to incite subsidiaries in other countries to follow. For example, this is the case in the meat packing industry where Alcan Canada helped Alcan United Kingdom to appraise the market potential and convince the U.K. meat packing industry of the advantage of Alcan's method. In the meat packing industry, as in any food-oriented business, one cannot run the risk of being wrong, and the transfer of know-how takes time. Therefore, whenever a product is launched in one part of Alcan, it has to first be successful in that country, before it has any chance of being adopted in another country.

One of the most interesting examples is taking place in the
packaging business with retortable containers. Aluminium A. G.
Rohrschach (Switzerland), one of Alcan's subsidiaries, is the worldwide leader, having developed and put on the market a heat steriliz-
able lid and body stock for food containers for unrefrigerated stor-
age. [21]

This means that one may soon be able to keep any food outside
the refrigerator for an extended period of time. This innovation is
typically European, as freezers are not common in Europe and the
incentive is greater to develop products that do not need freezers.
This convenience should also appeal to North Americans, and Alcan
Canada and Alcan United States are looking seriously at transferring
the Rohrschach technology. Meanwhile Toyo Aluminium K. K. , the
Japanese affiliate, has introduced that product already on the Japanese market. The Alcan packaging committee made up of representatives of the interested countries and the international product line coordinator (vice president, foil and packaging) agreed to share development expenses with Rohrschach in return for the know-how developed.

To summarize, the product strategies used in foil and packaging
originally involved few transfers, that is, the product strategies implemented were either MPS 13 = S1 or MPS 45 = S8 (Kh, Mh, Ph) for
any host country. There is presently a tendency toward much increased exchange of know-how under the leadership of worldwide
product coordinators. However, transfer is far from being rapid,
as the success in the innovating country has to be proven before any
of the operating managers elsewhere can be persuaded of its value.
Product strategies encountered are increasingly of the type MPS 8 -
S1 (Kp, Mp, Pp)-S4 (Kp, Mh, Ph) whenever the know-how is developed in Canada and transferred abroad or MPS 40 = S8 (Kh, Mh, Ph)-
S5 (Kh, Mp, Pp) when it is developed abroad and transferred to Canada,
while transfers among subsidiaries abroad correspond to the product
strategy MPS 5 = S8 (Kh, Mh, Ph).

Electrical Products

One of the early uses of aluminum was in cable for overhead
electrical transmission. Alcan has been involved in this product line
in Canada since the 1940s and in the United States it entered through
the acquisition of the Central Cable Corporation in 1963. Alcan has
not moved into other markets such as Europe, Japan, or elsewhere
in the world because competitors have preempted the markets there.

The transfer of know-how between the three centers of production (two in Canada, one in the United States) has not been extensive
and Alcan is only now starting with a laboratory established in the

TABLE 5.8

Alcan Aluminium Ltd.—General Pattern of Product Strategies, by Product Lines

Product Line	Main Know-how Centers	Main Markets	Main Production Centers	Main Set of Product Strategies Presently Implemented
Building products	Canada, United States, United Kingdom	Most of the world	Canada, United States, United Kingdom	MPS 13 = S1 in Canada only MPS 8 = S1-S4 whenever the know-how is transferred outside Canada MPS 45 = S8 for products developed, produced, and marketed outside Canada MPS 40 = S8-S5 whenever the know-how is transferred from any country to Canada
Foil and packaging	Canada, United Kingdom, Switzerland, Japan	Most of the world	Canada, United States, United Kingdom, Switzerland, Europe, Australia	MPS 13 = S1 in Canada only MPS 8 = S1-S4 whenever the know-how is transferred outside Canada MPS 45 = S8 for products developed, produced, and marketed outside Canada MPS 40 = S8-S5 whenever the know-how is transferred from any country to Canada
Electrical products	Canada, United States	Mainly Canada and United States	Canada, United States	MPS 13 = S1 in Canada only MPS 7 = S1-S3 for products marketed in Canada and exported to less developed countries MPS 45 = S8 in the United States only

Source: Compiled by the author.

109

TABLE 5.9

Alcan Aluminum Ltd. --Selected Products and Their Product Strategies

| | First State | | | | Diffusion of Product Worldwide | | |
| | Country of: | | | | United States | | |
Product Number	Development Know-how	First Market	First Production	First State	States	Market Lag	Production Lag
1	Canada	Canada	Canada	S1	--	--	--
2	Canada	Canada	Canada	S1	S4	96	96
3	Canada	Canada	Canada	S1	--	--	--
4	Canada	Canada	Canada	S1	--	--	--
5	Canada	Canada	Canada	S1	S4	24	24
6	United States	United States	United States	S8	S8	0	0
7	Canada	Canada	Canada	S1	--	--	--
8	United States	United States	United States	S8	S8	0	0

Explanatory notes:

a) The "S1" corresponds to the particular state encountered for each product.
b) Market lags and production lags are expressed in number of months since the first introduction of the product.
c) Dash indicates that there was neither marketing nor production for that product in this particular country.

United States. Therefore the main corresponding set of product strategies is, in Canada, MPS 13 = S1 (Kp, Mp, Pp) and in the United States, MPS 45 = S8 (Kh, Mh, Ph). Tariffs and regulations are such that there is practically no export from the United States to Canada, or the reverse. Therefore for some products originating in Canada the know-how may be transferred to the United States, or vice versa, but this has not been done extensively as yet. Nevertheless, Canada does export to some underdeveloped countries where the price is often supported by government grants, that is, product strategy MPS 7 = S1 (Kp, Mp, Pp)-S3 (Kp, Mh, Pp).

Summary of Growth and Product Strategies

Alcan has evolved over a half century (1925-75) from a primary producer of aluminum ingots that were to a great extent exported from Canada, to an integrated manufacturer of aluminum products. This drastic change was achieved by buying out a number of its customers in various countries. This resulted, initially, in a number of relatively autonomous business entities that Alcan is now progressively integrating. Alcan is integrating these units vertically by geographic area, creating a number of independent units. Alcan is also fostering coordination and exchange of technology among the

	Canada			Europe			Japan			Latin America		
	Diffusion of Product Worldwide											
States	Market Lag	Production Lag	States	Market Lag	Production Lag	States	Market Lag	Production Lag	States	Market Lag	Production Lag
S1	0	0	S3-S4	12	18	S3-S4	18	24	--	--	--
S1	0	0	S4	60	60	--	--	--	--	--	--
S1	0	0	S4	60	60	S3-S4	60	94	S4	94	94
S1	0	0	S4	72	72	--	--	--	--	--	--
S1	0	0	--	--	--	--	--	--	--	--	--
--	--	--	--	--	--	--	--	--	--	--	--
S1	0	0	--	--	--	--	--	--	--	--	--
S5	24	24	S8	94	120	--	--	--	--	--	--

Source: Compiled by the author.

various geographic units involved in the same product line. The transfer of technology is done by means of committee meetings and corporate staff coordinators. The pattern of product strategies presently implemented at Alcan is summarized in Table 5.8. Of the eight products selected for further study one is a building product, three are electrical products, and four are foil and packaging products. Their product strategies are presented in Table 5.9.

DYMO INDUSTRIES

Dymo Industries began its activities in California in 1958 with a few aggressive employees and $150,000 in capital. The objective was to market a unique labeling system and this resulted in the development of a hand-operated embossing tool utilizing an adhesive-back vinyl identification tape. The success of this product is revealed in the impressive growth record of Dymo that has carried it to sales in 1973 of $130 million, and today Dymo is a leader in visual communications and information transfer systems.

Dymo quickly capitalized on its initial product by expanding into the industrial, commercial, and consumer markets (the tape writer and label maker series). In the early 1960s Dymo acquired Roovers-Lotsch Inc. (the main acquisitions of Dymo are shown in Table 5.10), adding a full line of metal plastic and paper embossing

TABLE 5.10

Dymo Industries--Chronology of the Main Acquisitions

Year	Acquisition
1960	Roovers-Lotsch Corp. (Pennsylvania): Roovers-Lotsch has a 77-year history in the manufacture and national and international distribution of many types of embossing machines and supplies. This company provided a full line of metal, plastic, and paper embossing machines in both hand- and power-operated, heavy industrial models.
1960	Trig-A-Tape Corp: a manufacturer of portable lightweight hand-operated marking machines.
1963	Elliott Business Machines (Randolph, Mass.): a leading producer of addressing equipment; main plant in Randolph; other facilities in Toronto, Atlanta, Mexico, and Faltham (United Kingdom); entry of Dymo into that product line.
1964	Modulux Inc. (Newark, Calif.): a manufacturer of relocatable classrooms, cargo containers; entry of Dymo into that product line, but it later sold it to Kaiser Aluminum in 1969.
1964	Perin Products Corp. (Natick, Mass.): a leading manufacturer and distributor of specialty advertising and promotional products; entry of Dymo into that product line.
1964	Trans-Western Service Industries: one of the largest dry cleaning and laundry operations in the United States. It operates three dry cleaning and laundry plants servicing over 250 retail sales outlets; entry of Dymo into that business.
1966	Meto Gesellschaft Oscar Kind GmbH (Hirschhorn, West Germany): a leading European manufacturer and distributor of price marking tools and labels, which thrusts Dymo directly into the price marking field.
1971	Audac: a firm involved in credit verification terminals.
1972	Datascan Inc.: a leading manufacturer of automatic typesetting and photocomposition equipment. This acquisition has given Dymo a solid stake in this rapidly growing market.
1972	Farrington Manufacturing Co. (Virginia, New Jersey): Dymo acquired two profitable subsidiaries of Farrington, one of the world's market leaders in the imprinter field.
1972	Star Graphics Systems Co. (South Hackensack, N.J.): an electronic phototypesetting company; marked the entry of Dymo into the photocomposition field.
1973	Craftint Manufacturing Co. (Ohio): an important firm in the consumer-graphics industry in the United States.
1973	Promoflex: an in-store sign and display product line presently marketed in Europe only.

Source: Dymo Industries, Annual Report, various issues.

TABLE 5.11

Dymo Industries--General Pattern of Product Strategies, by Product Lines

Product Line	Main Know-how Centers	Main Markets	Main Production Centers	Main Set of Product Strategies Presently Implemented
Signs and labels	United States	Worldwide	United States, Belgium, Mexico, Japan, Australia	MPS 8 = S1–S4 between the United States and Europe MPS 7 = S1–S3 whenever host countries (besides Europe) are supplied by export from the United States MPS 1 = S1–S3–S4 whenever the product is introduced by export and later production MPS 15 = S4 whenever a host country is supplied from another
Retail systems	Germany, United States	Worldwide	Germany, United States	For the products developed in Germany MPS 55 = S8–S6 for exports from Germany to the United States MPS 51 = S8–S6–S5 for some products later manufactured in the United States MPS 45 = S8 from any host country to any other host country For the products developed in the United States MPS 7 = S1–S3 for products later exported from the United States MPS 1 = S1–S3–S4 for exports from the United States followed by production in Germany
Business systems	United States	Worldwide	United States, United Kingdom	MPS 7 = S1–S3 for products or basic components exported from the United States to supply other countries MPS 45 = S8 for other components designed and manufactured in the United Kingdom for some host country markets
Graphics systems	United States	United States and some other countries	United States	MPS 7 = S1–S3 for products exported from the United States
Dry cleaning	United States	United States	United States	MPS 13 = S1 for activity limited to the United States

Source: Compiled by the author.

TABLE 5.12

Dymo Industries--Selected Products and Their Product Strategies

Product Number	First State Country of:				Diffusion of Product Worldwide United States		
	Development Know-how	First Market	First Production	First State	States	Market Lag	Production Lag
1	United States	United States & Canada	United States	S1 S3	S1	0	0
2	Germany & United States	Worldwide	United States	S5,S7 S1,S3	S5 S1	0	0
3	United States	United States & Europe	United States & Europe	S1 S4	S1	0	0
4	United States	Europe	Europe	S4	S1	5	5

Explanatory notes:
  a) The "S1" corresponds to the particular state encountered for each product.
  b) Market lags and production lags are expressed in number of months since the first introduction of the product.
  c) Dash indicates that there was neither marketing nor production for that product in this particular country.
  d) The term "INF" (Infinite) means that production did not take place and is not envisaged.

machines in both hand-held and power-operated heavy industrial
models. Dymo also expanded into the addressing and labeling business with the acquisition in 1963 of Elliott Business Machines, Inc.,
a large manufacturer of addressing machines with sales of $9 million
and subsidiaries in Canada, Mexico, and the United Kingdom. In
1965, Dymo diversified into a new field through the acquisition of
Transwestern Service Industries, a dry cleaning and laundry operation. This was followed by a further move in the visual communication field with the acquisition of Meto Gesellschaft Oscar Kind GmbH
in 1966, a leading manufacturer and distributor of price marking
tools, coding equipment, and pressure sensitive labels. In 1972
Dymo further expanded into typesetting and photocomposition operations with the acquisition of Datascan Inc., and into the imprinter
field with the acquisition of two subsidiaries of Farrington Manufacturing Co.

Concurrently Dymo has regrouped its various activities in the
field of visual communication into five major business areas: (1) the
signs and labels group, which comprises the original product line;
(2) the retail systems group, which comes primarily from Meto, but
also includes Promoflex product lines; (3) the business systems
group which is composed of the Elliott, Farrington, Roovers product
lines, and Sten-c-label; (4) the graphics systems group, which includes the Stargraphics, Datascan, Craftint product lines; and (5) the
laundry and dry cleaning services.

| | | | | | | Diffusion of Product Worldwide | | | | | |
| Canada | | | Europe | | | Japan | | | Latin America | | |
States	Market Lag	Production Lag	States	Market Lag	Production Lag	States	Market Lag	Production Lag	States	Market Lag	Production Lag
S3	0	INF	S3-S4	12	14	S3	12	INF	S3	12	INF
S7	0	INF	S7	0	INF	S7-S8	0	12	S7	0	INF
S3			S3			S3-S4			S3		
S3	0	INF	S4	3	3	S3	12	INF	--	--	--
S3	5	INF	S4	0	0	S4	8	8	S3	6	INF

Source: Compiled by the author.

The first two groups accounted in 1973 for approximately 60 percent of sales and 84 percent of pretax income. With these two groups, Dymo holds a dominant position in the market. The other three groups account for 13 percent, 12 percent, and 13 percent of total Dymo sales respectively.[22]

As early as 1960, Dymo created a separate export sales department as a first step toward achieving international status, and in that year it also established distributor outlets in some twelve countries. The first major step abroad was taken in 1961 when a marketing center for the original Dymo product line (embossing tools and tapes) was established in Switzerland. Dymo acquired its first manufacturing facility outside the United States with the Elliott Business Machines takeover (1963), and it soon followed with manufacturing facilities for the Dymo product line in Belgium and the United Kingdom. By 1967, Dymo maintained, outside the United States and Canada, wholly owned production facilities in Belgium, Mexico, Japan, England, Germany, and Brazil. Additionally Dymo had interests in two joint ventures in Spain and Australia. International operations by 1967 covered full manufacturing and marketing operations of not only the Dymo and Elliott product lines, but also the Meto product line acquired in 1966. That year, international sales reached 25 percent of total sales.

The acquisition of Meto placed Dymo in the forefront, with price marking and pressure sensitive labels. The pressure sensitive label concept was developed in Europe in the early 1960s and

Meto had major patents in the technology. Dymo, using its international marketing sales force, not only extended the market for Meto products beyond the German border, but was also successful in marketing the products in the United States. Product acceptance came when the U.S. food industry was convinced of the overall cost saving it could achieve with initially more costly price marking tools.[23] As noted by Dymo officials:

> In just a year and a half since its acquisition by Dymo, sales volume at Meto increased by 50%. The Meto price marking and coding tools system was found at every level of retail distribution in Germany. In 1966-67, Dymo's international marketing team expanded distribution of the Meto line into major new markets: Latin America, Central America, Australia, [the] Orient.[24]

Pattern of Multinational Product Strategies

As the R and D activities at Dymo are carried out by each product group, the location of R and D reflects to a large extent the pattern of development and acquisitions. For example, the business systems group's R and D function is performed to a large extent at Elliott Business Machines in the United States, whereas the retail systems group's R and D is performed primarily in Germany. However, in response to the increased complexity of the various products, the corporate development laboratory in Berkeley has done research for a number of product groups.

The signs and labels group, with its development center in the United States, initially developed products to be sold in the U.S. market, that is, product strategy MPS 13 = S1 (Kp, Mp, Pp). As the group began to export its products, that is, product strategy MPS 7 = S1 (Kp, Mp, Pp)-S3 (Kp, Mh, Pp) it recognized the need to develop standardized products. Later with increased penetration of the European market it became economical to produce in Europe, that is, product strategy MPS 1 = S1 (Kp, Mp, Pp)-S3 (Kp, Mh, Pp)-S4 (Kp, Mh, Ph). Furthermore, for some of the later additions to Dymo's product line, the export stage is deleted from the strategy, that is, MPS 8 = S1 (Kp, Mp, Pp)-S4 (Kp, Mh, Ph). It has never proved economical for Dymo to import back to the United States a product that was developed, produced, and exported from the United States at the beginning of the product's life, thereby precluding the use of the international product cycle MPS 27 = S1-S3-S4-S2. The main reason for not using product strategy MPS 27 at Dymo is the low labor intensity of the products (that is, the transfer of production to low labor cost areas results in little cost savings). The rest of the world is supplied by exports from either its U.S. or European production center, with the exception of Mexico, Japan, and Australia. For these countries Dymo has established local assembly and manufacturing operations. The general pattern of product strategies showing the main centers of developments, production, and the markets for the sign and label group (and the other Dymo products) is presented in Table 5.11.

The retail systems group sells a smaller number of units than the signs and labels group. For economies-of-scale reasons,* most of this group's products are produced only in Germany where the main development center is located. This means that products which are exported follow either the product strategy MPS 45 = S8 (Kh, Mh, Ph) or product strategy MPS 55 = S8 (Kh, Mh, Ph)-S6 (Kh, Mp, Ph) in the case of exports to the United States.

For some products, certain parts are manufactured in the United States because the equipment is available there, that is, product strategy MPS 51 = S8 (Kp, Mh, Ph)-S6 (Kh, Mp, Ph)-S5 (Kh, Mp, Pp). Exports from Germany to any other host country correspond to product strategy MPS 45 = S8 (Kh, Mh, Ph). Dymo has also developed products in the retail systems group that use know-how in plastics which originated in the signs and labels development facility in the United States. This is one of the first examples of pooling of know-how on an international scale at Dymo.

In the business systems group, products are complex and high priced. A small number of units are sold and most products are produced in the United States for the domestic and export market, that is, product strategy MPS 7 = S1 (Kp, Mp, Pp)-S3 (Kp, Mh, Pp). Nonetheless some products are designed and manufactured in the United Kingdom for the European market, that is, product strategy MPS 45 = S8.

The graphics systems group has not penetrated foreign markets to the same extent as have other groups possibly because the printing industry outside the United States is less sophisticated. This group presently exports a limited number of products through distributors.

The product strategies implemented by Dymo for four selected products are presented in Table 5.12.

----

*Economies of scale are particularly great in molds and stampings. Dymo has found that it is economical to ship its molds from one plant to another.

Summary of Growth and Product Strategies

Our survey of the growth of Dymo shows that after initially developing operations abroad with the distinctive Dymo embossing tools, it diversified by several acquisitions in the United States and one in Europe. Dymo has had experience abroad only since 1964, but it has already implemented a variety of product strategies that go beyond the classic ones (that is, product strategies MPS 7 = S1-S3 and MPS 1 = S1-S3-S4). The primary reason for Dymo's early recognition of opportunities abroad is the international orientation and capacities of its top management, particularly the current president and chief executive officer, who had extensive experience in Europe, as vice president for international operations over the decade 1965-75.

GILLETTE COMPANY

The origins of the Gillette Company go back to 1901 when King C. Gillette, the inventor of the safety razor blade, revolutionized man's shaving habits. Gillette grew for half a century essentially as a safety razor company, before embarking in 1948 on a series of acquisitions that led to a diversification of its product line into toiletries, writing instruments, and personal care appliances. Today, Gillette is known as a leader in men's and women's personal care products with sales in excess of one billion dollars. Gillette spends more than $25 million in research and development, and $158 million to promote its products throughout the world, making Gillette one of the world's largest advertisers. The company's sales can be broken down as follows:

Product	Percent of Total Sales
Razors and blades	31
Toiletries and personal care products	32
Small electric appliances	22
Writing instruments	7
Other (lighters, surgical equipment. . .)	8

Almost from its very beginning Gillette has been a company with an international outlook. The company established its first

foreign subsidiaries in Canada and the United Kingdom in 1905; as
early as 1928 Gillette sold half of its production outside the United
States and in 1937 foreign earnings reached two-thirds of total earnings. In 1972, Gillette had 50 manufacturing facilities in 19 countries; 68 percent of its net assets were outside the United States and
of the 27,700 employees, 17,900 were employed by Gillette outside
the United States, making Gillette a truly multinational company.

Gillette's international operations were reorganized in 1960 to
reflect its major geographic markets. A domestic division was
formed to include Canada and the United States and this division was
departmentalized on a product group basis. The international division is organized along geographic lines: an Australian group, a
Latin American group, and European and British Commonwealth
groups.

Basic research and development is the responsibility of the
corporate laboratories; one is located in Boston, a second in Reading (Britain). A third laboratory, located in Rockville, Maryland,
has worldwide responsibility for the safety of the company's products.

The various Gillette product groups are presented with a chronology of acquisitions in each of these product groups in Table 5.13.

Razor and Blades Line

The razor and blades product line represents the foundation of
Gillette and still accounts for 31 percent of Gillette's total sales. It
is the company's most profitable product line. Gillette has maintained a solid commitment to achieve leadership in shaving technology and high visibility in the marketplace.

Strong competition has characterized the years of operation
from 1960 to 1975. Until 1960 the razor blade technology had re-
mained constant, but Wilkinson then gained market notoriety with its
introduction of a stainless steel teflon-coated blade that markedly
increased blade life and shaving comfort. Gillette was surprised by
this technological first, but only momentarily. It soon not only introduced a Super stainless steel blade but also the Techmatic--a
steel continuous band which is self-contained and uses thin steel for
a closer shave. Then in 1972 Gillette again made its technological
presence known through the introduction of Trac II, a twin blade system which presently is the best-selling razor in the United States.

Trac II was developed in the corporate laboratories in Reading
but first produced and sold in the United States. The international
diffusion of Trac II is similar to the diffusion of other Gillette razor
and blades products. Shortly after acceptance in the United States,
Trac II was introduced in Canada, the United Kingdom, and Germany--

TABLE 5.13

Gillette Co. --Chronology of the Main Acquisitions

Year	Acquisition

Razor and Blades Product Line

1929   Gillette acquired a controlling interest (67 percent) in Roth Buchner A.G., a Berlin company which manufactures and markets lower-priced razor blades. Gillette did this in response to the demand, in America and Europe, for a lower-priced blade.

1930   Autostrap Safety Razor Co. (United States): Gillette acquired Autostrap's subsidiaries in Canada, England, and Brazil.

1948   Gillette Safety Razor Co. of Mexico purchased and expanded a plant in Mexico City, which was to be used to produce razors and blades. This acquisition was the answer to increasing demand for Gillette products in Mexico.

1952   Gillette Safety Razor Co. of South America acquired all of the common stock of Efdelit, S.A., a leading Argentinian manufacturer of plastic products.

1952   Roth Buchner A.G., a German unit of Gillette, acquired a 100 percent interest in Zoellner-Werke GmbH (Germany).

1973   Acquisition of Bassat, S.A. in Spain.

1973   Start-up of a joint venture in Yugoslavia, with Yugoslavia Commerce. The new company would manufacture a specially selected brand of blades in that country, to supply Yugoslavia and certain export markets.

Toiletries and Personal Care Product Line

1948   Toni Co. (United States): this represented Gillette entry into the toiletry field.

1968   Colton Co. (United States): entry of Gillette into prestige toiletries and cosmetics products with Nine Flags Shaving Colognes and Foams.

1968   Evital S.P.A. (Italy): manufacturer of Eva of Rome. Gillette secured complete worldwide rights to the line of prestige cosmetics sold under the Eva of Rome trademark. Gillette sold its interest in Evital in 1971, because the division did not prove successful.

1970   North American Fashions Inc.: a leading U.S. manufacturer and distributor of wig products; North American and Toni were to work together in the hair field. These assets were sold to Len Sani (October 1974).

1973   Kanebo Ltd. (Japan): joint venture with one of the major Japanese companies. Gillette was to provide the aerosol technology, and Kanebo the expertise in manufacturing and distribution.

1973   Jafra Cosmetics Inc. (United States): a California manufacturer and distributor of skin care products.

Year	Acquisition

Writing Instruments Product Line

1955   Paper Mate Pen Co. (United States): Paper Mate is the nation's premier maker of ball-point pens.

1970   Autopoint Co. (United States): this acquisition expanded Paper Mate markets into commercial, industrial, and advertising specialty areas.

1973   Fritz Johansen Co. (Brazil): a manufacturer of pencils and other writing instruments and office and school supplies.

1973   Plumibol S.A. (Mexico): Gillette acquired 49 percent in this manufacturer of low-cost ball-point pens.

Diversified Companies Group

1962   Sterilon Co., maker of hospital supplies; in 1970 North American operations of Sterilon were sold due to a lack of profitability.

1967   A 94 percent interest in Braun A.G. (West Germany): this marked the entry of Gillette in the electric shaver business in Europe and other countries of the world where Braun is distributed. The electric shaver is not sold in North America, where Gillette has an agreement with Ronson. But Braun has diversified extensively (household appliances, electronic units, photographic equipment, hair dryers) and some of their products are sold in North America.

1971   S. T. Dupont (France): a group of companies purchased. A maximum of 48 percent interest was authorized by the French government initially, but was increased to 80 percent in 1973. With Dupont, Gillette acquired 100 percent of Anant S.A. Corp. (Switzerland) which holds exclusive rights to manufacture and sell Cricket disposable lighters outside France.

1971   Welcome Wagon International Inc. was purchased, and its affiliate Welcome Wagon Ltd. (Canada).

1972   Buxton Inc.: it has been the leading manufacturer of high quality personal leather goods for more than 75 years. It still is the first on the U.S. market, and its products are also sold in many foreign countries.

1972   Welcome Wagon acquired Felicitas B.V. of Holland, thus entering the community service business in continental Europe.

1974   Sunoroid Ltd. (Australia): manufacturer of sunglasses.

1973   Hydroponic Chemical Co. (United States): a home plant care business.

Source: Gillette, Annual Report, various issues.

three other highly developed countries. The reader is referred to Table 5.14 for the pattern of demand for Trac II and other shaving instruments. It shows that the demand for these instruments is directly related to the level of development of each area. Trac II is a growing product in the United States, but it is a newborn product in Latin America. This means that the first state of any product strategy for this product line must either be S1 (Kp, Mp, Pp) or S5 (Kh, Mp, Pp). In the case of Trac II it is S5 because the know-how was developed in the United Kingdom, whereas for the carbon double edge blade the first state is S1.

TABLE 5.14

Worldwide Pattern of Demand for Blades and Razor Systems

Market	Newborn	Growing	Mature	Declining
United States	Twin injector	Trac II	Stainless double edge	Carbon double edge
Western Europe		Trac II	Stainless double edge	Carbon double edge
		Techmatic		
Latin America	Trac II	Stainless double edge	Carbon double edge	
	Techmatic			
Africa and Asia	Stainless double edge	Carbon double edge		

Source: William D. Witter, "The Outlook for Personal Care Products," mimeographed (Gillette Co., 1974).

The first state (S1 or S5) depends upon corporate R and D strategy. Whereas production starts invariably in the United States close to the initial market, it is clear that Gillette does not limit itself in its R and D strategy. Sophisticated technology is confined to the corporate laboratories. Hence in most cases we will witness the

following two sets of product strategies for this product line:
(1) MPS 1 = S1-S3-S4, MPS 7 = S1-S3, MPS 8 = S1-S4; (2) MPS 31 =
S5-S7-S8, MPS 37 = S5-S7, MPS 39 = S5-S8. This general pattern
is presented in Table 5.15. The export stage from the United States
(that is, S3 and S7) is used because of the high economies of scale in
production that induce Gillette to first bring the U.S. plant to capacity
before starting manufacture in Europe and elsewhere. Razors and
blades being highly capital intensive, it is not economical to manufacture them abroad to supply the U.S. market, thereby precluding
the occurrence of the international product cycle.

Toiletries and Personal Care Products

Gillette entered the toiletries and personal care products field
on the one hand with the acquisition of the Toni Company in 1948 and
on the other hand with the diversification of interests of the razor
and blades division in the early 1960s toward men's grooming needs.

Product development is mainly done in the United States, where
the domestic division develops products in response to U.S. tastes.
Right Guard is a case in point. It was developed in the United States
for the male grooming market and a latent demand was uncovered for
this product as a family deodorant. The success of Right Guard,
domestically, signaled it as a product to be exploited internationally.
Gillette resourcefulness is indicated by the fact that the international
division marketed the deodorant in Latin America in a plastic squeeze
bottle to accommodate a lower-price demand. Toiletries have a low
value-to-weight ratio, they are bulky, difficult to ship and thus are
manufactured locally. This limits the range of states of any feasible
product strategy to S1 (Kp, Mp, Pp), S4 (Kp, Mh, Ph), S5 (Kh, Mp,
Pp), S8 (Kh, Mh, Ph). However, state S5 is not likely to occur due
to the sophistication of the U.S. market. In the case of Right Guard
the product strategy is MPS 8 = S1-S4. For Rujel, a skin care product developed in Italy for the European market, the strategy is MPS
45 = S8. The general pattern of product strategies observed for this
product line is MPS 8 = S1-S4, MPS 15 = S4, MPS 45 = S8.

It is expected that more toiletries and personal care products
will be developed abroad. International market sophistication in that
product line is growing. While three-quarters of the toiletry products presently sold in the international division now are developed in
the United States, this should diminish in the future.

TABLE 5.15

Gillette--General Pattern of Product Strategies, by Product Lines

Product Line	Main Know-how Centers	Main Markets	Main Production Centers	Main Set of Product Strategies Presently Implemented
Razor and blades	United States, United Kingdom	Worldwide	United States, Canada, United Kingdom, Argentina, Brazil, France, Germany, Mexico, Spain	MPS 1 = S1-S3-S4 MPS 7 = S1-S3 MPS 8 = S1-S4 MPS 39 = S5-S8 MPS 37 = S5-S7 MPS 31 = S5-S7-S8 } between the United States and the rest of the world; development is done in the United Kingdom and the product is initially launched in the United States
Toiletries and personal care products	United States, United Kingdom	Worldwide	United States, Canada, United Kingdom, Argentina, Brazil, France, Italy, Mexico	MPS 8 = S1-S4 MPS 45 = S8 } between the United States and the rest of the world for products developed, produced, and marketed outside the United States MPS 15 = S4 for products developed in the United States to be introduced in other countries
Writing instruments	United States, Italy, Mexico, France	Most of the world	United States, Canada, United Kingdom, France, Argentina, Mexico, Italy, Venezuela, Brazil	MPS 1 = S1-S3-S4 MPS 8 = S1-S4 } between the United States and the rest of the world MPS 45 = S8 for products developed, produced, and marketed outside the United States
Diversified companies Braun A.G.	Germany	Worldwide	Germany, Spain	MPS 55 = S8-S6 between Germany and the United States MPS 45 = S8 otherwise
Dupont	France	Most of the world	Puerto Rico, Mexico, Brazil	MPS 51 = S8-S6-S5 between France and the United States MPS 55 = S8-S6 and MPS 45 = S8 otherwise
Surgical	United Kingdom, Europe	Mainly Europe	United Kingdom, France	MPS 45 = S8 for products developed, produced, and marketed outside the United States

Source: Compiled by the author.

Writing Instruments

Gillette made its entry into writing instruments in 1955 with
the acquisition of the Paper Mate Pen Company of Santa Monica,
California, the leader in ball-point pens in the United States. Since
then Paper Mate diversified its product line with the Mark IV, a
chrome and gold plated pen and pencil set. In 1966, it successfully
introduced the Flair product, a pen with a tapered nylon tip that became a best seller in 1972. In 1970, Gillette acquired Auto Point
Company and introduced El Marko, a new line of ink markers.

The success of Gillette's domestic entry into the writing instrument product line led to the search for profitable opportunities
abroad. The first entry abroad occurred in Italy in 1967 and was
quickly expanded with manufacturing facilities; this entry is typical.
Gillette Italy initially introduced the Paper Mate pens by importing
them from Santa Monica. The success of the introduction led to the
importation of Flair pens; the marketing organization grew in Italy
to the point where in 1972 Gillette Italy developed and manufactured
low-priced pens for the local market. The whole of Europe is presently supplied by the Italian manufacturing facility. Gillette has
further increased its penetration in the lower-priced pen market with
two acquisitions--one in Mexico, the other in Brazil.

The pattern of product strategies in the writing instrument
product line corresponds to MPS 1 = S1 (Kp, Mp, Pp)-S3 (Kp, Mh,
Pp)-S4 (Kp, Mh, Ph); MPS 8 = S1 (Kp, Mp, Pp)-S4 (Kp, Mh, Ph);
MPS 45 = S8 (Kh, Mh, Ph). Essentially Gillette has exploited internationally an acquired technology (that is, a technology not initially
developed within the corporation) and relied for further expansion on
the dynamics of local managers in its Italian subsidiary.

Diversified Companies

The diversified companies of Gillette comprise a number of
firms of which the most important is the Braun Company, which accounted for 22 percent of total Gillette sales in 1973. The other companies include the S. T. Dupont Company, a highly successful firm
involved in lighters and luxury pens; Welcome Wagon, a community
service business; the Gillette surgical supplies unit; and Jafra Cosmetics.

Before Gillette acquired Braun in 1967, Braun was a family
owned German company, and a leader in the design and technology of
small electric appliances. Since its acquisition Braun's products
have obtained an expanded exposure abroad. As stated by the chair-
man of Braun, the Gillette affiliation has strengthened "the Braun

TABLE 5.16

Gillette Co. --Selected Products and Their Product Strategies

| Product Number | First State Country of: | | | | Diffusion of Product Worldwide United States | | |
	Development Know-how	First Market	First Production	First State	States	Market Lag	Production Lag
1	United Kingdom	United States	United States	S5	S5	0	0
2	United States	United States	United States	S1	S1	0	0
3	United States	United States	United States	S1	S1	0	0

Explanatory notes:

a) The "S1" corresponds to the particular state encountered for each product.
b) Market lags and production lags are expressed in number of months since the first introduction of the product.
c) Dash indicates that there was neither marketing nor production for that product in this particular country.
d) The term "INF" (Infinite) means that production did not take place and is not envisaged.

commitment internationally by providing us with experienced international company managers. Among Braun's twelve international operating subsidiaries, eight company managers have worked in Gillette backgrounds."[25]

In 1967 Braun sales were $69 million whereas in 1973 sales were $234 million of which more than half was accounted for by sales in the external market. Despite its large volume of exports Braun is basically a German firm having its development center and most of its production facilities in Germany. The corresponding Gillette product strategies are therefore MPS 55 = S8 (Kh, Mh, Ph)-S6 (Kh, Mp, Ph) between Germany and the United States and MPS 45 = S8 (Kh, Mh, Ph) in other cases.

The S. T. Dupont Company was a family owned, family run French business, manufacturing cigarette lighters for the domestic market. Gillette acquired 48 percent of the Dupont Company, and 100 percent of its sister company rights for marketing and manufacturing outside France in 1971. It increased its ownership of Dupont to 80 percent in 1973. Today the sales of lighters make them the fastest-growing products in Gillette worldwide operations.

Primarily due to the Cricket disposable lighter, output has been substantially expanded in France since the Gillette acquisition, and new facilities have been established in Puerto Rico, Mexico, and Brazil to supplement French production for the world market. This development underscores Gillette's ability (as was indicated with the writing instruments) to seize opportunities that were identified by Gillette's French management and exploit the firm's original product strength through its international marketing organization.

					Diffusion of Product Worldwide						
	Canada			Europe			Japan			Latin America	
States	Market Lag	Production Lag	States	Market Lag	Production Lag	States	Market Lag	Production Lag	States	Market Lag	Production Lag
S7	5	INF	S7–S8	8	17	S7–S8	8	INF	S8	20	20
S3–S4	3	60	S4	12	12	S4	132	132	S4	36	36
S3	12	INF	S3–S4	48	62	S3	30	INF	S3–S4	48	62

Source: Compiled by the author.

The product strategy of the Cricket lighter is MPS 51 = S8 (Kh, Mh, Ph)-S6 (Kh, Mp, Ph)-S5 (Kh, Mp, Pp) as it was first developed, marketed, and manufactured in France, later exported to the United States, and finally produced in Puerto Rico for the U.S. market. For the other countries the Cricket lighter was exported from one of the production centers. This is product strategy MPS 45 = S8 (Kh, Mh, Ph).

Summary of Growth and Product Strategies

The general pattern of product strategies for the various product lines at the Gillette Company illustrates the diversity of product strategies presently implemented by the company. Gillette went abroad with its unique razor blade, employing a classic strategy (that is, MPS 1 = S1-S3-S4 and MPS 7 = S1-S3 depending on the countries). Gillette still implements the strategy with a number of razors and blades systems, but the development of these systems may also occur in its U.K. laboratory. The company therefore employs a greater variety of product strategies (that is, MPS 31 = S5-S7-S8 and MPS 37 = S5-S7 depending on the countries). Gillette diversified into toiletries and personal care products and writing instruments, capitalizing on its worldwide distribution experience to extend the markets for these product lines. In the toiletries and personal care products Gillette relies on products developed in the United States and the United Kingdom, while production takes place close to the market (that is, MPS 8 = S1-S4, or MPS 15 = S4, or MPS 45 = S8). For the writing instruments Gillette has been able to use the classic strategy in penetrating international markets. In both of these product lines Gillette is presently moving toward products that are better tailored to needs abroad. It is developing toiletries for specific foreign markets and has acquired firms in the writing instrument product line. As of yet Gillette is not supplying the U.S. market with any of these products developed abroad. As noted above, Gillette also diversified into a number of related areas through a number of acquisitions abroad. These acquisitions have benefited from the experience of Gillette; Braun mainly from Gillette's worldwide management experience and Dupont mainly from Gillette's traditional expertise in the marketing of consumer goods. In this way Gillette has markedly increased its range of product strategies. The analysis of product strategies at Gillette is pursued with three selected products (two are from the razors and blades, and one from the toiletry product line) whose strategies are presented in Table 5.16.

INTERNATIONAL GROWTH OF THE FIRMS: FOUR CONCLUSIONS

The description of the growth of these five firms and the analysis of the main pattern of their multinational product strategies lead us to the following four conclusions.

The first conclusion is that in all cases, except one, the firms initially became involved internationally with a unique product that had been a success in their domestic market. They initially exported the product and as sales in international markets increased this led them to investment abroad. This corresponds to the classic product strategy MPS 1 = S1-S3-S4 (the only exception is probably Alcan, which initially was a primary producer as part of Alcoa, and started its involvement outside the United States by mining bauxite).

The second conclusion is that after having achieved a dominant position with their unique product internationally, the firms diversified their activities into other product lines. This diversification was achieved by internal development of products and/or acquisition of firms with different technologies.

The third conclusion is that the experience of the firm in a particular country led to the identification of opportunities in that market. Top management in all cases was instrumental in exploring these opportunities.

The fourth conclusion is that these firms developed a worldwide outlook and consequently they are able to see the potential of new technology on a world scale. It follows that the firm's products will eventually diffuse on a worldwide scale.

NOTES

1. See Hewlett-Packard in Perspective, 1970, p. 3. The company designs and manufactures more than 3,000 items including general purpose instruments (such as oscilloscopes, electronic counters, multifunction meters, power supplies and recorders); scientific instruments (including those for vibration, and nuclear and chemical measurement analysis); computational equipment (computers, calculators, computing counters, time sharing systems and related peripherals); microwave instruments, systems and components; a variety of communications instrumentation (analyzers, monitors, and fault testers); and electronic instruments and systems for medical diagnosis, monitoring, and research.

2. The international activities of the company are described in Hewlett-Packard, "Expanding International Markets," in Hewlett-Packard, Annual Report, 1969, pp. 9-22.

3. This section draws heavily on William R. Hewlett's address, "International Expansion: A Case Study," American Business Looks Abroad, Proceedings of the 19th Annual Stanford Business Conference, September 1960 (Palo Alto: Stanford University Press, 1961), pp. 92-103.

4. Ibid., p. 98. Hewlett emphasizes the importance of a sales force that understands the customer's technical problems and is able to make intelligent suggestions: "Domestically we had found to achieve this competence, we had to have intensive training programs for our representatives' sales engineers. In Europe, we have never had the opportunity to furnish this type of sales training. At best, we were fortunate if the principals visited us once every two or three years, and when they did, they were more interested in matters of policy than in technical questions."

5. Ibid., p. 99.

6. Ibid., p. 103.

7. Quoted in "The Challenge to Our International Trade," Measure, September-October, 1972, p. 10.

8. Ibid.

9. Interview with T. A. Christiansen, international trade relations manager, Hewlett-Packard, August 6, 1973.

10. Ibid.

11. Hewlett-Packard, Annual Report, 1972, p. 12.

12. Interview with Christiansen.

13. "Hewlett-Packard's New Post: The Reasons," Business International, November 21, 1969, p. 374.

14. The main sources of information for the history and growth of Massey-Ferguson come from E. P. Neufeld, A Global Corporation (Toronto: University of Toronto Press, 1969); see also series of studies by the Royal Commission on Farm Machinery (Canada) and the company's annual reports.

15. Neufeld, op. cit., pp. 16-17.

16. Ibid., p. 36.

17. Interview with C. W. Nygren, marketing manager, Massey-Ferguson, Spring 1974.

18. Alcan Aluminium, Annual Report, 1965, p. 5.

19. Alcan Aluminium, Annual Report, 1967, p. 5.

20. Culver, "Having It Both Ways," Compass, May 1973, p. 8.

21. Alcan Aluminium, Annual Report, Montreal, 1972, p. 6.

22. For further details, see Dymo Industries, "An Address by Claude L. Ganz, President and Chief Executive Officer," mimeographed (presented before the New York Society of Security Analysts, January 21, 1974).

23. See Dymo Industries, Annual Report, 1968, p. 6. Two products which achieved high U.S. acceptance are the Precision Pricer and the Speedrite Sign System.

24. Dymo Industries, Annual Report, 1967.

25. Report on the annual meeting of stockholders, Gillette Co., April 18, 1974, p. 17.

PART

III

**THE VARIETY
OF MULTINATIONAL
PRODUCT STRATEGIES
AND THEIR RATIONALE**

CHAPTER

6

THE VARIETY
OF STRATEGIES
IMPLEMENTED

The purpose of this chapter is twofold. First, we will attempt to consolidate the two sets of observations presented in Chapter 5, that is, the general pattern of product strategies by product lines and selected products, and their respective strategies. On the basis of this consolidation, we will proceed to evaluate the variety of multinational product strategies implemented by the five firms as compared with the feasible set identified in the typology.

Secondly, our intention is to appraise the relevance of foreign direct investment theories for business decision makers.

The first set of observations, by product lines, revealed a total of 87 observations of product strategies for the five firms and the 30 product lines studied. These data, classified by product strategy and by firm, are presented in Table 6.1.

The second set of observations resulted from our study of the 52 selected products for which data were shown (by firm) in Tables 5.3, 5.6, 5.9, 5.12, and 5.16. For each product in question, these tables contained the first state and various subsequent states relating to the international diffusion of the product. By combining the product's first state with the state corresponding to the country of diffusion, we obtain the specific product strategies for each of the 52 selected products as shown in Table 6.2.

For example, product 1 of Dymo Industries was developed in the United States. Therefore, the first state is S1 in the United States. The resultant multinational product strategies for this product are as follows:

MPS 7 = S1-S3 between the United States and Canada
MPS 1 = S1-S3-S4 between the United States and Europe
MPS 7 = S1-S3 between the United States and Japan
MPS 7 = S1-S3 between the United States and Latin America

133

TABLE 6.1

General Pattern of Product Strategies Implemented for the
30 Product Lines of the Five Firms Analyzed

Product Strategy	Hewlett-Packard	Massey-Ferguson	Alcan	Dymo	Gillette	Number of Times Observed
MPS 1 = S1–S3–S4	1, 2, 4, 5, 7, 8	3		2	1, 3	10
MPS 7 = S1–S3	1, 2, 3, 4, 5, 7, 8	2, 3	3	1, 2, 3, 4	1	15
MPS 8 = S1–S4	1	2, 3	1, 2	1	1, 2, 3	9
MPS 9 = S3–S4						0
MPS 10 = S3–S1						0
MPS 11 = S4–S1						0
MPS 12 = S4–S3						0
MPS 13 = S1	6		1, 2, 3	5		5
MPS 15 = S4	3			1	2	3
MPS 29 = S1–S3–S2–S4	3, 6					2
MPS 31 = S5–S7–S8						0
MPS 37 = S5–S7						0
MPS 39 = S5–S8					1	1
MPS 40 = S8–S5		2	1, 2			3
MPS 42 = S8–S7						0
MPS 43 = S5						0
MPS 45 = S8	1, 7, 8	1, 2, 3, 4, 5, 6, 7, 8	1, 2, 3	2, 3	2, 3, 4, 5, 6	21
MPS 51 = S8–S6–S5	1, 7, 8	8		2	5	6
MPS 55 = S8–S6	1, 7, 8	1, 4, 5, 6, 7, 8		2	4, 5	12
Total						87
Number of product lines by firm	8	8	3	5	6	30

Note: The numbers in the body of the table are product line numbers of the particular firm.

Source: Tables 5.2, 5.5, 5.8, 5.11, 5.15.

134

Two points with respect to our count of multinational product strategies merit further explanation. First, the initial state of some products is made up of several basic states as witnessed by S1 and S3 in Hewlett-Packard product 4, or S8 and S6 in Massey-Ferguson product 12, indicating that the product was simultaneously diffused in several countries. We have chosen not to double the number of product strategies by starting one subset of strategies for a given product with, for example, S1 and the other with S3. This decision is based on the fact that the lag between introduction in the two markets is positive. As a result of this market lag, a country will usually supply a given product for export shortly following initial production. Thus, the count is predicated on the use of S1 or S8 as the first state, but not S3 or S6.

Secondly, there are a few cases in which one product has more than one product strategy in a particular country. For example, several products at Hewlett-Packard were divided into two parts on the basis of the technical sophistication required to manufacture the product. Parts that require a sophisticated level of technology emanate from a unique production center and are destined exclusively for export, while less technologically demanding parts are manufactured in more than one location. For example, the double product strategy for Hewlett-Packard product 1 is a result of this division. Product strategy MPS 7 = S3 between the United States and Europe applies only to the technologically sophisticated component that requires a highly complex production process. The other component, produced through a process of low to medium complexity, is diffused in Europe by means of MPS 1 = S1-S3-S4. The count of product strategies thus results in two, as the two components are considered to be two distinct products within the definition of a product presented in Chapter 2. These further guidelines account for the 52 selected product strategies derived in Table 6.2. Three principal results can be derived from our analysis of the survey data shown in Tables 6.1 and 6.2.

ADEQUACY OF THE TYPOLOGY

The first result, concerning the variety of multinational product strategies, is that our typology (as given in Chapter 2) adequately covers the set of strategies observed in the firms. Eleven different product strategies are evident in our first set of 87 observations, by product lines. In the second set of observations, for the selected products, 19 different multinational product strategies result from the 191 observations. As we anticipated, the latter case provides better coverage of the typology. The 19 multinational product

TABLE 6.2

Multinational Product Strategies Employed by the Firms for the 52 Selected Products

Product Strategies	Hewlett-Packard	Massey-Ferguson	Alcan	Dymo	Gillette	Number of Observations
Know-how originates in the parent country						
MPS 1 = S1-S3-S4	1(2), 3(2), 5, 6(2), 8, 12(2), 13(2)	8	1(2), 3	1, 2	2, 3(2)	21
MPS 7 = S1-S3	1(4), 3(3), 4, 4 to 13(4), 14(3), 15(3), 16(4)	8(3)		2(3), 1(3), 3(2)	3(2)	70
MPS 8 = S1-S4			2(2), 3(2), 4, 5	3	2(3)	10
MPS 9 = S3-S4	2					1
MPS 10 = S3-S1	2					2
MPS 11 = S4-S1	17			4		2
MPS 12 = S4-S3	17			4(2)		3
MPS 13 = S1			7			1
MPS 14 = S3	2(3), 17(2)					5
MPS 15 = S4	17			4		2
MPS 29 = S1-S3-S2-S4	22(3), 23(3), 24(3)					9

136

Know-how originates in the host country

						Total
MPS 31 = S5-S7-S8		1			1(2)	3
MPS 37 = S5-S7		1(2)		2	1	5
MPS 39 = S5-S8		6		2(3)	1	3
MPS 40 = S8-S5		6(2)	8			2
MPS 42 = S8-S7		2(3)				2
MPS 45 = S8	18(3) 19(3) 20(3)	2(3) 3(3) 4(3) 5(3), 7 9(2) 10(3) 11(3) 12(3) 13(3)	6, 8			38
MPS 51 = S8-S6-S5	19	2, 3, 4, 5				1
MPS 55 = S8-S6	18, 19, 20	10, 11, 12, 13				11
Total number of MPS by firm	102	45	13	19	12	191

Note: The numbers in the body of the table are product numbers of the particular firm. The number in parentheses following some of the product numbers indicates the number of times a particular product strategy was used for that particular product.

Source: Tables 5.3, 5.6, 5.9, 5.12, 5.16.

137

strategies identified in the second set of observations include the 11
strategies of the first set. Thus, the second set results in almost
twice the number of observed strategies. The comparison between
the feasible set of strategies and the observed set is illustrated in
abridged form in Table 6.3.

TABLE 6.3

Variety of Product Strategies Observed Compared with
the Feasible Set Defined in the Typology of Strategies

Strategies	When the Know-how of the Product Originates in the Parent Country	When the Know-how of the Product Originates in the Host Country	Total
Feasible set	18	18	36
Observed set			
By product lines	6	5	11
By products	11	8	19

Sources: Tables 2.1 and 2.2, assuming the host country is the
low-cost producer; and Tables 6.1 and 6.2.

The reader should note that we have assumed, somewhat arbitrarily, that the parent country of the multinational firm (in this
case, the United States or Canada) was, in the long run, the high-
cost producer. This means that for our empirical study the feasible
set of strategies includes 36 multinational product strategies rather
than the 56 strategies identified in the typology as a whole (see Chapter 2 for details on the subset of strategies in this case). This
assumption appears to be valid in the study by product line, as no
contradictory strategies were observed; however, in the study of
selected products, five multinational product strategies were found
to be inconsistent with this assumption. These five strategies are
MPS 9, MPS 10, MPS 12, MPS 14, and MPS 42. Together they
account for only ten out of a total of 191 observations.

We also observed one multinational product strategy that falls
outside the feasible set defined in the typology; this is MPS 29 =
S1-S3-S2-S4. This exception was observed (Chapter 5) for high labor intensive components at Hewlett-Packard.

THE TYPOLOGY AND THE PFDI SERIES

Our second finding concerns the relationship between the set of observed multinational product strategies and the set expected on the basis of private foreign direct investment (PFDI) theories. The reader is reminded that our intention here is not in any way to provide a test of the various PFDI theories but, in a more modest way, to establish their relevance and shortcomings as applied to an individual firm's behavior.

From the survey data, we conclude that, as a whole, the set of observed multinational product strategies is consistent with the set that could be expected on the basis of available PFDI theories. That is, the bulk of the strategies observed fall within the set of expected strategies. However, the variety of observed multinational product strategies was not expected on the basis of the well specified PFDI theories.*

The data are presented in Tables 6.4 and 6.5. The first column of these tables corresponds to the set of feasible product strategies listed in the typology (as developed in Chapter 2); the second column presents the corresponding PFDI theories (as developed in Chapter 3). Note that we consider here only those theories that are well specified, that is, specific in terms of our framework. Consequently, we exclude the capital movements theory, the theory of tariffs, and the theory of currency areas discussed in Chapter 3. The third and fourth columns list the number of times a given product strategy was observed, first for product lines and secondly for selected products. These entries originate from the extreme right-hand column of Tables 6.1 and 6.2.

On the whole, the observed set of multinational product strategies is consistent with the PFDI theories; for each of the most frequently used strategies there is at least one corresponding PFDI theory. This is clearly shown in Table 6.6, which lists the most employed multinational product strategies. The figures included in the "frequency of occurrence" column correspond to the number of observations in the 30 product lines rather than those for the 52 selected products. This reduces the variety of product strategies

---

*The well specified PFDI theories are those that point to one or a few specific product strategies rather than broad subsets or the entire feasible set of product strategies. It is evident that without this qualification the PFDI theories are 100 percent adequate. For further discussion of the theories see Chapter 3, particularly the conclusion.

TABLE 6.4

Product Strategies Observed for a Product Whose Know-how
Originates in the Parent Country

Set of Feasible Product Strategies Listed in the Typology	Corresponding Private Foreign Direct Investment Theories	Number of Times Strategy Was Observed in the 30 Product Lines	Number of Times Strategy Was Observed in the 52 Products Selected
Subset starting with state S1 (Kp, Mp, Pp)			
MPS 1 = S1-S3-S4	ITKH, OLIGH	10	21
MPS 7 = S1-S3	--	15	70
MPS 8 = S1-S4	ITKH	9	10
MPS 13 - S1	--	5	1
MPS 16 = S1-S2-S4	ITKH	0	0
MPS 17 = S1-S4-S2	--	0	0
MPS 22 = S1-S2	OLIGV	0	0
MPS 27 = S1-S3-S4-S2	IPC	0	0
Subset starting with states S2 (Kp, Mp, Ph) or S4 (Kp, Mh, Ph)			
MPS 11 = S4-S1	--	0	2
MPS 15 = S4	--	3	2
MPS 18 = S2-S1-S4	--	0	0
MPS 19 = S2-S4-S1	--	0	0
MPS 20 = S4-S1-S2	--	0	0
MPS 21 = S4-S2-S1	--	0	0
MPS 23 = S2-S1	--	0	0
MPS 24 = S2-S4	--	0	0
MPS 25 = S4-S2	--	0	0
MPS 26 = S2	--	0	0
Others			
MPS 9 = S3-S4	--	0	1
MPS 10 = S3-S1	--	0	2
MPS 12 = S4-S3	--	0	3
MPS 14 = S3	--	0	5
MPS 29 = S1-S3-S2-S4	--	2	9
Total		44	126

Note: We assumed that the parent country is the high-cost producer. The subset called "others" corresponds to those product strategies that are not consistent with the assumption that the host country is the low-cost producer. We encountered five such cases. The various "well specified" PFDI theories are abbreviated as follows: imperfect international transfer of know-how (ITKH); international product cycle (IPC); oligopoly theory, horizontal (OLIGH), and vertical (OLIGV). A dash means that there is no "well specified" PFDI theory corresponding to the particular strategy.

Source: Tables 6.1, 6.2, and Chapter 3.

TABLE 6.5

Product Strategies Observed for a Product Whose Know-how
Originates in the Host Country

Set of Feasible Product Strategies Listed in the Typology	Corresponding Private Foreign Direct Investment Theories	Number of Times Strategy Was Observed in the 30 Product Lines	Number of Times Strategy Was Observed in the 52 Products Selected
Subset starting with state S8 (Kh, Mh, Ph)			
MPS 40 = S8-S5	--	3	2
MPS 45 = S8	OLIGV, OLIGH	21	38
MPS 50 = S8-S5-S6	--	0	0
MPS 51 = S8-S6-S5	OLIGV, OLIGH	6	1
MPS 55 = S8-S6	OLIGV, OLIGH	12	11
Subset starting with states S5 (Kh, Mp, Pp) or S6 (Kh, Mp, Ph)			
MPS 39 = S5-S8	--	1	3
MPS 43 = S5	--	0	0
MPS 46 = S5-S6-S8	--	0	0
MPS 47 = S5-S8-S6	--	0	0
MPS 48 = S6-S5-S8	--	0	0
MPS 49 = S6-S8-S5	--	0	0
MPS 52 = S5-S6	--	0	0
MPS 53 = S6-S8	--	0	0
MPS 54 = S6-S5	--	0	0
MPS 56 = S6	--	0	0
MPS 58 = S5-S7-S8-S6	--	0	0
Others			
MPS 31 = S5-S7-S8	--	0	3
MPS 37 = S5-S7	--	0	5
MPS 42 = S8-S7	--	0	2
Total		43	65

Note: We assumed that the parent country is the high-cost producer. The subset called "others" corresponds to those product strategies that are not consistent with the assumption that the host country is the low-cost producer. We encountered nine such cases. The various "well specified" PFDI theories are abbreviated as follows: imperfect international transfer of know-how (ITKH); international product cycle (IPC); oligopoly theory, horizontal (OLIGH), and vertical (OLIGV). A dash means that there is no "well specified" PFDI theory corresponding to the particular strategy.

Source: Tables 6.1, 6.2, and Chapter 3.

observed but emphasizes the most frequently used product strategies, as our observations by product line already represent the most
likely used product strategy for any particular product line.

TABLE 6.6

Most Frequently Implemented Product Strategies and the
Corresponding Private Foreign
Direct Investment Theories

Product Strategy	Corresponding PFDI Theory	Frequency of Occurrence of the Product Strategy
MPS 45 = S8	OLIGH, OLIGV	21/87 = 23
MPS 7 = S1–S3	--	15/87 = 17
MPS 55 = S8–S6	OLIGH, OLIGV	12/87 = 13
MPS 1 = S1–S3–S4	ITKH, OLIGH	10/87 = 11
MPS 8 = S1–S4	ITKH	9/87 = 10
MPS 51 = S8–S6–S5	OLIGV, OLIGH	6/87 = 7
Total percentage of observations explained by the six product strategies above		73/87 = 85
Total percentage of observations explained, excluding MPS 7		58/72 = 81

Note: The various PFDI theories are abbreviated as follows:
imperfect international transfer of know-how (ITKH); international
product cycle (IPC); oligipoly theory, horizontal (OLIGH), vertical
(OLIGV). A dash means that there is no "well specified" PFDI
theory corresponding to the particular strategy.

Source: Tables 6.4 and 6.5, first and second columns.

The only strategy listed in Table 6.6 that is an exception is
MPS 7 = S1–S3, which does not involve production in the host country
and thus does not enter into the realm of PFDI theories. Therefore,
we conclude that the well specified PFDI theories, collectively, are
adequate to cover the observed set of strategies. Their individual
effectiveness, however, will be explored below.
We observed a number of strategies that were part of the
feasible set defined in the typology but that were not expected to be
used on the basis of the well specified theories. Using the specific
product data presented in Table 6.4 we observe from the 52 selected

products that nine multinational product strategies are not consistent with well specified PFDI theories. These nine product strategies are as follows:

MPS 7 = S1 (Kp, Mp, Pp)-S3 (Kp, Mh, Pp)
MPS 13 = S1 (Kp, Mp, Pp)
MPS 11 = S4 (Kp, Mh, Ph)-S1 (Kp, Mp, Pp)
MPS 15 = S4 (Kp, Mh, Ph)
MPS 9 = S3 (Kp, Mh, Pp)-S4 (Kp, Mh, Ph)
MPS 10 = S3 (Kp, Mh, Pp)-S1 (Kp, Mp, Pp)
MPS 12 = S4 (Kp, Mh, Ph)-S3 (Kp, Mh, Pp)
MPS 14 = S3 (Kp, Mh, Pp)
MPS 29 = S1 (Kp, Mp, Pp)-S3 (Kp, Mh, Pp)-S2 (Kp, Mp, Ph)-
         S4 (Kp, Mh, Ph)

Some of these multinational product strategies correspond to activities that are not unique to the MNF and hence have understandably been excluded from the PFDI literature. This is the case for MPS 13, MPS 14, and MPS 7. The first corresponds to the production in and for the parent country alone, while the second represents exports from the parent country only, and the third is a combination of the two previous strategies.

In none of these cases is there production outside the parent country. The six remaining strategies are truly multinational product strategies unique to the MNF, as they involve direct investment abroad. These strategies account for 19 cases out of 191 observations of multinational product strategies for the 52 selected products.

Similarly, Table 6.5 lists the multinational product strategies for the case where the know-how originates in the host country; here we observe five strategies that are not specifically mentioned in the PFDI theories. These strategies were used in 15 of the 191 observations in our study. The five strategies are as follows:

MPS 40 = S8 (Kh, Mh, Ph)-S5 (Kh, Mp, Pp)
MPS 39 = S5 (Kh, Mp, Pp)-S8 (Kh, Mh, Ph)
MPS 31 = S5 (Kh, Mp, Pp)-S7 (Kh, Mh, Pp)-S8 (Kh, Mh, Ph)
MPS 37 = S5 (Kh, Mp, Pp)-S7 (Kh, Mh, Pp)
MPS 42 = S8 (Kh, Mh, Ph)-S7 (Kh, Mh, Pp)

In summary, we have observed a total of 11 different multinational product strategies (the 6 derived from Table 6.4 and the 5 derived from Table 6.5) that are not accounted for by the well specified PFDI theories. These 11 strategies were used in 34 (19 + 15) out of 191 observations, or in almost 20 percent of the cases. This result corroborates our previous conclusion that PFDI theories are insufficient for the analysis of business strategy.

THE RELEVANCE OF THE INTERNATIONAL
PRODUCT CYCLE

Our third discovery is the lack of a strategy corresponding to the international product cycle theory within the observed set. This is surprising in view of the fact that we considered this strategy, designated as MPS 27 = S1-S3-S4-S2, to be a classic one owing to its widespread acceptance as a pattern followed by U.S.-based multinational firms.

This theory, or, more appropriately, this model gains its appeal from the adaptation of one of the most important marketing concepts, the product life cycle, to the different environmental conditions characteristic of a multi-country world. The originality of the international product cycle model stems from the fact that it explains the U.S. trade pattern that suggests that a product initially exported will later be produced abroad and finally imported into the United States. That is to say, a given product at the initial stage of its life cycle may require a high proportion of skilled labor. Once the product becomes standardized, it will be forced to meet competition on a cost basis and hence will require a more capital-intensive production process. These conditions are likely to be more effectively fulfilled abroad. We shall attempt to determine those reasons that hinder observation of the international product cycle model in operation.

The unique product definition inherent to this study could conceivably account for this result. Our study is based on a technological definition of a product. A product is composed of a specific set of technological features or elements of know-how. Previous empirical studies have defined a product in terms of Standard Industrial and Trade Classification (SITC) or Standard Industrial Classification (SIC) at the two-digit or four-digit level. This classification, even at the four- or six-digit level, is an industry rather than a product classification. It is based on the end use of the product and rarely coincides with a technological definition as used in this study. Seev Hirsch, for example, in his study of the U.S. electronics industry uses the four-digit SIC classification, and defines products as "government and industrial products," "special purpose tubes," "components and accessories," "consumer products," and "receiving tubes."[1] The group of "government and industrial products" (SIC 3662), which accounts for approximately half of U.S. exports in electronics, includes a large diversity of products such as television sets and electronic calculators. Even within the category "television," black and white television sets are technically quite different from color. While our study included one electronics firm, Hewlett-Packard, we failed to observe a case corresponding to the international product cycle strategy, although we encountered close substitutes among the firm's electronic components. Thus, it appears quite possible that our definition of a product limits the likelihood of observing strategies that correspond to the international product cycle strategy. It is quite evident that an appropriate test of the international product cycle model is one that does not distort the notion of product as defined in the model. For this reason, the research presented here provides new insights into business strategy that have relevance for policy makers in the fields of industrial strategy and international economics.

A further explanation of the absence of the international product strategy may be our exclusive concern, in this study, with trade within the multinational firm; the final stage of the cycle, import back into the United States, could be performed by other firms. To assess the validity of this hypothesis, Table 6.7 indicates the share of U.S. imports accounted for by U.S.-based MNFs. It shows that, in the aggregate, imports from foreign subsidiaries of U.S. MNFs represent a small percentage of U.S. imports, except in paper and transportation equipment. Thus, it suggests that the final stage of the international product cycle may not occur extensively within the MNF. However, because of the SITC definition of product used in these trade statistics, it is impossible to ascertain whether the MNFs are supplying the United States from domestic production at the end of the cycle or are forfeiting this task to foreign competitors.

The latter case does in fact occur in the mini-calculator market. Hewlett-Packard limits itself to the sophisticated segment of the market and leaves the low price segment to competitors, often foreign.

In terms of our study, these are two products of the same product line, as the sophisticated version requires additional elements of know-how. As noted in Chapter 5, the strategy implemented for those highly labor-intensive elements of this product that are manufactured in Singapore closely resembles the international product cycle strategy.

A third explanation as to why the international product cycle strategy was not observed may relate to the fact that the pace of innovations is such that when a product has reached a stage where it would be profitable to import it back into the United States, the U.S. demand is already shifting toward newer products. That is, the final stage of the cycle is preempted by a new substitute. This was indeed the case for the razor blade product line at Gillette.

Furthermore, the international product cycle may be inappropriate for capital-intensive industries. It is less feasible for such firms to realize production economies by shifting production to areas abroad where labor costs are lower. We therefore wanted to deter-

mine whether the firms selected were in high capital-intensive industries. This is done in Table 6.8, which presents the ratio of
capital to labor in a number of manufacturing industries. The average capital-to-labor ratio for the 19 industries included is 15.6. The
five firms in our study belong to industries whose capital-to-labor
ratios are as follows:

Firms	Industry	Industry Capital--to-Labor Ratio
Hewlett-Packard	Electrical machinery	9.41
Massey-Ferguson	Machinery (except electrical)	17.5
Alcan	Fabricated metals	12.0
Dymo	Machinery (except electrical)	17.5
Gillette	Fabricated metals	12.0
Average for the five industries		13.6

We can conclude from the above figures that the ratio of capital to
labor for the five firms in our study is not biased toward capital-
invensive firms; rather, they tend to be labor-intensive relative to
the average.

In addition, during the interviews a number of managers
pointed out that lower labor costs in several countries were more
than compensated for by higher materials costs or that the percentage
of labor in the value of the product was small. As a result, in most
cases, costs abroad were not lower than those in the United States or
Canada.* As many multinational firms are in R and D-intensive
industries, they appear at the same time to be in relatively high
capital-intensive industries, as indicated in Table 6.8. This limits
their gains from production abroad.

According to our observations, we are tempted to conclude
that the international product cycle is more myth than reality. The
evidence reveals that it is not so common a phenomenon as we had
anticipated and that its observation is likely to depend on the researcher's definition of a product. A manager is prone to demand
that a pertinent definition take into account the distinctive features
of a product. These features are, for the most part, technological,
as has been suggested by Posner, Vernon and others. Most of the

---

*Owing to host country policies requiring multinational firms
to export part of their local production, we increasingly observe the
last stage of the cycle. But even in this case firms may not follow
the international product cycle strategy, but may, instead, bypass
stages.

empirical tests, however, were not consistent with the definition of
product as it was developed and are therefore of limited use.

TABLE 6.7

Share of U.S. Imports Accounted for by
U.S.-Based Multinational Firms
(millions of dollars, 1968)

Product	Total U.S. Imports	U.S. Imports from Foreign Subsidiaries of U.S.-Based MNFs	Share of U.S. Imports Accounted for by U.S.-Based MNFs
Food	1,992	211	10.6
Paper	976	745	76.3
Chemicals	1,135	189	16.6
Rubber	277	30	10.8
Primary and fabricated metals	4,559	398	8.7
Machinery, excluding electrical	2,197	338	15.3
Electrical machinery	1,495	90	6.0
Transport equipment	4,298	2,485	57.8
All	16,929	4,486	26.5

Sources: Trade by Commodities, Series C, Organisation for
Economic Cooperation and Development, Imports, January-February
1968; Survey of Current Business, October 1970.

It is paradoxical that we were not able to observe the international product cycle--a model based on the marketing principle of
the product life cycle--while the PFDI theories, based on economics,
are readily discernible. The essence of this dilemma is that the
product life cycle can be applied to the multicountry world in a variety of ways. Each market has particular features that will determine the position of a product in its country's product life cycle at a
particular time. By comparison with other countries, one can position the various cycles relative to one another. However, the international product cycle model is only one way of relating the cycles
of two countries, and our study shows that other substitute paths of
diffusion are not only feasible but are often preferred to the inter-

TABLE 6.8

Estimates of Capital-Labor Ratios for
U.S. Manufacturing Industries, 1971

Industry	Gross Book Value of Assets ($ million)	Number of Man Years (1,000)	Capital/Labor
Transportation (37)	20,828	1,621	12.85
Electrical machinery (36)	15,616	1,659	9.41
Instruments (38)	4,112	382	10.8
Chemicals (28)	36,749	849	43.3
Drugs (283)	3,051	135	22.6
Chemicals (other than drugs)			
Machinery, except electrical (35)	21,011	1,744	17.5
Rubber and plastics (30)	8,212	544	15.1
Stone, clay, and glass (32)	12,023	583	22.3
Petroleum and coal (29)	16,619	141	11.8
Fabricated metal (34)	15,321	1,279	12.0
Primary metal (33)	43,027	1,169	36.8
Nonferrous metal (333)	3,252	59	55.1
Ferrous metal (331-332)	31,869	768	41.5
Leather (31)	766	273	2.8
Printing and publishing (27)	9,913	1,049	9.5
Tobacco (21)	968	67	14.4
Food (20)	13,902	1,574	15.8
Textile (22)	10,373	907	11.4
Furniture and fixtures (25)	2,391	436	5.5
Lumber and wood (24)	5,967	530	11.2
Paper (26)	20,122	632	31.8
Apparel (23)	2,814	1,319	2.1
All 19 industries	277,419	17,426	15.6
5 industries with highest R and D effort	19,663	1,251	18.77
14 other industries	12,458	750	14.46

Note: Industries are ranked in decreasing order of R and D effort, measured by the ratio of R and D expenses to sales in 1962. Industrial classification is the Standard Industrial Classification (SIC). The SIC number appears next to the corresponding industry.

Source: U.S. Department of Commerce, Bureau of the Census, Annual Survey of Manufactures, 1970-71, pp. 123 and 151.

national product cycle strategy by U.S.- and Canadian-based MNFs. Depending on the particular case, we observed the use of 11 different paths of diffusion, or multinational product strategies, for products developed in the parent country of the firm. The manager is therefore faced with a strategic decision composed of two distinct elements: the choice of a particular path as well as the timing of entrance into a new state of a particular path or strategy. Thus, planners need to consider a variety of alternative paths for the products developed in their parent country.

It is important to note that numerous studies that have previously borrowed from the international product cycle model still retain their validity. The reason for this is that many of them have not been concerned with the entire sequence of decisions involved in that model. For example, comparative studies that focus on the pattern of consumption between two countries in terms of lags or of demand, or the income elasticity of demand, have suffered no loss of relevance; nor have those that focus on lags in production between countries due to different stages of development.

The international product cycle model is a complex model involving the interaction of the technology, marketing, and production aspects of a product. An awareness of this interaction is integral to an understanding of the true nature of the model and its implications for international trade at the product level.

The model was in fact a major source of reference for the author, as it was one of the classic strategies identified in the initial stages of research. Our discovery that firms use a variety of alternative paths to diffuse their product confirms Vernon's intuition that the international product cycle model is losing much of its relevance as a model (see Chapter 1).

CONCLUSION

The description of the activities of multinational firms, using the typology presented in Chapter 2, leads us to conclude that the framework of multinational product strategies is useful in enabling us to analyze MNF activities from a new perspective.

By identifying the evolution of the product strategies we have been able to describe not only the variety of strategies that these firms presently implement, but also their development from initial moves abroad to their present state. A number of similarities in growth pattern across firms were introduced in Chapter 5 and will be dealt with in greater detail in Chapter 7.

By pulling together the observations in the five firms we observed a large variety of multinational product strategies, 19 in all.

All but one fall within the feasible set thereby confirming the comprehensiveness of the typology. The observed set, however, did not completely encompass the feasible set as we encountered 19 out of 35 feasible strategies corresponding to the case where the parent country of these firms (that is, the United States or Canada) was the high-cost producer in the long run. We had assumed that this case would prevail. In fact, however, we observed a few multinational product strategies that corresponded to the case where the parent country is the low-cost producer in the long run. No doubt further studies using this framework would uncover the use of multinational product strategies that were not observed here and thereby increase the coverage of the feasible set.

Furthermore, the adequacy of the typology lies in its operational value, which has been substantiated by the empirical study.

Finally, the typology as a research tool should lead us to increased knowledge in the field. To this end we have shown in this chapter that the greater variety of alternative multinational product strategies available gives the decision maker greater choice than we had initially anticipated. Consequently, the choice of an appropriate strategy is a more complex question that will be explored in Chapter 7.

We have also shown the relevance of private foreign direct investment theories, which we introduced previously to appraise the typology. We found that collectively the theories cover the most frequently used strategies; however, the well specified theories do not cover a number of multinational product strategies.

Finally, we have focused on one theory in particular, the international product cycle theory, since contrary to expectation we did not observe the corresponding strategy MPS 27, previously thought to be classic.

We did not observe the last stage of the cycle--the import back to the parent country of a product that was initially exported. Among the possible reasons for this result, the most important is the product definition used in this study. The study shows that a number of other strategies are available for products developed in North America and that these substitute paths are often preferred. For this reason a second objective of this research is to explore the rationale behind the variety of multinational product strategies.

NOTE

1. Seev Hirsch, "The United States Electronics Industry in International Trade," National Institute Economic Review, November 1965, pp. 92-97; using the four-digit SIC, Hirsch defines products in the electronics industry such as "government and industrial products," "special purpose tubes," "components and accessories," "consumer," "receiving tubes."

7

THE RATIONALE
BEHIND THE
VARIETY OF
STRATEGIES

Our aim in this chapter is to delineate the rationale behind
specific multinational product strategies employed by the firms in our
study. We want to know the determinants of, for example, Hewlett-
Packard's decision to introduce its frequency counter in Japan
through direct production in that country and on the other hand, its
decision to introduce spectrum analyzers in the same country by importing them from the United States. Or why did Gillette diversify
into new product areas such as writing instruments or electrical
equipment with acquisitions in specific host countries? It is clear
that different sets of circumstances influence which strategies firms
may implement. In light of the exploratory nature of this aspect of
the study our objective is to present some preliminary observations
about specific determinants of the strategies employed by the five
firms under consideration. Our approach is to move from a general
set of determinants to the specific relevance of a subset of those determinants to the firms in our study.

The analysis throughout this chapter is based on partial corre-
lations of the various country, firm, and product characteristics.
While it is obvious that multiple correlation would have provided
more detailed information, the data used for this exploratory study
did not lend themselves to this treatment. For example, it is probable that a number of characteristics that we have attributed to the
product are in fact intimately related to the firm's ability to diffuse
its product effectively. Thus, the distinction between product and
firm characteristics, as presented in this chapter, is not so definitive as multiple correlation would have provided.

We hypothesize that the behavior of the individual firm is determined by three sets of characteristics:

1. characteristics specific to the firm's environment
2. characteristics specific to the firm
3. characteristics specific to the firm's product

The first set of characteristics includes such factors as the stage of economic development, barriers to trade, host country investment climates, and so on. The firm is assumed to have no control over this set. The second set of characteristics--those specific to the firm--includes the international experience of the firm, the number of years abroad, and management's business philosophy and operating policies. The third set--product characteristics--include, for example, the complexity of the production process, economies of scale in production, and the ability of the product to be traded. This third set is obviously different for each product of the firm.

This hypothesis would appear to be a statement of the obvious; of course such things as management's philosophy and the ability of goods to be traded are important, one might argue. That is exactly the point! It is disconcerting to note that the literature has not dealt with these three sets in any coherent and systematic fashion. At best the environmental variables or characteristics have been stated.[1] This may be due in part to the fact that one generally needs a framework for analysis before an investigation of a phenomenon can proceed. It should be evident that the framework of the product strategy typology reveals the extreme importance of investigating international growth at the firm and product level. This is the contribution of our framework--the delineation of both new and obvious areas for further research. This chapter introduces some of these areas.

It is clear from the empirical study in Chapter 5 that our thrust has not been to shed further light on the set of characteristics related to the firm's environment and indeed, scant mention is made of this set. By the nature of our in-depth analysis of specific firms we are far better equipped to suggest hypotheses relating specific firm and specific product characteristics to a particular set of multinational product strategies. In fact we will show that the firm's specific characteristics are most important in determining the location of know-how (that is, whether the product strategies will emanate from the set where the know-how originates in the parent or in the host country) while the specific product characteristics play an important role in determining where production will be located in response to market needs (that is, whether the product strategy is an export one using MPS 7 = S1-S3 or MPS 55 = S8-S6, or one involving first export, then production abroad, using MPS 1 = S1-S3-S4 or MPS 51 =

S8-S6-S5, or one involving immediate diffusion by direct production
using MPS 8 = S1-S4 or MPS 40 = S8-S5).

FIRM CHARACTERISTICS

In Chapter 4, we hypothesized that firm characteristics, particularly the experience of the firm internationally, were a major
determinant of the type of multinational product strategies implemented. We will now develop our argumentation further based on
the description of the similarities in the growth of the five multinational firms studied. The pattern of international expansion that
emerges from these similarities is presented below, using the
Gillette Company as an illustration. Further support for the importance of firm characteristics is provided by relating the present
pattern of multinational product strategies of the five firms to their
international experience.

Figure 7.1 presents the pattern of international expansion of the
multinational firm in schematic form. It shows that the firm follows
a series of steps from a domestic firm (step 1) to implementing its
initial move abroad (steps 2 and 3). Step 3 represents a major phase
in the establishment of the firm abroad, as it means that resources
will be committed exclusively to the host country B. A number of
products are diffused internationally following these steps until management recognizes profitable opportunities peculiar to the host country. When this occurs it is likely to lead to further international
expansion either through steps 4 to 6 following path 1 whenever this
involves acquisition of technology; or steps 7 to 10 following path 2
whenever the technology is developed internally. This pattern was
followed in the case of the international expansion of the Gillette
Company as seen in the illustration below.

We recall that Gillette initially went abroad at the beginning of
the century, after having successfully marketed carbon blades in the
United States (step 2). It exported the blades first to a number of
European countries (step 2), and later established a plant in the
United Kingdom in 1920 to supply Europe (step 3). This was followed
by its first acquisition in 1929 of a German firm (step 4). The latter
was a manufacturer of low-priced blades that Gillette bought in response to American and European demand for this type of product,
thereby implementing step 5. By 1929 Gillette had accumulated
enough experience to recognize host country opportunities in Europe
through its U.K.-based operations.

Gillette leadership in blades was so strong that as long as it
defined its business as a manufacturer of razor blades, there was
little reason for further acquisitions or internal development in some

FIGURE 7.1

Pattern of International Expansion of the Firm

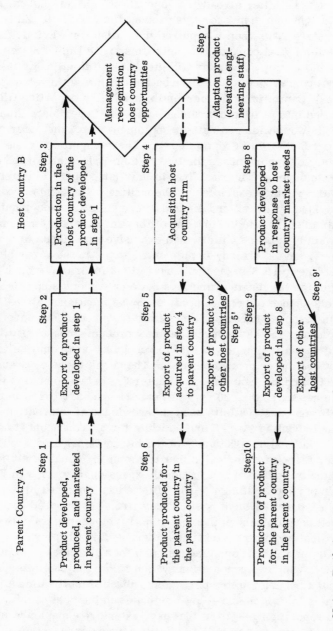

Note: Path 1—entry into new technology through acquisition (steps 1 to 6).
      Path 2—entry into new technology through internal development (steps 1, 2, 3, 7, 8, 9, 10).

Source: Compiled by the author.

host countries. When Gillette changed its business philosophy, however, and diversified into toiletries and personal care products,
new opportunities arose for expansion abroad. The Toni Company,
acquired by Gillette, already had operations abroad; that is, Gillette
went straight into step 3 for this product line. Gillette did not reach
step 4 before 1968 when it acquired the Italian firm Evital. As part
of Gillette, Evital expanded its activities to the United States, thereby
implementing step 5. (Later Gillette divested itself of Evital because
it did not correspond to the distribution and marketing strength of
Gillette.) Capitalizing further on its marketing expertise Gillette
diversified into writing instruments with the Paper Mate Company.
It used its worldwide strength to implement step 2 and later established production in Europe (step 3). The recognition by the Italian
subsidiary of opportunities for the medium-priced end of the line led
Gillette to develop a market first in Italy (step 8), and later in Europe
(step 9a). Further examples in the writing instruments product line
are provided by Brazil and Mexico where Gillette made acquisitions
in order to enter into the low end of the line, thereby implementing
step 4. In both cases Gillette had extensive experience in those
countries, having already implemented step 3 in the razor blades
product line in 1948 in Mexico, and in 1943 in Brazil. Much of the
rationale for the length of the lags between various steps lies in
Gillette's change of business philosophy as mentioned above.

In response to competition Gillette has become a more aggressive company and has entered into new product lines abroad, capitalizing on management's ability to recognize opportunities in countries where the company operates. The acquisitions of Braun A.G.
and S. T. Dupont (examined in Chapter 5), in two countries where
Gillette has more than 30 years of experience, are cases in point.
In the Braun case, Gillette used its knowledge of international markets, implementing steps 5 and 5a, while for S. T. Dupont it used
steps 5, 5a, and 6. The study of the international expansion of
Gillette, therefore, indicates that the company consistently followed
one of the two paths of international expansion described in Figure
7.1. In particular it shows that Gillette has a marked preference
for path 1 (acquisition of host country firms) as opposed to path 2
(internal development in the host country) evident in its policy of
diversification into related fields (discussed in Chapter 5).

On the basis of our discussion of the Gillette case we arrive
at the following two propositions which relate the characteristics of
the firm's behavior to the particular subset of multinational product
strategies for which know-how originates in the host country.

Proposition 1--MNFs that have extensive experience in a host
country (as opposed to MNFs with little experience in the specific
country) are more likely to develop products in the host country that

are designed for this market, and acquire firms in the host country in order to diversify into new product lines. Our study of the other four firms confirms the importance of operating in the host country as a prerequisite for exploiting new opportunities in that market.

Proposition 2--MNFs are likely to be consistent worldwide in their policy of internal development or acquisition of know-how: that is, if they pursue a policy of diversification of products by acquisition in the parent country, they are likely to follow a similar course in host countries thus implementing path 1; and if they introduce new products in their parent country by internal development they are likely to follow a similar course worldwide thus implementing path 2.

This second proposition represents an extension of Jon Didrichsen's work to the worldwide activities of the firm.[2] The conclusion that he drew from his study of the development of 50 large diversified American corporations, is that the firms consistently followed one strategy of growth in the United States, either acquisition or internal development of know-how.

We can add further credence to the importance of firm characteristics as determinants of multinational product strategies if, rather than analyzing the pattern of any one firm through time, we compare instead the present pattern of product strategies of the five MNFs in our study. If the length of time a firm has operated outside its parent country is an adequate index of its experience, we should find that the firms that have been abroad longer will tend to implement to a greater extent product strategies in which know-how originates in the host countries. This is because they have had more opportunities to implement steps 4 to 6, or steps 8 to 10. We use as an index of the international experience of the firm the number of years elapsed since the firm set up its international division. An index of the relative importance of the set of product strategies with know-how originating in the parent country, versus the product strategies with know-how originating in the host country, is provided by the ratio R, the ratio of the number of products found in the first set to the number found in the second; the product line data are used here rather than the product-specific data, because the product lines are a better approximation of the relative importance of the various activities of the firm. The results are shown in Figure 7.2.

We can see from this figure that Massey-Ferguson, which established its international division in 1909, has ratio R = .3, while the two younger MNFs, Hewlett-Packard and Dymo Industries, have a ratio R = 2.0. Gillette, which set up its international division in 1920, and Alcan, which did so in the 1930s have a ratio R = 1.0 and R = 1.2 respectively. This lends support to our hypothesis that as the firms gain experience abroad they increasingly implement product strategies originating in host countries.

FIGURE 7.2

The General Pattern of Multinational Product Strategies
Through Time for the Five Firms

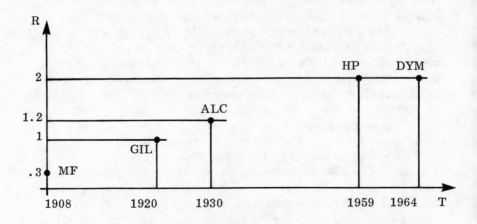

$$R = \frac{\text{Number of product strategies originating in the parent country}}{\text{Number of product strategies originating in the host country}}$$

(from the product line data)

T = Year the international division was set up for that company

HP = Hewlett-Packard; MF = Massey-Ferguson; ALC = Alcan;
DYM = Dymo; GILL = Gillette

Company	HP	MF	ALC	DYM	GIL
T	1959	1908	1930	1964	1920
R	18/9=2	5/16=.3	6/5=1.2	8/4=2	7/9=.8

Source: Compiled by the author.

In addition, our study suggests that the product strategy selected, in particular the location of development of the know-how, is
influenced by management's philosophy and the firm's policy toward
product development (internal development or acquisition of know-how).

PRODUCT CHARACTERISTICS

Based on our interviews with managers of the five firms we
developed a list of product characteristics that were seen by the

managers as important in their choice of a particular product strategy. This step was intended to determine which characteristics play a role in inducing a firm to export one product and produce another locally.[3]

These product characteristics are the following:

1. the type of product
2. the novelty of the product
3. the size of the demand
4. economies of scale in production
5. complexity of the production process
6. labor intensity in production
7. tradeability index
8. competitive situation

Table 7.1 presents the product characteristics for the 52 selected products in this study. However, before we define these characteristics and explore the interrelationship among them and the product strategies, it is appropriate to make the following comments concerning the limitations of the study.

In the analysis of the relationship between product characteristics and corresponding product strategies we must take into account the fact that a given product is diffused in various countries through a variety of product strategies. For example, product 1 of Gillette was diffused in Canada with MPS 37 = S5–S7 and in Europe with MPS 31 = S5–S7–S8. In other words, there are environment, or country effects in the strategy selection by management which must be neutralized in order to highlight product–specific effects. The way we have done this is to compare the different products across the same country pattern. This should become clear from Table 7.2. For example, note the country pattern United States/ Canada–Europe presented in column 4 (in view of quite similar characteristics of the two parent countries, the United States and Canada, we have grouped them together); there are three different multinational product strategies employed in the diffusion process, MPS 7, MPS 1, and MPS 8. These strategies are contrasted on the basis of the products classified in that column (17 for MPS 7, 10 for MPS 1, and 5 for MPS 8); in other words, we do not contrast products for MPS 7 in column 5 with products for MPS 1 and MPS 8 in column 4.

The second comment concerns the choice of only three multinational product strategies used in this analysis (MPS 7, MPS 1, and MPS 8). The reasons are straightforward. At any point in time for any given product, these three strategies are the main alternative strategies among which management must choose, given that

Table 7.1

Product Characteristics for Selected Products

Company	Product Number[a]	Type of Product[b]	Size of Demand[c]	Technological Novelty[d]	Novelty of Performance[e]	Level of Fixed Investments[f]	Complexity of the Production Process[g]	Labor Intensity in Production[h]	Tradeability Index[i]	Intensity of Competition[j]
Hewlett-Packard	1	Ind	Hi	MAJ	MN	Lo	Hi*, Me	Lo	Me	Hi
	2	Ind	Hi	TN	TN	Hi	Hi*, Me	Hi	Hi	Hi
	3	Ind	Me	TN	TN	Me	Hi*, Me	Me	Me	Me
	4	Ind	Hi	TN	TN	Me	Me	Me	Hi	Lo
	5	Ind	Me	TN	TN	Me	Hi*, Me	Me	Hi	Lo
	6	Ind	Hi	MAJ	MN	Me	Hi*, Me	Me	Hi	Lo
	7	Ind	Me	MAJ	MN	Me	Hi	Me	Hi	Lo
	8	Ind	Hi	TN	MN	Me	Hi*, Me	Me	Hi	Lo
	9	Ind	Lo	TN	MN	Me	Hi	Me	Hi	Lo
	10	Ind	Lo	TN	TN	Me	Me	Me	Hi	Me
	11	Ind	Me	MIN	SIM	Me	Hi	Me	Hi	Me
	12	Ind	Hi	MAJ	TN	Me	Hi*, Me	Me	Hi	Lo
	13	Ind	Hi	MIN	SIM	Me	Hi*, Me	Hi	Hi	Lo
	14	Ind	Me	TN	MN	Me	Lo	Me	Hi	Me
	15	Ind	Lo	MIN	TN	Me	Lo	Me	Hi	Me
	16	Ind	Me	MIN	SIM	Lo	Me	Hi	Me	Me
	17	Ind	Hi	TN	MN	Lo	Hi	Lo	Hi	Hi
	18	Ind	Hi	TN	MN	Hi	Hi	Hi	Hi	Hi
	19	Ind	Lo	TN	TN	Hi	Me*, Lo	Me	Hi	Lo
	20	Ind	Lo	MAJ	MN	Lo	Lo	Me	Hi	Me
	21	Ind	Lo	TN	MN	Me	Hi	Me	Hi	Lo
	22	Ind	Hi	TN	MN	Me	Me	Hi	Hi	Lo
	23	Ind	Me	TN	MN	Hi	Hi	Hi	Hi	--
	24	Ind	Hi	TN	MN	Lo	Lo	Me	Hi	Hi
Massey-Ferguson	1	Ind	Hi	MIN	MN	Lo	Lo	Lo	Lo	Hi
	2	Ind	Hi	MAJ	MN	Hi	Hi	Lo	Lo	Me
	3	Ind	Hi	MIN	MN	Hi	Hi	Hi	Hi	Hi
	4	Ind	Hi	TN	TN	Hi	Hi	Lo	Hi	Me
	5	Ind	Hi	TN	TN	Me	Me	Lo	Hi	Hi
	6	Ind	Hi	MAJ	MN	Lo	Me, Lo	Lo	Me	Hi

a (Product)	b (Type)	c (Demand)	d (Tech. novelty)	e (Novelty of perf.)	f (Fixed inv.)	g (Complexity)	h (Labor int.)	i (Tradeability)	j (Competition)
7	Ind	Lo	MIN	SIM	Hi	Me	Hi	Hi	Me
8	Ind	Hi	TN	MN	Hi	Lo	Hi	Hi	Hi
9	Ind	Lo	TN	TN	Lo	Lo	Hi	Me	Me
10	Ind	Me	MIN	TN	Me	Me	Me	Me	Me
11	Ind	Lo	TN	TN	Lo	Me	Lo	Me	Me
12	Ind	Me	TN	TN	Me	Me	Me	Me	Me
13	Ind	Lo	TN	TN	Me	Lo	Lo	Me	Hi
Alcan Aluminum									
1	Co	Me	TN	MN	Lo	Lo	Lo	Lo	Hi
2	Co	Lo	MIN	MN	Lo	Me	Me	Lo	Lo
3	Co	Hi	MIN	TN	Lo	Lo	Lo	Lo	Hi
4	Co	Hi	MIN	MN	Me	Hi	Lo	Hi	Me
5	Ind	Me	MAJ	TN	Lo	Lo	Lo	Lo	Hi
6	Ind	Hi	TN	TN	Lo	Me	Lo	Lo	Me
7	Co	Hi	TN	TN	Lo	Me	Lo	Lo	Me
8	Co	Hi	TN	TN	Lo	Lo	Lo	Lo	Hi
Dymo Industries									
1	Co	Hi	MIN	SIM	Lo	Lo	Lo	Me	Hi
2	Ind	Lo	MIN	SIM	Lo	Lo	Lo	Me	Lo
3	Ind	Lo	TN	MN	Hi	Me	Me	Me	Lo
4	Co	Hi	MIN	SIM	Lo	Lo	Lo	Hi	Me
Gillette									
1	Co	Hi	MAJ	MN	Hi	Hi	Lo	Hi	Me
2	Co	Hi	MAJ	MN	Me	Lo	Lo	Lo	Me
3	Co	Hi	MAJ	MN	Hi	Hi	Me	Hi	Hi

*The part of the product which is more complex is produced in one location only, close to the R and D center; the other components, not so complex, are produced in several countries.

aProduct number corresponds to the number of the product referred to in Tables 5.3, 5.6, 5.9, 5.12, 5.16.
bType of product: Ind = industrial; Co = consumer.
cSize of demand: Hi = high; Me = medium; Lo = low.
dTechnological novelty: TN = totally new; MAJ = major modification; MIN = minor modification.
eNovelty of performance: TN = totally new; MN = markedly new; SIM = similar performance.
fLevel of fixed investments: Hi = high; Me = medium; Lo = low.
gComplexity of the production process: Hi = high; Me = medium; Lo = low.
hLabor intensity in production: Hi = high; Me = medium; Lo = low.
iTradeability index: Hi = high value; Me = medium; Lo = low.
jIntensity of competition: Hi = high; Me = medium; Lo = low.
Source: Compiled by the author.

TABLE 7.2

Diffusion of Products Using Particular Product Strategies, by Countries

Multinational Product Strategies (MPS)	Canada--U.S.	U.S.--Canada	U.S./Canada--Europe	U.S./Canada--Japan	U.S./Canada--Latin America
MPS 7 = S1-S3	MF8	HP1, HP3 to HP16, HP21, DY1, DY2, DY3, GL3	HP1, HP3 to HP16, HP21, DY2	HP1, HP4 to HP16, HP21, DY1, DY3, GL3	HP1, HP4 to HP13, HP16, MF8, DY1, DY2
Number of Product Strategies	1	20	17	18	15
MPS 1 = S1-S3-S4	--	GL2	HP1, HP3, HP5, HP6, HP12, HP13, MF8, GL3, AL1, DY1	HP1, HP3, HP8, HP9, HP12, HP13, AL1, AL3, DY2	GL3
Number of Product Strategies	0	1	10	9	1
MPS 8 = S1-S4	AL2, AL5		GL2, AL2, DY3, AL3, AL4	GL2	GL2, GL3
Number of Product Strategies	2	0	5	1	2

Note: Hewlett-Packard is HP; Massey-Ferguson, MF; Alcan, AL; Dymo, DY; Gillette, GL. Numbers alongside company names are product numbers from Tables 5.3, 5.6, 5.9, 5.12, 5.16. For example, HP1 refers to Hewlett-Packard product number 1. MPS 7 = S1 (Kp, Mp, Pp)-S3 (Kp, Mh, Pp), MPS 1 = S1 (Kp, Mp, Pp)-S3 (Kp, Mh, Pp)-S4 (Kp, Mh, Ph), MPS 8 = S1 (Kp, Mp, Pp)-S4 (Kp, Mh, Ph).

Source: Compiled by the author.

the know-how originates in the parent country. (If the know-how
originated in the host country, management would have to decide
between MPS 55, MPS 51, and MPS 40). Furthermore, this exploratory analysis has revealed that a sufficient number of products
were found to have been diffused for only these three strategies.

Type of Product

A product is defined as either a consumer or an industrial
product. A number of managers pointed out that their product, an
industrial product, had features such that it could be sold as a standardized product worldwide. This was true for Hewlett-Packard
and also for Massey-Ferguson. For consumer goods, where taste
and other cultural factors matter to a greater extent, a standardized
approach does not work as often. Gillette does not use a standardized approach in toiletries, and Alcan does not use a standardized
approach in building products, or foils and packaging. Table 7.3
presents the characteristic "type of product" scored across the
three multinational product strategies--the results are striking:
MPS 7 is consistently the preferred strategy for industrial products.
This applies to the three diffusion cases shown. Furthermore,
MPS 8 is the preferred strategy for consumer products in those
three cases.

The results, though striking, were nevertheless expected.
Industrial products do not generally suffer from the effect of particular country traits (measurements excepted) which force product
adaptation. With consumer products, however, it is frequently necessary; hence local production is the preferable state.

The Novelty of the Product

The importance of a product's novelty was suggested by management and it involves two concepts: one relates to technology, the
other to functional performance. It was suggested in the interviews
that management's view of a product relates to the degree of difference in technological sophistication between the firm's present product and its previous product in this product line. For example,
when solid state circuitry replaced tube electronics, solid state
products represented a totally new technological innovation. On the
other hand, the increase of horsepower in a new tractor model essentially represents a minor technological change. Managers were
asked to score their products on a three-point technology scale (see

Appendix D): In terms of technology, for your firm, is this product totally new?, a major change of an existing product?, a minor change of an existing product?

TABLE 7.3

The Type of Product As It Relates to the
Product Strategy Selected

| Product Strategy | Type of Product | | Ratio |
	Consumer (1)	Industrial (2)	(1)/(1) + (2)
Diffusion from the United States/Canada to Europe			
MPS 7 = S1–S3	0	17	.0
MPS 1 = S1–S3–S4	3	7	.3
MPS 8 = S1–S4	4	1	.8
Diffusion from the United States/Canada to Japan			
MPS 7 = S1–S3	2	16	.1
MPS 1 = S1–S3–S4	2	7	.2
MPS 8 = S1–S4	1	0	1.0
Diffusion from any country to any other			
MPS 7 = S1–S3	5	65	.1
MPS 1 = S1–S3–S4	7	14	.3
MPS 8 = S1–S4	8	2	.8

Note: Numbers in the body of the table are the number of times a particular product strategy was observed.
Sources: Tables 6.4 and 7.1.

Performance was differentiated in an essentially similar fashion: In terms of performance, for your firm, is this product totally new? markedly new? similar to the performance of an existing product?

It should be pointed out that a major technological innovation may not imply any performance change whereas very minor technological changes may result in major performance differences. The increase in horsepower may mean that the tractor might tow implements, which heretofore was impossible. The relevant data are presented in Table 7.4.

For the case involving diffusion from the United States or Canada to Europe, it can be seen that as the degree of technological novelty decreases from being totally new (TN) to a minor change (MIN), the use of MPS 7 = S1-S3 or MPS 1 = S1-S3-S4 decreases only very slightly; and that in the case of MPS 8 = S1-S4 its use increases from 8 percent to 30 percent as the degree of technological novelty decreases. For example, when the product is totally new, MPS 8 = S1-S4 is used only once (8 percent), and when the product represents a major change (MAJ), MPS 8 = S1-S4 is used once (12 percent), while it is used three times (or 30 percent of the cases) when the products introduced incorporated minor technological change. The data on the diffusion of products from the United States or Canada to Japan suggest that the use of MPS 7 = S1-S3 or MPS 1 = S1-S3-S4 is independent of the degree of technological novelty. We cannot draw any conclusion for MPS 8 = S1-S4. Thus the degree of technological novelty appears to have an impact only on MPS 8 = S1-S4.

The data in Table 7.4 for the "novelty of performance" of a product and its relation to product strategies appears equally inconclusive as MPS 7 and MPS 1 again appear to be independent of the performance measurement.

The Size of the Demand

The size of the demand is defined for any one product as the ratio of the number of units of that product sold worldwide to the number of units of other products sold by the company in the world market. Managers were asked: What volume of sales was anticipated over the life of the product? How does it compare to the other products of your firm? The measurement is in terms of management's subjective evaluation on a three-point scale, high-medium-low.

In any one country as the size of demand increases one would expect that, ceteris paribus, export to that country would be replaced by the transfer of production to the market. Table 7.5 shows the data for product strategies in relation to the size of demand. This table indicates that in one case, as the demand increases, the frequency of MPS 7 declines. This is not as obvious in two other cases, yet the frequency of MPS 7 declines. This supports the above assumption that in all probability the location of production does change.

TABLE 7.4

The Novelty of the Product As It Relates to the Product Strategy Selected

| | Novelty of the Product | | | | | | | | | | | |
| | Technological | | | | | | Performance | | | | | |
Product Strategy	TN	Percent	MAJ	Percent	MIN	Percent	TN	Percent	MN	Percent	SIM	Percent
Diffusion from the United States/ Canada to Europe												
MPS 7 = S1–S3	8	61	4	44	5	50	6	60	7	50	4	66
MPS 1 = S1–S3–S4	4	31	4	44	2	20	3	30	5	25	2	25
MPS 8 = S1–S4	1	8	1	12	3	30	1	10	4	25	0	0
Total	13	100	9	100	10	100	11	100	16	100	6	100
Diffusion from the United States/ Canada to Japan												
MPS 7 = S1–S3	7	64	5	62	6	66	5	71	9	60	4	67
MPS 1 = S1–S3–S4	4	36	2	25	3	34	2	29	5	33	2	33
MPS 8 = S1–S4	0	0	1	13	0	0	0	0	1	7	0	0
Total	11	100	8	100	9	100	7	100	15	100	6	100

Note: Numbers in the body of the table refer to the number of times a particular product strategy was observed. Degrees of novelty are, in terms of technological novelty of this product relative to the previous product of the firm, totally new (TN), major change (MAJ), minor change (MIN); in terms of performance novelty of this product relative to the previous product of the firm, totally new (TN), markedly new (MN), similar (SIM).

Source: Tables 6.4 and 7.1.

TABLE 7.5

The Size of Demand As It Relates to the
Product Strategy Selected

Product Strategy	Size of Demand		
	High	Medium	Low
Diffusion from the U.S./			
Canada to Europe			
MPS 7 = S1–S3	6	6	5
MPS 1 = S1–S3–S4	7	3	1
MPS 8 = S1–S4	3	0	2
Number of observations	16	9	8
Frequency of MPS 7	6/16 = .28	6/9 = .36	5/8 = .63
Diffusion from the U.S./			
Canada to Japan			
MPS 7 = S1–S3	8	5	5
MPS 1 = S1–S3–S4	4	2	3
MPS 8 = S1–S4	1	0	0
Number of observations	13	7	8
Frequency of MPS 7	8/13 = .62	5/7 = .72	5/8 = .63
Diffusion from any country			
to any other			
MPS 7 = S1–S3	32	22	16
MPS 1 = S1–S3–S4	15	5	1
MPS 8 = S1–S4	6	1	3
Number of observations	53	28	20
Frequency of MPS 7	32/53 = .60	22/28 = .79	16/20 = .80

Sources: Tables 7.1 and 7.2.

Economies of Scale in Production

Economies of scale in production is a product characteristic
that was often referred to by the executives interviewed. However,
executives had some difficulty in classifying their products on a
three-point scale along this dimension (defined intuitively). It was
decided therefore to operationalize this definition by using the level
of fixed investments as an index of economies of scale; this is certainly not a good proxy for economies of scale but the two characteristics presumably would often appear together, since high fixed

investments will be amortized with high volumes of production. Managers were asked: Considering the initial fixed investments for production, how do these compare with other products of your firm?

The answers were again classified on a three-point scale (high-medium-low). The data relating to the level of fixed investments are presented in Table 7.6.

TABLE 7.6

The Level of Fixed Investment for Production As It Relates
to the Product Strategy Selected

Product Strategy	Level of Fixed Investment		
	High	Medium	Low
Diffusion from the U.S./			
Canada to Europe			
MPS 7 = S1-S3	0	14	3
MPS 1 = S1-S3-S4	2	5	3
MPS 8 = S1-S4	1	2	2
Total	3	21	8
Frequency of MPS 8	1/3 = .33	2/21 = .10	2/8 = .25
Diffusion from the U.S./			
Canada to Japan			
MPS 7 = S1-S3	2	13	3
MPS 1 = S1-S3-S4	0	5	4
MPS 8 = S1-S4	0	1	0
Total	2	19	7
Frequency of MPS 8	0/2 = 0	1/19 = .05	0.7 = 0
Diffusion from any country			
to any other			
MPS 7 = S1-S3	7	53	10
MPS 1 = S1-S3-S4	3	11	7
MPS 8 = S1-S4	1	4	5
Total	11	68	22
Frequency of MPS 8	1/11 = .1	4/68 = .06	5/22 = .23

Sources: Tables 7.1 and 7.2.

An analysis of the frequency of product strategies in this table does not indicate any definitive pattern. Furthermore, there are few observations for the high or low investment cases. Nevertheless, it does appear that the product strategy MPS 7 is the likely strategy for a medium level of investments whereas MPS 8 and MPS 1 are equally likely in low investment cases. We would have expected that the lower the investment requirements, that is, the smaller the economies of scale the easier it would be for the firm to relocate its production centers and therefore to produce abroad. However, the data are very inconclusive.

Complexity of the Production Process

Managers were asked: Do you consider the production process as highly complex? That is, does it require a large number of skilled personnel, and close communication with development people relative to other products of your firm? Table 7.7 presents their responses to this question.

TABLE 7.7

The Complexity of the Production Process As It Relates
to the Product Strategy Selected

Product Strategy	Complexity of Production Process		
	High	Medium	Low
Diffusion from the U.S./ Canada to Europe			
MPS 7 = S1–S3	11	3	3
MPS 1 = S1–S3–S4	1	6	3
MPS 8 = S1–S4	1	1	1
Frequency of MPS 7	$11/13 = .85$	$3/10 = .30$	$3/7 = .43$
Diffusion from the U.S./ Canada to Japan			
MPS 7 = S1–S3	10	4	3
MPS 1 = S1–S3–S4	1	5	3
MPS 8 = S1–S4	0	0	1
Frequency of MPS 7	$10/11 = .91$	$4/9 = .44$	$3/6 = .50$

Sources: Tables 7.1 and 7.2.

It can be seen that the frequency of MPS 7 = S1–S3 (where the product is only exported) corresponds to 85 percent of the cases for the product diffused to Europe, and 91 percent of the cases for those diffused to Japan, while it is used for only 43 percent and 50 percent

of the cases respectively when the complexity of the production process is low. The rationale is that a high degree of complexity in
the production process is associated with the need to be in close
communication with the development people. This results in one
production center close to the development center that supplies
worldwide demand.

Labor Intensity of Production

When discussing with executives why they transferred production abroad, very few mentioned labor cost as a factor. Lower
wages abroad, they argued, were more than offset by losses in pro-
ductivity, and in any event, European wage levels were now very
close to those in North America. Nevertheless, labor intensity data
were gathered for the 52 products. Managers were asked: Do you
consider the production process (for this product) as labor intensive
relative to other products of your firm? Answers were again classified on a three-point scale. The data are shown in Table 7.8.

One would expect from a consideration of classic trade theory
that MPS 7 = S1-S3 would be used frequently when the production is
capital intensive. The data suggest the contrary, that the labor
intensive products are exported.

A number of attempts have been put forward to explain this result which corresponds to what is known as the Leontieff paradox.
We add here, on the basis of our discussion with executives, that
labor costs generally represent only a small percentage of the total
costs of production. Labor costs were close to 15 percent of total
costs at Massey-Ferguson, and between 5 percent and 15 percent at
Hewlett-Packard except for electronic components where they
reached 60 percent. Managers viewed labor costs as having generally a minor effect on their selection of product strategies.

Tradeability Index

The index of tradeability chosen for our study is the value-to-
weight ratio of the product. Managers were asked: What is the
value-to-weight ratio of the product. Managers were asked: What
is the value-to-weight ratio of this product? (The value is measured
as the factory price, the index measured in $/lb.) How does it com-
pare for this product relative to other products of the firm?

The first part of the question provided an objective index. For
Massey-Ferguson the tradeability index varies from $1/lb. to $10/lb.
By comparison the index at Hewlett-Packard is near $100/lb. These

figures were complemented by the subjective index in the second
part of the question. The data, presented in Table 7.9, indicate
that product strategy MPS 7 is used for products having a high tradeability index.

TABLE 7.8

Labor Intensity in Production As It Relates to the
Product Strategy Selected

Product Strategy	Labor Intensity		
	High	Medium	Low
Diffusion from the U.S./			
Canada to Europe			
MPS 7 = S1–S3	3	12	2
MPS 1 = S1–S3–S4	2	5	3
MPS 8 = S1–S4	0	2	2
Number of observations	5	19	8
Frequency of MPS 7	3/5 = .60	12/19 = .63	2/8 = .25
Diffusion from the U.S./			
Canada to Japan			
MPS 7 = S1–S3	3	13	2
MPS 1 = S1–S3–S4	1	4	2
MPS 8 = S1–S4	0	0	1
Number of observations	4	17	7
Frequency of MPS 7	3/4 = .75	13/17 = .76	2/7 = .28
Diffusion from any country			
to any other			
MPS 7 = S1–S3	14	46	10
MPS 1 = S1–S3–S4	3	10	8
MPS 8 = S1–S4	0	3	7
Number of observations	17	59	25
Frequency of MPS 7	14/17 = .82	46/59 = .78	10/25 = .40

Sources: Tables 7.1 and 7.2.

The Competitive Situation

The competitive situation for any product is defined as the intensity of competition faced by the product, as compared to the intensity of competition faced by other products of the firm. The managers
were asked to answer the following question: How would you charac-

terize the competitive situation for this product compared to the other major products in your firm?

TABLE 7.9

Tradeability Index As It Relates to the
Product Strategy Selected

Product Strategy	Tradeability Index		
	High	Medium	Low
Diffusion from the U.S./ Canada to Europe			
MPS 7 = S1–S3	14	3	0
MPS 1 = S1–S3–S4	6	4	1
MPS 8 = S1–S4	1	1	3
Frequency of MPS 7	14/21 = .66	3/8 = .37	0/4 = 0
Diffusion from the U.S./ Canada to Japan			
MPS 7 = S1–S3	15	3	0
MPS 1 = S1–S3–S4	4	3	2
MPS 8 = S1–S4	0	0	1
Frequency of MPS 7	15/19 = .78	3/6 = .50	0/3 = 0
Diffusion from any country to another			
MPS 7 = S1–S3	55	15	0
MPS 1 = S1–S3–S4	11	6	4
MPS 8 = S1–S4	1	1	8
Frequency of MPS 7	55/67 = .80	15/22 = .68	0/12 = 0

Sources: Tables 7.1 and 7.2.

Our expectation for this characteristic is that the greater the competitive situation, the more likely the firm is to produce its products close to the market. From a marketing viewpoint, which includes the servicing, the visibility, and the market feedback aspects, this would appear to be a desirable state. Table 7.10 indicates that this is the situation based on management's view of the competitive environment. In fact, the views expressed in the interviews are very much along the lines that extremely competitive activity in a market represents an opportunity for profits as opposed to a threat of losses. Whereas a classic analysis would suggest not

committing investment resources in a competitive market before a
market share has been achieved, the firms interviewed tend in fact,
to favor the opposite view.   They meet competition head-on.

TABLE 7.10

Competitive Situation As It Relates to the
Product Strategy Selected

Product Strategy	Intensity of Competition		
	High	Medium	Low
Diffusion from the U.S./			
Canada to Europe			
MPS 7 = S1–S3	1	4	12
MPS 1 = S1–S3–S4	5	1	4
MPS 8 = S1–S4	2	1	1
Frequency of MPS 7	1/8 = .12	4/6 = .66	12/17 = .70
Diffusion from the U.S./			
Canada to Japan			
MPS 7 = S1–S3	3	3	12
MPS 1 = S1–S3–S4	3	1	5
MPS 8 = S1–S4	1	0	0
Frequency of MPS 7	3/7 = .23	3/4 = .75	12/17 = .70

Sources: Tables 7.1 and 7.2.

Strategies and Product Characteristics:
Some Propositions

It is commonly assumed that the manager bases his decision to
export only (MPS 7), to produce close to the market (MPS 8), or to
export first and then produce close to the market (MPS 1), on factors
such as demand and cost considerations related to economies of scale
in production, transportation costs, and differential labor costs between countries. In this study we used these product characteristics
as viewed by the managers of the firms. Our analysis leads us to conclude that these traditional product characteristics have some effect
on the product strategies chosen by management. The lack of evidence of a clear relationship observed with our index of economies of
scale is probably the result of our crude measurement of this dimension. In addition, some other product characteristics appeared to
affect significantly the type of product strategy selected. Managers

suggested that the following three product characteristics were also important in their strategic plans: the type of product, the complexity of the production process, and the competitive situation.

This comparison of the product characteristics that influence the choice of a particular multinational strategy, either MPS 7, MPS 8, or MPS 1, can be summarized in the following propositions.

Proposition 1--The MNF is likely to diffuse a product internationally by export, selecting the multinational product strategy MPS 7 = S1-S3 whenever (a) a standardized product is acceptable worldwide (most likely, an industrial product); (b) the size of demand is small in comparison to economies of scale in production; (c) the production process is highly complex; (d) the tradeability index is high; (e) the product is a leader in its industry--the firm is in a strong competitive situation.

Proposition 2--The MNF is likely to diffuse a product internationally first by export and then by production abroad, selecting the multinational product strategy MPS 1 = S1-S3-S4 whenever (a) a standardized product is acceptable worldwide (most likely, for an industrial product); (b) the size of demand is medium or large in comparison to economies of scale in production; (c) the production process has a medium or low degree of complexity; (d) the tradeability index is high or medium; (e) the product is a leader in its field.

Proposition 3--The MNF is likely to diffuse a product internationally by production, only selecting the product strategy MPS 8 = S1-S4 (bypassing export) whenever (a) the product needs to be adapted to the sociocultural environment (for consumer goods); (b) demand is high in comparison to economies of scale in production; (c) the production process has a low or moderate degree of complexity; (d) the product has a low tradeability index; (e) the product is faced with a strong competitive situation in various markets.

Due to the small number of observations gathered for each of the remaining multinational product strategies, it was impossible to develop similar propositions for them. This is an unfortunate outcome which results from our decision to control the selection of the firms rather than the particular multinational product strategies to be studied.

The rationale for these strategies was explained as the particular strategy was observed, and presented for the corresponding firm. In addition, as we mentioned above, the choice of MPS 1, MPS 7, or MPS 8 when the know-how for the product originates in the parent country is similar to the situation when a product has been developed outside the parent country and one ponders whether to use MPS 51, MPS 55, or MPS 40.

In a few cases of strategies where the first state was export (state S3 or S5) followed by marketing in the country of initial production (state S1 or S8) it appeared to result from strong initial competitive pressures in the export market. Here, contrary to what we observed above, competition was met by rapid introduction of the product by another country rather than by production close to the market.

We also observed that in a few cases the firm bypassed the export stage in view of the sizable market it could reach and the quasi-certainty of that market. That is, the decision maker discounts the savings from avoiding tariff and transportation costs in the short run, versus the possibility of higher costs of production with a low level of initial demand. In addition, production close to the market may bring increased demand due to better customer service and image. [4]

NOTES

1. Besides the literature on foreign direct investment dealt with in Chapter 3 of this study, the other work of importance is Robert Stobaugh, "Where in the World Should We Put That Plant?" Harvard Business Review, January-February 1969, pp. 31-37.

2. Jon Didrichsen, "The Development of Diversified and Conglomerate Firms in the United States 1920-1970," Business History Review, Summer 1972, pp. 202-19.

3. For a typical treatment see Raymond Vernon, Manager in the International Economy (Englewood Cliffs, N.J.: Prentice-Hall, 1968), p. 203. In general, this question is viewed as a locational one, involving the trade-off among the size of demand, economies of scale in production, and tariffs and transportation costs.

4. For further information see Georges Leroy, "Multinational Product Planning: An Innovation-Diffusion Perspective," unpublished working paper delivered at the Multinational Product Management Workshop, January 1976, Marketing Science Institute, Cambridge.

This study provides an analytical framework for appraising the strategies of multinational firms. Using a typology of multinational product strategies, we were able to show that the strategies actually chosen depend not only on a number of environmental characteristics, but also on characteristics of the firm itself, especially its experience as a multinational enterprise, and on a number of product characteristics.

The notion of multinational product strategy, the central concept of this study, has been used to analyze alternative patterns of innovation and diffusion in terms of the location and development of the product, the location of the market of the product, and the location of production of the product over geographic space and time. The typology of these patterns, defined as strategies and developed in Chapter 2, resulted in the identification of 56 feasible multinational product strategies--28 strategies for which the product's technology or know-how originates in the parent country, and 28 for which the know-how originates in one of the host countries.

The typology of multinational product strategies includes two classic paths of international expansion by the firm. The first corresponds to the following sequence of actions: (1) domestic production and consumption, (2) domestic production for an export market, (3) production and consumption abroad. The typology furthermore includes as one of the multinational product strategies a second classic path, Vernon's international product cycle model. This model postulates that U.S.-based MNFs not only follow the first classic path but extend that path with the addition of a fourth stage wherein the product at the end of its life cycle is imported to the United States from the more economical production center located abroad. However, the typology also defines a number of other

alternative strategies not generally discussed in the international
business literature. In that sense the typology developed in Chapter
2 represents a unique and broader framework for the analysis of the
product's diffusion along the axis mentioned.

The multinational product strategies of five firms (three U.S.-
and two Canadian-based MNFs) active in a variety of manufacturing
industries have been studied at great length. It was revealed that
while these firms followed the first classic path in their initial ventures abroad, they subsequently implemented a great variety of
multinational product strategies. Our analysis of the general pattern of strategies for 30 product lines reveals that these firms presently implement 11 different multinational product strategies. The
study of 52 selected products which complemented the general analysis, broadens this finding to 19 different multinational product
strategies. Among these, 11 have their know-how originating in the
parent country, while 8 correspond to strategies whose know-how
originates in host countries.

The list of multinational product strategies presented in Chapter 6 provides an impressive array of nonclassic paths presently
implemented by these firms. This result added to the one contained
in Appendix B, confirms the value of the typology in identifying a
variety of paths. The most notable among these is the subset of
multinational product strategies whose know-how originated in the
host countries. The usefulness of the typology as an analytical tool
is clearly established not only because it identifies a variety of nonclassic strategies, but also because it reveals that the international
product cycle strategy is not commonly implemented. These findings
have a number of consequences relating to the probable reasons for
the implementation of such a variety of strategies.

A second set of findings indicated that private foreign direct
investment (PFDI) theories, discussed in Chapter 3, are only broadly
consistent with our findings. However, these theories were developed to explain one particular stage of involvement of the firm: the
setting up of production outside the parent country. That is, the
theories may or may not consider the entire flow of activities included in a multinational product strategy.

The strategy concept used here is basically a management
concept, while the PFDI theories attempt to explain the PFDI phenomenon in the aggregate--from an economic viewpoint. These two
differences explain some of the difficulties involved in matching
PFDI theories with multinational product strategies. The study
shows that the various PFDI theories, collectively, correspond to
the most frequently used strategies, thereby adequately covering the
observed set of multinational product strategies. Nevertheless, a
number of strategies could not be matched specifically (on a one-to-

one basis) with a theory. This lack of specificity of some of the theories was found to be a major drawback.

This study suggests that one well-specified theory, the international product cycle, was rarely implemented. Among the four possible explanations advanced to explain this limited usage the most important relates to our unique use of a product definition based on technology. While studies based on macrodata (trade data) may uncover a cycle, with our definition of product based on technology, rather than an industry definition as used in trade data, we did not observe cases where a product initially exported from the United States was imported back by the same firm toward the end of its life. Were this last stage performed by competitors, the international product cycle would still be reflected in macrotrade data if not in the behavior of the individual firm. While this certainly occurs with a number of products, this study shows that, rather than using one particular strategy, the manager may choose among a variety of strategies that are substitutes for each other.

The application of the concept of the product life cycle to international business is therefore not as straightforward as it seemed: the international product cycle may be present in the aggregate without being observable for individual products. The firm may, for example, use a strategy that incorporates the first stage of the international product cycle for some of its products, while for others it jumps from the first to the last stage of the cycle. This research suggests that although an interesting and provocative theory, the international product cycle theory may have limited relevance for the description of innovation-diffusion paths of products inside multinational firms. This finding does not imply that numerous studies based on the international product cycle concept are obsolete, as a number of them deal with particular aspects of the cycle that may still be relevant. What this research shows is the importance for decision makers of choosing a strategy from among a feasible set that offers a large variety of possibilities, thus increasing the need for a proper strategy formulation.

A third set of findings focuses on the rationale and conditions under which a particular multinational strategy is preferred. The variety of multinational product strategies implemented is affected by a number of specific national, firm, and product characteristics. Traditionally, the literature has emphasized alternative patterns of multinational investment in terms of national or environmental characteristics and some product characteristics. That is, the role of other characteristics such as firm and product characteristics has been overlooked in the determination of a strategy. However, the present study suggests that a firm like Massey-Ferguson, with long experience as an MNF, implements to a much greater extent than others strategies where the product know-how originates in a number of host countries. We observed,in fact, a strong relationship between the experience of the firm abroad and the extent to which it implements multinational product strategies originating in host countries. Discussion with product managers and executives who had exposure in the development and the international diffusion of products indicated that the experience of their firm in a particular country was instrumental in the identification of production, marketing, and know-how development or acquisition opportunities. Two other characteristics of the firm, management philosophy and policy toward development of new products, were also observed to have a significant effect on the product strategy selected. This finding runs contrary to much of the literature that does not recognize the importance of the firm as an entity.

Management's rationale for selecting a multinational product strategy also included a number of specific product characteristics. In addition to the economies of scale in production, the labor intensity, and the value-to-weight ratio, this study indicates that management takes into account the type of product (consumer or industrial), the degree of complexity of the production process, and the competitive environment, when deciding on a product strategy. This led us to generate in Chapter 7 a number of propositions relating some of the most frequently used multinational product strategies to a number of firm and product characteristics. These propositions, resulting from this exploratory study, represent a preliminary attempt to systematize the decision making involved in one of the most important decisions that corporate planners must make.

RESEARCHERS' AND MANAGERS' PERSPECTIVES ON STRATEGY

For researchers, analyzing international management from a dynamic standpoint, in terms of multinational product strategy,is a new and promising field of research. It permits the integration of various important functional dimensions of the firm (development, production, and marketing) to study the process of innovation-diffusion itself, and to relate it to other dimensions such as finance, personnel, and organizational structure. We have shown that the concept of multinational product strategy, and the typology, are not only conceptually sound, but operational, and empirically relevant. At a time when one investigates alternative means of international technology transfer this research framework is a useful one. Further attention, in particular, should be devoted to the development of a contingency theory of multinational product strategies that will be helpful for the management of international business operations.

Also noteworthy is the fact that as the firm's international experience increases, it modifies its strategies to reflect a better
perception of the world environment. In essence, two firms, one
MNF with international experience and one without, will not necessarily implement the same MPS for a given product. The emergence
of a weltanschauung is likely to lead the firm to a better recognition
of host country opportunities, and according to our findings it is
likely to lead to certain product development activities abroad. The
nature of international business, which has shifted since the early
1950s from trade-related activities to production investment activities, appears to be now entering into a third phase with international
development implications. This third dimension will become increasingly important as countries continue to establish industrial
policies of their own that stress development. In this area researchers in international economics will be able to benefit from the work
carried on in international business stressing the microdimensions
of firm behavior (intrafirm decision making) rather than industrial
organization patterns and market structure.

Organizational Dimensions of Strategy Selection

The concept of multinational product strategy incorporates two
crucial elements of the firm's competitiveness: the development
and diffusion of products on a world scale through exports of products or through the transfer of technology. We were able to indicate
the various paths available, and show that some of them were implemented only as the firm gained experience, thus raising the question of whether some firms could under certain circumstances
profitably bypass some stages of this development. This is likely
to depend to a large extent on the intelligence capabilities of the
firm, that is, on the organization of information that could decrease
the perceived risk of any commitment abroad. The central concept
of this research, the multinational product strategy, is likely to
imply in a number of minds that the product innovation-diffusion was
planned. A number of managers disagreed; the researcher view of
strategy, they argued, imposed a clear vision of the future, while
in fact one needed to be more pragmatic. During the interviews, we
encountered a variety of approaches, as illustrated by the following
two opposite cases or scenarios of multinational product strategy
planning and organization.

In firm A, a product is developed in response to some market
need that is perceived in the parent country of the firm. The product so developed is tested and introduced on that market. As it is
successful, the manager of a subsidiary abroad (that is, from

country 2) shows interest in the product and decides to introduce it.
Some tests of this new market are conducted, that lead to the need
to modify the product, to adapt it to the country 2 market need. The
subsidiary manager who in country 2 is quite autonomous is then
free to decide whether he wants to import a product that he has been
able to have modified, or to manufacture it locally. Other foreign
subsidiaries may follow suit and decide to adopt the product, which
leads them to go through similar steps as the one described above.
After one, but more often two or three years, the product is sold in
several countries as subsidiary managers become convinced of the
profitability of the product.

In firm B, the case is quite the opposite. A product is developed in response to the need of several countries to push toward a
more advanced product, because of competition or consumer dis-
satisfaction. A product specification is then agreed upon which
meets the approval of subsidiary managers. As the firm is most
often a leader, the most stringent specifications will be agreed on.
One country is likely to test it first but others will start production
and marketing soon after. The product is a standardized one and is
likely to be introduced worldwide practically instantaneously. This
is more likely to be so whenever the firm is structured with worldwide product managers, or when worldwide product coordinators are
able to use relatively strong persuasive means.

In essence, then, we have described above two opposite managerial views on the multinational product strategy. Firm A considers the series of moves from country to country as ad hoc moves
where little multinational planning is done. That is, the multinational product strategy is viewed by managers as a researcher tool,
identifying a pattern ex post facto. For firm B the sequence of steps
identified in the multinational product strategy are really part of the
planning process. Firm B may have the choice to decide in which
country the development of product X will take place, and it will decide in which countries it will be produced and sold--that is, the
successive (likely) steps over the life of the product. For firm B
the concept of multinational product strategy is a familiar one.

It is quite clear that the benefits from using the multinational
product strategy concept for planning purposes vary from product to
product. For example, firms manufacturing industrial products appear to make greater use of it, which reflects their ability to select
the standardized product segment of the market where large economies of scale may be present.

In this research we were able to observe firms in various po-
sitions between the two extreme cases. In some instances it was
clear that the international product planning had not reached a satisfactory level of expertise, particularly with regard to the transfer of

the in-house technology of various parts of the firm. In others, the
firm had succeeded in establishing communication channels that allowed free flow of information, and encouraged the exchange of experience between various centers of the firm.

Furthermore, the study enabled us to see the need for corre-
spondence between the planning and organization functions in the
firm at the product strategy level. It is now commonplace to say
that structure should be designed so as to achieve the desired strategy in an efficient manner. However, we know that in practice this
is no easy task. The coordination of the innovation and worldwide
diffusion activities was achieved by the various firms in different
ways. Some used a "linking pin" approach with international product
coordinators in a purely advisory capacity while in other firms their
recommendations were close to being orders. In still other firms
the coordination was achieved by the structure which relies on a
product manager who has direct responsibility for a given product
or product line worldwide.

We also observed a few cases where innovation and diffusion
aspects were not carried out in an optimal way because of the constraints imposed by the organization. A case was described whereby
one of the firms increased markedly its efficiency by altering its
structure, and shifting toward the use of worldwide product managers.

The concept of multinational product strategy, which was initially viewed as imposing an elaborate rationale framework on what
is largely an intuitive decision process of the businessman, should
increasingly be seen by managers as a pertinent dimension in any
study of their product strategy as it integrates a number of critical
dimensions of the product that need to be viewed as a whole.

Public Policy Implications

Public policy makers may find this research relevant as it
describes the evolution of the strategies of a number of multinational
firms, tracing the various phases of their development as the firms
gain international experience and meet environmental changes.
These firms are emerging as leaders in managing resources on a
worldwide scale, thus affecting other firms including those that are
still national in scope.

The observed pattern of development in multinational firms
selected for this study indicates that their involvement in any particular country is likely to be first in terms of market opportunity
recognition, then production, and, only later, product development
activities in the host countries. If this is the sequence of commitments that is preferred by the firm, then countries limiting foreign

direct investment altogether may also reduce the involvement of multinational firms in local product development.

The third stage of involvement, the development of products in the host country, appears to be taking place when certain conditions are met: The first is that the presence of the firm in that host country has enabled it to appraise the distinctive aspects of the host country market opportunity; secondly, this opportunity cannot be adequately fulfilled using present parent company know-how; and it requires thirdly that the host country be able to supply research talents of its own. These conditions have only been present in some developed countries; this suggests that whenever any of these conditions are lacking, government incentives may be needed.

The strength of these multinational firms was not only related to the nature of their products, but also to their ability to diffuse these products worldwide. In view of the fact that most technological innovations have a short life, the speed of international diffusion may be critical to the ability of the innovative firm to penetrate international markets. Our study indicates that market lags and production lags were relatively small in the multinational firms. One can therefore question the ability of national firms to be as efficient. Obviously firms have and still are reaching the international stage by capitalizing on an innovative product but this may prove to be more and more difficult as they have to compete against established multinationals. Governments may therefore have to provide incentives for the international diffusion of products commercialized by national firms. In this study we have described a number of cases where an innovative firm had confined its activities to its country of origin up until a multinational firm discovered the worldwide potential of its products, thus indicating the need to devise better incentives for drawing firms into the international arena.

DESCRIPTION OF MULTINATIONAL PRODUCT STRATEGIES

Multinational Product Strategies Originating in the Parent Country (MPS 1 to MPS 29)

MPS 1 = S1 (Kp, Mp, Pp)-S3 (Kp, Mh, Pp)-S4 (Kp, Mh, Ph)
The firm first develops the know-how in the parent country and produces and markets the product in that country. It then exports the product abroad to the host country market and later transfers production to the host country in order to supply that market.

MPS 2 = S3 (Kp, Mh, Pp)-S4 (Kp, Mh, Ph)-S1 (Kp, Mp, Pp)
The firm has developed the know-how and produces the product in the parent country, to be first exported to the host country market; then it transfers production of the product to the host country. Finally the firm decides to supply the parent country market from its production facilities in that country.

MPS 3 = S4 (Kp, Mh, Ph)-S1 (Kp, Mp, Pp)-S3 (Kp, Mh, Pp)
The know-how for the product originates in the parent country, but the product is first manufactured and marketed in the host country. Then it is manufactured and marketed in the parent country and later this production center exports to the host country market.

MPS 4 = S4 (Kp, Mh, Ph)-S3 (Kp, Mh, Pp)-S1 (Kp, Mp, Pp)
The know-how originates in the parent country but the product is first manufactured and marketed in the host country. Then production starts in the parent country, the production from that plant being exported to the host country market, and later the market is developed in the parent country.

Note that a multinational product strategy (MPS) represents successive entries into new basic states; a firm may at any point in time be in several basic states. For further details see Chapter 2.

MPS 5 = S3 (Kp, Mh, Pp)–S1 (Kp, Mp, Pp)–S4 (Kp, Mh, Ph)
Know-how is developed in the parent country, and production starts there too but the product is exported to the host country market. Then the product is supplied to the parent country market and finally the host country market is supplied by local production.

MPS 6 = S1 (Kp, Mp, Pp)–S4 (Kp, Mh, Ph)–S3 (Kp, Mh, Pp)
The firm develops the know-how and produces and markets the product in the parent country. Then production is transferred to the host country for that market; later the firm starts supplying the host country by imports from the parent country.

MPS 7 = S1 (Kp, Mp, Pp)–S3 (Kp, Mh, Pp)
The firm develops the know-how and produces and markets the product in the parent country. Then the product is exported to the host country.

MPS 8 = S1 (Kp, Mp, Pp)–S4 (Kp, Mh, Ph)
The firm develops the know-how and produces and markets the product in the parent country. Then the product is introduced in the host country market by production close to the market.

MPS 9 = S3 (Kp, Mh, Pp)–S4 (Kp, Mh, Ph)
The product is developed and produced in the parent country in order to supply the host country's market. Then production starts in the host country for that market.

MPS 10 = S3 (Kp, Mh, Pp)–S1 (Kp, Mp, Pp)
Development and production of the product take place in the parent country and the product is first exported to the host country. Then the product is marketed in the parent country from the parent country production center.

MPS 11 = S4 (Kp, Mh, Ph)–S1 (Kp, Mp, Pp)
The know-how originates in the parent country but production is carried out first in the host country for that market and later the product is manufactured in the parent country for that market.

MPS 12 = S4 (Kp, Mh, Ph)–S3 (Kp, Mh, Pp)
The product is developed in the parent country, but production and marketing take place in the host country.

Later, production is started in the parent country and the product is exported to the host country.

MPS 13 = S1 (Kp, Mp, Pp)
Product development, production, and marketing take place only in the parent country market.

MPS 14 = S3 (Kp, Mh, Pp)
Product development and production take place in the parent country, but the product is exported to the host country.

MPS 15 = S4 (Kp, Mh, Ph)
Product know-how originates in the parent country while production takes place in the host country for that market.

MPS 16 = S1 (Kp, Mp, Pp)-S2 (Kp, Mp, Ph)-S4 (Kp, Mh, Ph)
The know-how originates in the parent country and production takes place there in order to supply the parent country's market. Then production starts in the host country and the product is exported back to the parent country. Later, the host country market is supplied from local manufacture.

MPS 17 = S1 (Kp, Mp, Pp)-S4 (Kp, Mh, Ph)-S2 (Kp, Mp, Ph)
The product is developed, produced, and marketed in the parent country; then manufacturing starts in the host country in order to supply the market. Later, the product is imported into the parent country.

MPS 18 = S2 (Kp, Mp, Ph)-S1 (Kp, Mp, Pp)-S4 (Kp, Mh, Ph)
The product is developed and marketed in the parent country, but manufacturing operations initially take place in the host country, and then production starts in the parent country. Later, production is transferred partially or totally to the host country in order to supply that market.

MPS 19 = S2 (Kp, Mp, Ph)-S4 (Kp, Mh, Ph)-S1 (Kp, Mp, Pp)
The product is developed and marketed initially in the parent country, while production takes place in the host country; then the product is marketed in the host country. Later, production starts in the parent country in order to supply that market.

MPS 20 = S4 (Kp, Mh, Ph)-S1 (Kp, Mp, Pp)-S2 (Kp, Mp, Ph)
The know-how originates in the parent country and production is carried out in the host country for that market.

Then production starts in the parent country for distribution in that market. Later, the parent country market is supplied by imports from the host country.

MPS 21 = S4 (Kp, Mh, Ph)-S2 (Kp, Mp, Ph)-S1 (Kp, Mp, Pp)
The know-how originates in the parent country and production is carried out in the host country for that market. Then the product is imported into the parent country and finally production is started in the parent country to supply that market.

MPS 22 = S1 (Kp, Mp, Pp)-S2 (Kp, Mp, Ph)
The know-how is developed in the parent country and production takes place there to supply that market. Then manufacturing operations are carried out in the host country and the product is imported back into the parent country.

MPS 23 = S2 (Kp, Mp, Ph)-S1 (Kp, Mp, Pp)
The product is developed in the parent country and production takes place in the host country for export to the parent country. Then the manufacturing operations are started in the parent country to supply this market.

MPS 24 = S2 (Kp, Mp, Ph)-S4 (Kp, Mh, Ph)
The product is developed in the parent country and initially produced in the host country and exported to the parent country. Then the product is marketed in the host country for that market.

MPS 25 = S4 (Kp, Mh, Ph)-S2 (Kp, Mp, Ph)
The know-how is developed in the parent country, but the product is initially manufactured and marketed in the host country. Then the product is exported to the parent country.

MPS 26 = S2 (Kp, Mp, Ph)
The know-how originates in the parent country, but the parent country market is supplied by imports from the host country.

MPS 27 = S1 (Kp, Mp, Pp)-S3 (Kp, Mh, Pp)-S4 (Kp, Mh, Ph)-S2 (Kp, Mp, Ph)
The product is developed, manufactured, and marketed in the parent country. Then it is exported to the host country. Later manufacturing operations start in the host country for that market. Finally the product is exported to the parent country.

MPS 28 = S4 (Kp, Mh, Ph)-S2 (Kp, Mp, Ph)-S1 (Kp, Mp, Pp)-S3 (Kp, Mh, Pp)

While the know-how comes from the parent country, production and marketing take place initially in the host country. Then the product is exported to the parent country. Later, production starts in the parent country in order to supply that market, and finally the product is exported to the host country.

*MPS 29 = S1 (Kp, Mp, Pp)-S3 (Kp, Mh, Pp)-S2 (Kp, Mp, Ph)-S4 (Kp, Mh, Ph)

The product is developed, manufactured, and marketed in the parent country. Then it is exported to the host country. Later, manufacturing operations start in the host country in order to supply the parent country market. Finally the production center in the host country supplies the host country market.

Multinational Product Strategies Where Product Know-how Originates in the Host Country (MPS 31 to MPS 58)

MPS 31 = S5 (Kh, Mp, Pp)-S7 (Kh, Mh, Pp)-S8 (Kh, Mh, Ph)

While the product is developed in the host country, production and marketing are carried out initially in the parent country. Then the product is exported to the host country and later manufacturing operations start in the host country in order to supply that market.

MPS 32 = S5 (Kh, Mp, Pp)-S8 (Kh, Mh, Ph)-S7 (Kh, Mh, Pp)

The product is developed in the host country, production and marketing take place in the parent country. Then production starts in the host country in order to supply that market; later the host country imports the product.

MPS 33 = S7 (Kh, Mh, Pp)-S5 (Kh, Mp, Pp)-S8 (Kh, Mh, Ph)

The know-how originates in the host country, production is carried out in the parent country, and the product is exported to the host country market; the parent country

---

*Note that this multinational product strategy MPS 29 is not on the list of the feasible strategies identified in the typology defined in Chapter 2. This exception is presented here as it was encountered in the analysis of Hewlett-Packard multinational product strategies.

market is later supplied by its initial production center. Finally manufacturing operations start in the host country in order to supply this market.

MPS 34 = S7 (Kh, Mh, Pp)–S8 (Kh, Mh, Ph)–S5 (Kh, Mp, Pp)
The product is developed in the host country, production is carried out in the parent country, and the product is exported to the host country. Then production starts in the host country to supply that market. Finally the market of the parent country is supplied by local production in that market.

MPS 35 = S8 (Kh, Mh, Ph)–S5 (Kh, Mp, Pp)–S7 (Kh, Mh, Pp)
The product is developed, manufactured, and sold in the host country; then production starts in the parent country in order to supply that market. Finally the product is exported to the host country from the parent country.

MPS 36 = S8 (Kh, Mh, Ph)–S7 (Kh, Mh, Pp)–S5 (Kh, Mp, Pp)
The product is developed, manufactured, and sold in the host country; then production is started in the parent country in order to supply the host country market. Later, the product is marketed in the parent country.

MPS 37 = S5 (Kh, Mp, Pp)–S7 (Kh, Mh, Pp)
The product is developed in the host country, but production and marketing initially take place in the parent country. Then the product is exported to the host country in order to supply that market.

MPS 38 = S7 (Kh, Mh, Pp)–S5 (Kh, Mp, Pp)
The product is developed in the host country but is initially produced in the parent country for export to the host country. Later, the product is sold in the parent country market.

MPS 39 = S5 (Kh, Mp, Pp)–S8 (Kh, Mh, Ph)
The know-how of the product is developed in the host country but initial production and marketing take place in the parent country. Then manufacturing starts in the host country in order to supply that market.

MPS 40 = S8 (Kh, Mh, Ph)–S5 (Kh, Mp, Pp)
The know-how, production, and marketing of the product all take place originally in the host country; then production starts in the parent country in order to supply that market.

MPS 41 = S7 (Kh, Mh, Pp)-S8 (Kh, Mh, Ph)
   The product is developed in the host country, produced in
   the parent country for exports to the host country; then
   production starts in the host country to supply that market.

MPS 42 = S8 (Kh, Mh, Ph)-S7 (Kh, Mh, Pp)
   The product know-how originates in the host country and
   the product is manufactured and sold initially in that country. Then production starts in the parent country for export to the host country market.

MPS 43 = S5 (Kh, Mp, Pp)
   While the product know-how originates in the host country,
   production is carried out in the parent country in order to
   supply that market only.

MPS 44 = S7 (Kh, Mh, Pp)
   The product is developed in the host country, produced in
   the parent country, and exported for the host country
   market.

MPS 45 = S8 (Kh, Mh, Ph)
   The product is developed, manufactured, and marketed in
   the host country for that market.

MPS 46 = S5 (Kh, Mp, Pp)-S6 (Kh, Mp, Ph)-S8 (Kh, Mh, Ph)
   The product know-how originates in the host country but
   production and marketing take place initially in the parent
   country. Then production starts in the host country and
   the product is exported to the parent country. Finally demand starts in the host country and is supplied locally.

MPS 47 = S5 (Kh, Mp, Pp)-S8 (Kh, Mh, Ph)-S6 (Kh, Mp, Ph)
   The know-how comes from the host country but production
   and marketing are first carried out in the parent country.
   Then production starts in the host country in response to
   that market opportunity. Finally the product is exported
   to supply the parent country market.

MPS 48 = S6 (Kh, Mp, Ph)-S5 (Kh, Mp, Pp)-S8 (Kh, Mh, Ph)
   The product is developed and manufactured in the host
   country for export to the parent country. Then production
   starts in the parent country to supply its own market.
   Finally the host country market develops and is supplied
   by local production.

MPS 49 = S6 (Kh, Mp, Ph)-S8 (Kh, Mh, Ph)-S5 (Kh, Mp, Pp)
The product know-how originates and the production takes place initially in the host country; the product is exported to the parent country. Then the host country market develops, and is supplied by local production. Finally production is started in the parent country in order to supply that market.

MPS 50 = S8 (Kh, Mh, Ph)-S5 (Kh, Mp, Pp)-S6 (Kh, Mp, Ph)
The know-how, production, and marketing originally take place in the host country. Then production is transferred to the parent country in order to supply this market. Finally the parent country market is supplied by exports from the host country production facilities.

MPS 51 = S8 (Kh, Mh, Ph)-S6 (Kh, Mp, Ph)-S5 (Kh, Mp, Pp)
Know-how, production, and marketing of the product take place originally in the host country. Then the product is exported to supply the host country market. Finally production starts in the parent country for the parent country market.

MPS 52 = S5 (Kh, Mp, Pp)-S6 (Kh, Mp, Ph)
While the know-how is developed in the host country production takes place initially in the host country to supply this market. Then production is transferred to the host country and the product is exported to the parent country.

MPS 53 = S6 (Kh, Mp, Ph)-S8 (Kh, Mh, Ph)
The know-how is developed in the host country and production takes place in that country for export to the parent country. Then the market develops for this product in the host country and is supplied from local production.

MPS 54 = S6 (Kh, Mp, Ph)-S5 (Kh, Mp, Pp)
The know-how is developed and production for the product takes place in the host country, the product is exported to the parent country. Later, production starts in the parent country to supply this market.

MPS 55 = S8 (Kh, Mh, Ph)-S6 (Kh, Mp, Ph)
The product know-how is developed and production and marketing take place initially in the host country. Then the product is exported to the parent country.

MPS 56 = S6 (Kh, Mp, Ph)
> The product know-how is developed and production initially takes place in the host country for export of the product to the parent country.

MPS 57 = S8 (Kh, Mh, Ph)-S6 (Kh, Mp, Ph)-S5 (Kh, Mp, Pp)-S7 (Kh, Mh, Pp)
> The product know-how is developed and production and marketing of the product take place initially in the host country. Then the product is exported to the parent country; later, production starts in the parent country in order to supply this market. Finally the product is exported to the host country market.

MPS 58 = S5 (Kh, Mp, Pp)-S7 (Kh, Mh, Pp)-S8 (Kh, Mh, Ph)-S6 (Kh, Mp, Ph)
> While the product know-how originates in the host country, production and marketing take place in the parent country. Then the product is exported to the host country, and later production starts in the host country to supply this market. Finally the product is exported to the parent country from this new production center in the host country.

EXAMPLES OF MULTINATIONAL PRODUCT STRATEGIES

Data Source Number	Company	Country of Parent	Product Developed or Acquisition	Country of Development	Multinational Product Strategy
1	ASEA	Sweden	More efficient way of conducting electric power over long distance.	U.S.	S8–(S5 ?)
2	BASF	Germany	Acquisition of Wyandotte Chemicals, the largest producer in the U.S. of polyols for urethanes, that allows BASF to enter the polyols field.	U.S.	S8–(S5 or S6 ?)
3	Carborundum	U.S.	Acquisitions to expand in consumer goods W. T. Copeland (U.K.), maker of Spode china. Barthmann Cristall (Germany), cut crystal manufacturer.	U.K. Germany	S8–(S6 ?) S8–(S6 ?)
4	Colgate–Palmolive	U.S.	Manual washing device, all plastic, hand-powered washer.	? (likely U.S.)	?
5	CPC International	U.S.	Acquisition of C. H. Knorr, maker of packaged soups and flavor cubes, that are now sold worldwide.	Germany	S8–S6–S5
6	Crane	U.S.	Acquisition DEV Engineering Co., manufacturer of butterfly valves, adding new product to Crane line.	U.K.	S8–?
			Heatnaire Ltd., a pioneer in warm air heating systems.	U.K.	S8–?
7	Dymo Industries	U.S.	Acquisition Meto Gesellschaft, leader in price marking tools; Dymo entered the field with this acquisition.	Germany	S8–S6
			Other Dymo product strategies Dual tract machine	U.S.	S4–S1

APPENDIX B (continued)

Data Source Number	Company	Country of Parent	Product Developed or Acquisition	Country of Development	Multinational Product Strategy
8	General Instrument	U.S.	Laboratory in Naples designed a plastic package that helped the company cut its semiconductor prices by 60 percent.	Italy	?
9	Gillette	U.S.	Acquisition Braun, manufacturer of appliances; Gillette gained entry into the electric shaver market.	Germany	S8–S6
			Dupont, manufacturer of lighters.	France	S8–S6
10	Guest, Keen and Nettlefolds	U.K.	Acquisition BKL Alloys, moving into aluminum technology.	U.S.	S8 ?
			Round Brook Bearing Corp., entering the powder metallurgy field.	U.S.	?
11	Gulf	U.S.	Acquisition Shawinigan Chemical, a leader in carbon block; Gulf entered the field through this acquisition.	Canada	S8–?
12	Hewlett-Packard	U.S.	Microwave division: spectrum analyzer signal generator	U.S. U.S.	S1–S3 S1–S3–S4
			VHF, UHF, HF signal.	U.S.	S3–S1–S4
			Santa Clara division: electronic counter Fourier analyzer.	U.S.	S1–S3–S4
				U.S.	S1–S3
			Scotland division: microwave link analyzer.	U.K.	S8–S6
13	Hoechst	Germany	Research laboratory set up, employing 120 persons in U.K.	U.K.	?
14	Honeywell	U.S.	Development of fiber-control devices in its subsidiaries in France and Germany.	France	?
			Development of computer hardware in France and Italy.	France Italy	

15	International Business Machines	U.S.	Development abroad started in 1958. Among the products developed abroad are the following: IBM 360–20 IBM 360–40 Experimental thin film memory unit for electronic computers (IBM laboratory in Zurich). IBM 2750 and 3750 electronic private business telephone exchange.	Germany U.K. Switzerland Europe	 S8 ?
16	International Telephone and Telegraph	U.S.	Acquisition Rimmel Ltd.; ITT entered the cosmetics field.	U.K.	S8 ?
17	Ling–Temco–Vought	U.S.	The "kid," an amphibious, all-purpose vehicle.	U.S.	S3 ?
18	Litton Industries	U.S.	Acquisition Triumph Adler, for its technology in electric typewriter.	Germany	S8–S6
19	J. Lyons	U.K.	Acquisition Baskin-Robbins; entered ice cream field.	U.S.	S8
20	Minnesota Mining and Manufacturing	U.S.	Beverage operations of Squible Co. Acquisition Ferrania	U.S. Italy	S8 ?
21	Massey–Ferguson	Canada	Development of the first reaper thresher or combine by three Australians connected with Massey-Harris. The first combine was made in Canada for the Australian market only.	Australia	S7–S6–(S5 ?)
			Development of the self-propelled combine by T. Caroll working for Massey-Harris in Argentina. Caroll undertook the work in Toronto and sent the prototype into the field in Argentina. A total of 925 of these	Canada	S3-(S4 ?)

195

Data Source Number	Company	Country of Parent	Product Developed or Acquisition	Country of Development	Multinational Product Strategy
			number 20 combines were manufactured in Canada. A lighter, smaller, low-cost model was developed meanwhile. So emerged the famous number 21 self-propelled combine that was to penetrate the rich U.S. corn belt.	U.K.	S8-S6
			Acquisition of Ferguson, and gained a solid entry into the tractor field (something it was not able to do previously).	U.K.	S8-S6-(S5?)
			Acquisition of Perkins, one of the world's largest producers of high-speed diesel.	U.S.	S8-(S7 or S6?)
22	Omron Tateisi Electronics	Japan	Laboratory in California to tap U.S. research brainpower, and develop new products for the American market.	U.S.	S8-(S7?)
23	Parker	U.S.	Acquisition of Imperial Industries, thereby gaining entry into camping equipment.	Canada	S8-(S7 or S6?)
24	Philips	Netherlands	Development of the portable tape recorder in its Austrian subsidiary, leading to extensive Philips involvement in the musicassette.	Austria	S8-S6-(S5?)
25	Plessey	U.K.	Acquisition of Alloys Unlimited, entering into alloys field, a technology practically unknown in Europe.	U.S.	S8-S6-(S5?)
26	Sandvik Steel	Sweden	Its U.S. subsidiary developed a "throwaway" carbide cutting edge that was later transferred to European operations.	U.S.	S8-(S5?)
27	Sperry Rand	U.S.	Acquisition of a German firm by its Vickers division which entered gear pumps thereby.	Germany	S8-(S?)
28	Volkswagenwerk	Germany	Acquisition of Delanari Engineering (Texas), a company specializing in air conditioning.	U.S.	S8-(S?)

Note: For a number of products, it was impossible to know precisely, from the secondary sources, which product strategy was used. Question marks indicate those states that were uncertain.

Sources (numbers are those in first column):

1) "Making U.S. Technology More Competitive," Business Week, January 15, 1972, p. 45.

2) "BASF Strengthens Position in U.S.," Business International, September 2, 1969, p. 290.

3) "Carborundum Gets Its Global Growth Through Acquisitions and Multiple Sourcing Policy," Business Week, December 19, 1970, p. 69.

4) Warren J. Keegan, "Five Strategies for Multinational Marketing," European Business, January 1970, p. 38.

5) "C.P.C.: Momentum from a Foreign Affiliate," Business Week, December 19, 1970, pp. 64-69.

6) Crane Co., Annual Report, 1962, p. 3 and 1963, p. 6.

7) Dymo, Annual Report, 1967.

8) "Know-how Jumps the Language Barrier," Business Week, December 19, 1970, pp. 121-22.

9) Philip R. Cateora and John M. Hess, International Marketing (Homewood, Ill.: Irwin, 1971), p. 257.

10) "An Old Ironmonger Gets New Muscle," Business Week, September 25, 1971, pp. 66-67.

11) "Gulf Oil Canada Limited," Financial Post, December 18, 1973, p. 4.

12) Personal interviews with various managers at Hewlett Packard.

13) Dirk Schaeffer, "Y Exporter, oui, y investir peut-etre," Vision, March 1973, p. 63.

14) "Know-how Jumps the Language Barrier," Business Week, December 19, 1970, pp. 121-22.

15) "Inside IBM's Management," Business Week, July 14, 1973; John Dunning, ed., The Multinational Enterprise (London: George Allen and Unwin, 1971), p. 77; "IBM Has Now Seven R and D Centers in Europe," Business Europe, March 22, 1967, p. 91; James Biran Wuinn, "Technology Transfer by Multinational Companies," Harvard Business Review, November-December 1969, p. 147; "Know-how Jumps the Language Barrier," Business Week, December 19, 1970, p. 22.

16) "ITT Uses Complex Share Technique to Buy British Cosmetics Company," Business Europe, November 26, 1971, p. 384; "The Electronics Technology Gap: (IV)," Business International, August 15, 1969, p. 262.

17) Vern Terpstra, International Marketing (New York: Holt, Rinehart and Winston, 1972), pp. 248, 259.

18) Seymour Tilles, "How to Evaluate Corporate Strategy," Harvard Business Review, July-August 1963, p. 118; "The Model Conglomerate Tries to be an Operating Company," Business Week, December 1, 1973, pp. 66-73; "Litton is Ordered by FTC to Divest Itself of German Typewriter Firm Acquired in '69," Wall Street Journal, March 15, 1973.

19) "International Outlook, Britain," Business Week, December 8, 1973, p. 54; "1973 Shapes Up As a Top Merger Year, Two-Way Street," Business Week, January 13, 1973, p. 19.

20) "A Force To Be Reckoned With," Business Europe, February 15, 1967, p. 50.

21) Personal interviews with various managers at Massey-Ferguson.

22) "When East Comes West: A Period of Adjustment," Business Week, March 24, 1973, p. 57.

23) "Parker Co. Finds That the Sleeping Bag is Mightier Than the Pen in the Summer," Wall Street Journal, July 30, 1973.

24) "Philips: A Multinational Copes with Profitless Growth," Business Week, January 13, 1973, pp. 63-69; "In Depth: A Family Business Grows Up," Multinational Business, no. 11972.

25) Lawrence G. Franko, European Business Strategies in the United States (Lausanne: Business International, Research Report 71-2), p. 8.

26) Ibid., p. 8.

27) "How the RCA Line Paid off for Univac," Business Week, February 24, 1973, p. 56.

GENERAL FIRM QUESTIONNAIRE

1. What have been the major directions of growth for the firm
    over the past 15 years (in terms of products; in terms of
    markets)?

2. Regarding the company's R and D centers, where are they
    located? What are their relationships one to the other, and
    how is the needed coordination achieved?

3. What is the R and D intensity of the firm? What percent of
    sales is spent on R and D? What percentage of the total R
    and D budget is spent abroad?

4. What are the main characteristics of the production function
    of the firm? Are the production centers specialized?

5. What are the main characteristics of the worldwide organiza-
    tional structure of the enterprise (production divisions; geo-
    graphic structure; product manager with worldwide responsi-
    bility; major profit centers; role of corporate staff)? Have
    there been recent changes? Why?

6. What has been the pattern of product innovation-diffusion on a
    worldwide scale? Examples?
    Who asks for the product or the know-how to be transferred
    from one country to another?
    What is the company's policy toward standardization of prod-
    ucts worldwide, modules, products adapted to market clusters?

7. Are there cases where the company has:
    Developed a product in the home country in response to spe-
    cific needs of another country?
    Developed products in your home country, or another country,
    and produced them in both countries without exporting?
    Developed a product in the home country, produced in that
    country, then exported to markets abroad, produced it locally,
    and then imported it back into the home country?
    Developed a product in the home country for that market, then
    started production abroad and later imported it back into the
    home country?

Interviewer note:
    Selection of products to be investigated in depth

Product line A sales volume	Product line B sales volume	Product line C sales volume

Product:

1.

2.

3.

4.

5.

6.

7.

8.

9.

PRODUCT QUESTIONNAIRE

COMPANY _____   PRODUCT NAME_____

DIVISION_____   TYPE: - industrial_____
                                    - consumer_____

BRIEF DESCRIPTION OF PRODUCT_____

SIC NUMBER   _____

YEAR PRODUCT INTRODUCED ON
THE MARKET   _____

NUMBER OF YEARS PRODUCT KEPT ON THE MARKET - (ACTUAL
OR EXPECTED)

_____   _____

IS IT STILL SOLD ON THE MARKET? YES _____ NO _____

IF YES, WHAT ARE THE PRINCIPAL MARKETS WORLDWIDE?

_____

_____

Main Features of the Product

a) What are the main components of this product?

b) Which of the components are new as compared with the previous
    products developed by your firm?

c) What is the effect of this technological change on the performance
    of the product?

d) In terms of <u>technology</u>, for your firm: is this product
    . totally new?   _____
    . a major change of an
      existing product?   _____
    . a minor change of an
      existing product?   _____

e) In terms of <u>performance</u>, for your firm: is this product
    . totally new?   _____
    . markedly new?   _____
    . similar to the performance
      of an existing product?   _____

f)   What is the value-to-weight ratio of this product?
     (in $/lbs)   _____
     (If no figure is available, circle the most appropriate
     description below.)
     Tradeability index:
     High   Medium   Low

Development of the Product

a)   What factors led to the perceived need to develop a new product?
     . competition in a particular market, which one
     . emanated from engineering and development department;
     . other.

b)   How were the product specifications determined?
     i)   Please describe the process by which product specifications
           were established. That is, what were the successive steps
           that led to the final choice of product specifications?
     ii)   Did these specifications come from more than one country?
           If yes, which inputs came from which countries?
     iii) How were these different product specifications gathered?
           (meetings; trips; written memos; informal contacts; other).
     iv)   How does the final product differ from the one that was (or
           would have been) developed for the U.S. market?
     v)   In general, is it the company policy to have
           . one standardized product worldwide?   _____
           . one product with specific adapta-
             tations for some markets?   _____
           . one product for each country?   _____
           . or some other strategy?   _____
     vi)   For this product, what degree of standardization did you
           adopt?

c)   What were the target markets (countries) at the time the product
     was launched?
     i)   Was a worldwide assessment of demand made? Explain.

d)   What volume of sales was anticipated over the life of the prod-
     uct? How does it compare to other products of your firm?
     i)   What has been the actual volume of sales (units and value)
           each year over the relevant time span?
     ii)   How well do you know the general characteristics of the
           market for this type of product? (See response in the
           following form.)

Knowledge of respondent

Market characteris- tics in Europe-- versus--those in parent country	little	much less	little less	same	better
	___	_____	_____	___	____

Market characteris- tics in Japan-- versus--those in parent country					
	___	_____	_____	___	____

iii) What has been the relative accuracy of demand forecasts in other countries relative to those done for the parent country market? (Seek answer in form similar to above.)

iv) In what way does your ability to forecast demand in a particular country influence your entry strategy?

e) How would you characterize the competitive situation with respect to this product?

   i) How strong was the competition in this product line when it was first introduced abroad vis-a-vis the parent country?

   ii) How do the competitive pressures for this product compare to other major products in your firm?

   iii) Are the main competitors of your firm in Europe and Japan basically the same firms as in the U.S. market?

Location of Product Development

Did the main know-how inputs for this product come from one country alone, or from a cooperative venture between two or more subsidiaries?

If cooperative venture, why was it used in this case?

What in your opinions are the key elements in the success of such cooperative ventures?

a) In which country was the product developed?
In the case of product modification, was the modification developed in the same country as the previous product itself? Explain.

b) Why was it developed in that country?
(Main skills required were in this country only; main market was there; main production facilities there; need to adapt to local conditions; country has relatively cheap skilled labor; other.)

i)   How were the needed skills first developed there?
     (Originated in the firm; acquisition of firm; manufacturing
     led to product development; image in host country better;
     government incentives; other.)
ii) Were there alternative locations where it could have been
     developed as the necessary skills were available there also?

Production and Market Locations

a)   In what country was the product produced first? Why?
b)   Characteristics of the production process
     i)   Considering the initial fixed investments for production,
          how does this product rank in comparison with other prod-
          ucts of your firm?
                    (High, Medium, Low)
     ii) Do you consider the production process as highly complex?
          That is, does it require a large number of skilled personnel,
          and close communication with development people relative
          to other products of your firm?
     iii) How do you rank the labor intensity of the production process
          for this product relative to other products of your firm?
                    (High, Medium, Low)
     iv) How does the cost of production for this product compare in
          Parent country/Europe: lower   same   higher
          Parent country/Japan: lower   same   higher
c)   In what country was the product marketed first? What factors
     determined this choice?
d)   In what countries was the product subsequently introduced?

	Market time lag (months)	Production time lag (if no production indicate source of import)	Product strategy
Europe			
Latin America			
Canada			
Japan			

e)   How was the product introduced in each major country?
     i)   If by export only, was this direct or indirect? What were
          the reasons for this choice (uncertainty about market
          size; small-size market initially; other)?
     ii) If by direct production, was this by the firm itself? Was it
          through a licensing agreement? What were the reasons for
          this choice   (environmental constraints; lower costs of pro-
          duction; high tariffs; competition; government pressures;
          other)?

    iii) If by export first and then production, what were the prin-
cipal factors behind this choice   (increased market size;
changed cost factors; business risks; increased competition; resources available; other)?

f) What important changes took place as the product matured?

    i)   How strong is competition now (in 1974, or at the end of
the product's life) relative to competition at the time of
introduction of product?

	less intense	similar	somewhat higher	very intense
in U.S.				
in Europe				
in Japan				

g) Did you shift the production location as the product matured in
order to supply some particular markets?
(If you shifted the supply of a part of the product only, go to
question (h). If yes, where was production shifted? Time lag?

    i)   Do you supply the U.S. market from _____?
Why?

    ii) Do you supply the European market from _____?
Why?

    iii) Do you anticipate supplying the U.S. market from a low-
wage country in the future?

h) Did you shift the manufacture of some components of the product
to another country?
If yes, which components? When? Value (component/product)?
For each such component transferred:

    i)   What factors lead up to the decision to transfer the produc-
tion of that particular component   (low technological
sophistication; lowest costs of production abroad; high
tariff for import of that component; shift in quantity demanded; other)?

    ii) Do you supply or plan to supply the U.S. market with this
component manufactured abroad?

Planning of the Product Strategy

a) What were the main steps in the planning of the introduction of
this product in the various production locations and markets at
the time the product was first produced? (main steps; planning
horizon; who decided what?).

b) Have alternative product development locations been considered?

c) How are the various development centers coordinated (if any)?

d)   At what point in time after the initial start of production were other production locations planned?

e)   What kind of product moves did you effect that were not anticipated at the start? Why?

f)   What are the main advantages that stem from planning this series of moves?

g)   In general, how could one best describe the strategy employed in developing, producing, and marketing of this product?

Interviewer note:

Books

Aharoni, Yair. The Foreign Investment Decision Process. Boston: Division of Research, Harvard University, 1966.

Andrews, Kenneth R. The Concept of Corporate Strategy. Homewood, Ill.: Dow Jones-Irwin, 1971.

Ansoff, H. Igor. Corporate Strategy: An Analytic Approach to Business Policy for Growth and Expansion. New York: McGraw-Hill, 1965.

Bauer, Raymond A., and Kenneth J. Gergen. The Study of Policy Formation. New York: The Free Press, 1968.

Beaufre, General. Introduction a la Strategie. Paris: Librairie Armand Colin, 1965.

Behrman, Jack N. "Some Patterns in the Rise of the Multinational Enterprise." Research paper no. 18. Chapel Hill: University of North Carolina Press, 1968.

Brooke, Michael Z., and H. Lee Remmers. The Strategy of Multinational Enterprise: Organization and Finance. London: Longman, 1970.

Chandler, Alfred D. Strategy and Structure. Cambridge: The M.I.T. Press, 1962.

Daniels, J. D. Recent Foreign Direct Manufacturing Investment in the United States. New York: Praeger, 1973.

Dunning, John H. Studies in International Investment. London: George Allen and Unwin, 1969.

_____, ed. The Multinational Enterprise. London: George Allen and Unwin, 1971.

Dymsza, William A. Multinational Business Strategy. New York: McGraw-Hill, 1972.

Fayerweather, John. International Business Management: A Conceptual Framework. New York: McGraw-Hill, 1969.

Franko, Lawrence D. European Business Strategies in the United
States. Research Report 1971-2. Lausanne: Business International.

_____. Joint Ventures Survival in Multinational Corporations.
New York: Praeger, 1971.

Hart, Liddell B. Strategy: The Indirect Approach. London: Faber,
1967.

Horst, Thomas. At Home Abroad, A Study of the Domestic and Foreign Operations of the American Food-Processing Industry.
Cambridge: Ballinger Publishing Co., 1974.

Hufbauer, G. C. Synthetic Materials and the Theory of International
Trade. Boston: Harvard University Press, 1966.

Iversen, Carl. Aspects of the Theory of International Capital Movement. Copenhagen: Levin and Munksgaard, 1935.

Katz, Daniel, and Robert L. Kahn. The Social Psychology of Organization. New York: John Wiley and Sons, 1966.

Keegan, Warren J. Multinational Marketing Management. New York:
Prentice-Hall, 1974.

Kindelberger, Charles P. American Business Abroad: Six Lectures
on Direct Investment. New Haven: Yale University Press,
1969.

Knickerbocker, Frederick T. Oligopolistic Reaction and Multinational Enterprise. Boston: Harvard University Press, 1973.

Lawrence, Paul R., and Jay W. Lorsh. Organization and Environment. Boston: Harvard University Press, 1967.

Learned, E. P., C. R. Christiensen, and K. R. Andrews. Problems of General Management. Business Policy, Irvin, 1961.

Luce, Duncan R., and Howard Raiffa. Games and Decisions: Introduction and Critical Survey. New York: John Wiley, 1957.

Mansfield, E. Research and Innovation in the Modern Corporation.
    New York: Norton, 1971.

Neufeld, E. P. A Global Corporation. Toronto: University of
    Toronto Press, 1969.

Penrose, Edith T. The Growth of the Firm. Oxford, England:
    Basic-Blackwell, 1959.

Polk, J., I. W. Meister, and L. A. Veit. U.S. Production Abroad
    and the Balance of Payments: A Survey of Corporate Invest-
    ment Experience. New York: National Industrial Conference
    Board, 1966.

Robinson, Richard D. International Business Policy. New York:
    Holt, Rinehart and Winston, 1964.

_____. International Management. New York: Holt, Rinehart
    and Winston, 1967.

Root, Franklin R. International Trade and Investment. 3rd ed.
    Cincinnati: South-Western Publishing Co., 1973.

Safarian, A. E. Foreign Ownership of Canadian Industry. 2d ed.
    Toronto: University of Toronto Press, 1973.

Schwartzman, David. Oligopoly in the Farm Machinery Industry.
    Royal Commission on Farm Machinery, Study no. 12. Ottawa:
    Information Canada, 1970.

Schwendiman, John S. Strategy and Long-Range Planning for the
    Multinational Corporation. New York: Praeger, 1973.

Simon, Herbert A. Administration Behavior. New York: Macmillan
    Co., 1947.

Steiner, George A., and Warren M. Cannon. Multinational Cor-
    porate Planning. New York: Macmillan Co., 1966.

Stopford, John M., and Louis T. Wells. Managing the Multinational
    Enterprise. New York: Basic Books, 1972.

Terpstra, Vern. International Marketing. New York: Holt, Rine-
    hart and Winston, 1972.

Tilton, John E. International Diffusion of Technology: The Case of
    Semi-Conductors. Washington, D.C.: The Brookings Institu-
    tion, 1971.

Vernon, Raymond. The Economic Environment of International
    Business. New York: Prentice-Hall, 1972.

_____. Manager in the International Economy. Englewood Cliffs,
    N.J.: Prentice-Hall, 1968.

_____. Sovereignty at Bay. New York: Basic Books, 1971.

_____, ed. The Technology Factor in International Trade. New
    York: National Bureau of Economic Research, 1970.

Vicas, Alex G. Research and Development in the Farm Machinery
    Industry. Royal Commission on Farm Machinery, Study no. 7.
    Ottawa: Information Canada, 1970.

Wells, Louis T. The Product Life Cycle and International Trade.
    Boston: Harvard University Press, 1972.

Zenoff, David B., and Jack Zwick. International Financial Manage-
    ment. New York: Prentice-Hall, 1969.

                                    Articles

Aharoni, Yair. "On the Definition of a Multinational Corporation."
    Quarterly Review of Economics and Business, Autumn 1971.

Bruck, N. K., and F. A. Less. "Foreign Investment Capital Con-
    trols and the Balance of Payments." Institute of Finance
    Bulletin, no. 48/49 (April 1968).

Buzzel, Robert D. "Can You Standardize Multinational Marketing?"
    Harvard Business Review, November-December 1968.

Caves, Richard E. "International Corporation: The Industrial Eco-
    nomics of Foreign Investment." Economica, February 1971.

Didrichsen, Jon. "The Development of Diversified and Conglomerate
    Firms in the United States 1920-1970." Business History Re-
    view, Summer 1972.

Dunning, John H. "The Determinants of International Production."
In "La Croissance de la Grande Firme Internationale."
Colloques Internationaux C.N.R.S., no. 549 (1973).

Gilmore, F. F., and R. G. Brandenburg. "Anatomy of Corporate
Planning." Harvard Business Review, November-December
1962.

Gruber, W. H., D. Mehta, and R. Vernon. "The R and D Factor
in International Trade and International Investment of United
States Industries." Journal of Political Economy, February
1967; Survey of Current Business, October 1964, p. 11.

Holton, Richard H. "Marketing Policies in Multinational Corporations." California Management Review 13, no. 4 (Summer
1971).

Keegan, Warren J. "Multinational Product Planning: Strategic
Alternatives." Journal of Marketing, January 1969.

McManus, John. "The Theory of International Firm." In Multinational Firm and the Nation State, ed. Gilles Paquet. Toronto:
Collier-Macmillan, 1972.

Mintzberg, Henry. "Research on Strategy Making." Working Paper.
Montreal: McGill University, 1972. Unpublished.

Penrose, Edith T. "Foreign Investment and the Growth of the Firm."
The Economic Journal 262 (June 1956).

Rutenberg, D. "Organizational Archetypes of a Multinational Company." Management Science, February 1970.

Skinner, Wickham C. "Management of International Production."
Harvard Business Review, September-October 1964.

Stobaugh, Robert B. "Where in the World Should We Put that Plant?"
Harvard Business Review, January-February 1969.

Vernon, Raymond. "International Investment and International
Trade in the Product Cycle." Quarterly Journal of Economics,
May 1966.

Other Publications

Leroy, A. P. "Multinational Product Planning: An Innovation-
   Diffusion Perspective." Unpublished working paper delivered
   at the Multinational Product Management Workshop, Marketing
   Science Institute, Cambridge, Mass., January 1976.

U.S. Congress, Senate. Implications of Multinational Firms for
   World Trade and Investment and for U.S. Trade and Labor.
   Report of the Committee on Finance of the United States Senate
   and its subcommittee on International Trade on Investigation
   no. 332-69, under Section 332 of the Tariff Act of 1930.
   Washington, D.C.: Government Printing Office, 1973. 93rd
   Congress, 1st Session.

GEORGES LEROY is Associate Professor in the Faculty of Management at McGill University. He taught previously at the Ecole des Hautes Etudes Commerciales in Montreal.

After earning an engineering degree from his native land, France, he spent a year studying business administration in Aix en Provence, and received a Fulbright Award to study at Stanford University. He later worked as project analyst at TEMPO, General Electric Center for Advanced Studies, in Santa Barbara, before joining the staff of the Ecole des Hautes Etudes Commerciales.

He is the author of several articles on international business, and he has presented seminars in management and international business. He is a consultant to various firms engaged in overseas operations.

Dr. Leroy holds a degree of Ingenieur de l'Institut National des Sciences Appliquees, in France, a Master of Science (engineering, economic planning) from Stanford University, and a Ph.D. from the University of California at Berkeley.

THE EUROPEAN APPROACH TO U.S. MARKETS:
Product and Promotion Adaptation by European
Multinational Corporations
                                    James J. Ward

FOREIGN DISINVESTMENT BY U.S. MULTINATIONAL
CORPORATIONS: With Eight Case Studies
                                    Roger L. Torneden

MANAGING MULTINATIONAL CORPORATIONS*
                                    Arvind V. Phatak

MARKETING MANAGEMENT IN MULTINATIONAL FIRMS
                                    Ulrich E. Wiechmann

MULTINATIONAL CORPORATIONS AND GOVERNMENT:
Business-Government Relations in an International Context
                            edited by Patrick M. Boarman
                            and Hans Schollhammer

STRATEGIC AND LONG-RANGE PLANNING FOR THE
MULTINATIONAL CORPORATION
                                    John Snow Schwendiman

*Also available in paperback as a PSS Student Edition.